WHOSE *Monet?*

An Introduction to the American Legal System

ASPEN PUBLISHERS

WHOSE *Monet?*

An Introduction to the American Legal System

John A. Humbach

Professor of Law
Pace University School of Law

Wolters Kluwer
Law & Business

AUSTIN   BOSTON   CHICAGO   NEW YORK   THE NETHERLANDS

Aspen Publishers
Attn: Permissions Department
76 Ninth Avenue, 7th Floor
New York, NY 10011-5201

To contact Customer Care, e-mail customer.care@aspenpublishers.com, call
1-800-234-1660, fax 1-800-901-9075, or mail correspondence to:

Aspen Publishers
Attn: Order Department
PO Box 990
Frederick, MD 21705

Printed in the United States of America.

1 2 3 4 5 6 7 8 9 0

ISBN 978-0-7355-6557-9

Library of Congress Cataloging-in-Publication Data
Humbach, John A.
Whose Monet? : an introduction to the American legal system / John
    A. Humbach.—1st ed.
    p.   cm.
    ISBN 978-0-7355-6557-9
    1. Actions and defenses—United States. 2. Civil procedure—United
States. I. Title.
KF8863. H86   2007
347.73′5—dc22

                                                              2007005974

About Wolters Kluwer Law & Business

Wolters Kluwer Law & Business is a leading provider of research information and workflow solutions in key specialty areas. The strengths of the individual brands of Aspen Publishers, CCH, Kluwer Law International and Loislaw are aligned within Wolters Kluwer Law & Business to provide comprehensive, in-depth solutions and expert-authored content for the legal, professional and education markets.

CCH was founded in 1913 and has served more than four generations of business professionals and their clients. The CCH products in the Wolters Kluwer Law & Business group are highly regarded electronic and print resources for legal, securities, antitrust and trade regulation, government contracting, banking, pension, payroll, employment and labor, and healthcare reimbursement and compliance professionals.

Aspen Publishers is a leading information provider for attorneys, business professionals and law students. Written by preeminent authorities, Aspen products offer analytical and practical information in a range of specialty practice areas from securities law and intellectual property to mergers and acquisitions and pension/benefits. Aspen's trusted legal education resources provide professors and students with high-quality, up-to-date and effective resources for successful instruction and study in all areas of the law.

Kluwer Law International supplies the global business community with comprehensive English-language international legal information. Legal practitioners, corporate counsel and business executives around the world rely on the Kluwer Law International journals, loose-leafs, books and electronic products for authoritative information in many areas of international legal practice.

Loislaw is a premier provider of digitized legal content to small law firm practitioners of various specializations. Loislaw provides attorneys with the ability to quickly and efficiently find the necessary legal information they need, when and where they need it, by facilitating access to primary law as well as state-specific law, records, forms and treatises.

Wolters Kluwer Law & Business, a unit of Wolters Kluwer, is head-quartered in New York and Riverwoods, Illinois. Wolters Kluwer is a leading multinational publisher and information services company.

TO EVA

ACKNOWLEDGMENTS

These materials were inspired by, and portions of them adapted from, *Introduction to the Study of Law* by Professor Robert J. Nordstrom of the Ohio State University College of Law. That book stands out in my recollection as the best I read in law school, and he as my finest teacher.

*****

I wish to express my gratitude to my colleagues, Professors Donald L. Doernberg and Steven H. Goldberg, for their immensely helpful comments and constant encouragement, and to John R. Horan, Esq., who generously made available to me the litigation papers from the original case.

Cover photograph is reprinted with the generous permission of the law firm of Shearman & Sterling. Jeremy G. Epstein, Esq., a member of that firm, and a recognized expert and published scholar in the field of art law, led the representation of Wildenstein & Co., Inc., and he played an important role in the ultimately successful defense of Mrs. Baldinger in the case.

INTRODUCTORY NOTE

The lawsuit that is described in this book is an actual case. In that case, the trial judge determined the facts after a "bench" trial (*i.e.*, without a jury). In the present description, however, several procedural wrinkles have been added and the trial process is presented in terms of a jury trial, so that students will begin to become familiar with that most important of the common-law institutions: the jury. In editing the courts' opinions, some minor textual modifications have been made in order to make the procedural posture of the substantive discussion consistent with a trial by jury. For the sake of easier readability, however, these textual modifications (which occur mainly in the opinions' introductory and conclusory paragraphs) have generally not been indicated.

Other than introducing the jury trial and related trial-level motions, the procedural course and substantive outcomes in the case follow the original.

CONTENTS

WHOSE *Monet?*

An Introduction to the American Legal System

United States Courthouse in Manhattan with permission of cardcow.com

*t*his is not a book to teach you law. The next three years will be devoted to that. The purpose of these materials is more fundamental. They are intended to help make your adjustment to law school a little easier. Sometimes new law students find this adjustment to be a bit confusing. For instance, you will probably notice fairly quickly that your assigned readings and classroom discussions generally are for a very different purpose than those in typical undergraduate courses. Also, the rate at which new material is presented may seem, compared with college, to be pretty intensive. You are likely to wonder, early on, "What is really important here? What do I really have to know?"

One of the most important things you will be learning in law school is how to approach legal problems the way a lawyer does, to think like a lawyer. This means, among other things, to look closely at each new set of facts to see how they might be *analogous* to the facts of legal cases decided in the past and, at the same time, keeping a sharp eye out for ways they might be *distinguished* from prior cases. The ability to recognize analogies and detect distinctions is a basic legal skill. You will soon find out that much of what you read (for example, the facts of your assigned cases) is not meant so much for permanent retention as for immediate *use*. You will learn to spot analogies, distinctions, and legal issues by *practicing* these skills on actual and hypothetical sets of facts, and you have to know the facts of the assigned cases so you can "learn by doing" when you get to class. Long experience has shown that learning by doing is one of the most effective ways to develop your proficiency at approaching legal problems in a lawyer-like way. It is the method we use in law school.

Many students come to law school with some "peculiar" preconceptions of how they will learn law. During the first few weeks, especially, these preconceptions can be a stumbling block to the learning process. One erroneous notion is that law school mostly involves memorization—cramming your mind full with rules, with facts from historical cases, and with statutes and agency regulations. In fact, however, learning the law's *conceptual structure* is much more important. Another erroneous preconception is that the key thing is to get down in your notes essentially everything your professor says. In reality, the key thing is that you *comprehend* what is said, and classroom stenography can, if overdone, be an impediment instead of an aid. Perhaps these and similar misconceptions are reflected most strikingly in a common wrong idea many new students have about law examinations. (It may seem early to be already discussing examinations, but it is not too early to discuss success in law school, and final exams are inevitably a part of that.) The wrong idea runs something like this:

> The examination day has arrived. You and your classmates are seated in a large room, each of you with a blank sheet of paper and a pen. You are allowed a certain number of hours and, in that time, you are supposed to write down as many "laws" in the subject as you can remember. At the end, the papers are collected and graded. The students writing the most correct "laws" receive grades of "A"; the next _____% receive a "B"—and so on.

This description could hardly be less true. There are of course some things you will need to remember, but what really counts is your ability to *use* what you remember — to pick out relevant facts, to recognize the applicable legal rules and standards, and to state in a lawyer-like way how courts would, or should, apply the law to the sets of facts presented. In this connection, learning to use the law to advocate for particular positions or outcomes is crucial. For even though lawyers often encounter factual situations in which the law's application is fairly predictable (the "rule of law" could never work otherwise), you will find that there is little demand for lawyers to spend their valuable time analyzing these "easy" cases. The situations that particularly call for the legal-analysis skills of lawyers (and of law students) are precisely those in which the law and its application are not so cut and dried. Thus, your main task in the next several years will be to absorb the law's core vocabulary and conceptual structure and to evolve your skills and abilities to put law and fact together, to solve legal problems, particularly in situations of uncertainty as to what the courts may do. In short, you will be developing a specialized professional capacity — the capacity "to think like a lawyer," and to act accordingly. It is toward developing this capacity that your classroom preparation and instruction will be aimed. In these materials you will find an introduction, a first look at the kinds of things that are to come.

To present a picture of the law's typical operation and the lawyer's role in it, the following pages offer a fairly close look at an actual case, one that arose in New York a few years ago. We will trace the various legal problems that this case raised as it was litigated through the court system. Let's start with the following news story:

Painting by Claude Monet is ordered returned to original owner, notwithstanding good faith purchase

New York, N.Y., Sept. 1987—Edith Marks Baldinger must return a painting by Claude Monet entitled "Champs de Ble a Vetheuil" to Gerda Dorothea DeWeerth, a Federal District Court in New York has ruled.

Mrs. DeWeerth's father purchased the painting in 1908, and kept it in his house in West Germany. DeWeerth inherited the painting in 1922. In 1943, DeWeerth sent the Monet to her sister in Southern Germany for safekeeping. In 1945, some American soldiers were quartered in the sister's house; soon after the soldiers departed, the disappearance of the painting was noted. DeWeerth's efforts to locate the painting were unsuccessful.

By 1956, the Monet had made its way to the United States. Wildenstein & Co., Inc., an art gallery in New York City, acquired the work on consignment from an art dealer from Switzerland. Baldinger purchased the Monet from Wildenstein in June 1957.

Eventually, DeWeerth learned of the gallery's connection with the painting and, in 1982, obtained a state court order directing Wildenstein to reveal the identity of the possessor. The instant action followed.

Judge Vincent L. Broderick first determined that New York law governed all issues in the case. Under New York law, DeWeerth's action was timely since it was instituted within three years of the accrual of the cause of action, i.e., when DeWeerth demanded the return of the property and the demand was refused. Furthermore, DeWeerth had undertaken a "diligent, although fruitless effort" to find the Monet, and did not unreasonably delay her demand for the return of the work.

Judge Broderick then found that DeWeerth had an immediate and superior right to the possession of the painting. Baldinger could trace her title back to the art dealer, but there was no evidence as to how the dealer came into possession of the Monet.

Excerpted with permission from Entertainment Law Reporter © 1987 Entertainment Law Reporter Publishing Company, September 1987.

There is nothing in this news account that would cause any great amount of excitement among most readers of the local daily newspaper. Yet, for the people behind this story the odyssey of Claude Monet's impressionist painting of a wheat field was a matter of enormous importance. The resulting lawsuit went on for a number of years and, very likely during its slow progress, it often dominated the thoughts of the people whose lives were caught up in it, probably making for many restless nights. Law is a serious business.

As you read the unfolding legal story behind this news account, and discuss it in class, keep in mind that law school orientation has several goals. The immediate goals are to help you understand what it is that your professors will be trying to do for you during the coming semesters and, also very important, what they will expect from you.

Law school orientation is not, however, merely your introduction to law school. It is your beginning in your new profession — the profession of law. Over the next several years you will prepare for your new professional role not merely by "learning law," but, just as importantly, by acquiring a deep professional sense of what it means to be a lawyer, and of the vital role of law and legal process in our democracy. While most lawyers' time is spent not in lawsuits but in activities such as transactions and counseling, where the goals are precisely to *avoid* litigation, these materials will follow the tasks of lawyers who are engaged in a lawsuit. The reason for this choice is that, during your first months of law school, *your* primary task will be to read and understand the decisions that courts have rendered in lawsuits, specifically in appeals. (Law students and even some of their professors sometimes ask why so much of law school is devoted to reading, analyzing, and learning to deal with appellate cases when a relatively small part of actual law practice is spent on appeals. The answer of course is because, in our legal system, appellate decisions are where the *law* is.)

In any event, the main focus of the discussion in these materials will be on those aspects of litigation that are essentially similar to lawyers' core activities in virtually all areas of practice: gathering facts, ascertaining the law, preparing documents, counseling the clients, and strategically applying legal materials to the solution of practical problems. As you follow the steps that the lawyers took in the course of one particular lawsuit, you will begin to form a more definite idea of what it is that lawyers do (and should do), the ways we serve our clients, and the benefits we can provide to the people of the society in which we live, and from whom we earn our livings.

Finally, the case discussed in these materials presents opportunities for you to consider the ethical or moral dimension of the lawyer's job — and the tension that sometimes exists between a lawyer's duty to the client, on one hand, and the lawyer's professional and individual duty to promote justice. In our lawsuit over the Monet *Champs de Blé à Vétheuil*, for instance, you will see that the appellate court's ultimate decision was, bluntly, to cancel a woman's property rights in a painting, which had been in her family for decades, and to declare somebody else to be the owner. The appeals court did this even though, by that point in the case, there was no longer any serious legal question that the woman who lost was the rightful owner of the painting under the applicable state law. She ended up with nothing.

The court had legal reasons, of course. It explained that its holding was based on a normal and often cited legal principle ("finality"), according to which courts generally decline to correct their mistakes once a judgment becomes final. There is much to be said for finality — lawsuits cannot go on forever. Nonetheless, whatever the virtues of finality you still might wonder how it can be "justice" to take away an innocent person's property rights when the applicable law makes the ownership clear. The court appears to have "stayed within all the rules," but did it do the right thing?

The reason for bringing this to your attention now is this: You are preparing to become a lawyer. Like many law students, you are very likely drawn to law (at least in part) because you place a high value on "justice." If so, good. But here is the question: Do you think you will be able to do a better job of achieving justice than the legal professionals who litigated and decided the case of the stolen Monet? Undoubtedly, it is too early for you to say, but it is not too early to ask. On the contrary, the earlier the better, and you are urged to ask yourself this question repeatedly as you read the materials that follow, and as you continue your progress through law school. You may not always be able to give a great answer, but you will surely become a better lawyer for trying.

THE LAWYER'S TASK:
FACTS AND LAW

*O*ne day, out of a clear blue, Edith Baldinger received a demand from somebody in Germany directing that she give up one of her most prized possessions, a painting by Claude Monet. The person making the demand, Gerda DeWeerth, claimed to be the true owner. The Monet painting was very valuable, worth more than half a million dollars, so this startling claim by a perfect stranger was no trifling matter. Because a woman from thousands of miles away had got into her head that she owned the Monet, Mrs. Baldinger suddenly found she was on the verge of being sued—and would be forced to defend herself at law. She was about to be sued by a person she had never even heard of and certainly had never knowingly harmed. To top it all off, Mrs. Baldinger had bought the painting in complete honesty, had paid a fair amount of money for it, and had possessed it for many, many years without even a hint that somebody else might have rights to it.

Mrs. Baldinger needed a lawyer. She needed to find out what her legal rights were, and she needed advice as to what to do next. And, of course, she needed somebody to take the proper steps to assert her rights and protect her legal interests in court once a lawsuit was commenced.

To provide legal consultation and advice, she chose Edward M. Sills, Esq.,[1] a member of the New York bar then associated with the large and highly regarded law firm of Paul, Weiss, Rifkind, Wharton, and Garrison, in New York City. Once Mrs. Baldinger had retained Mr. Sills and his firm as her legal counsel, Mr. Sills had at least two important jobs:

(1) to ascertain the *facts* relevant to Mrs. Baldinger's legal rights; and

(2) to ascertain the legal principles, the *law*, applicable to those facts

Let's look at these jobs one at a time.

THE FACTS

[A]fter a case has been tried and the evidence has been sifted . . . , a particular fact may be a clear and certain as a piece of crystal or a small diamond. A trial lawyer, however, must often deal with mixtures of sand and clay.   *—Justice John Paul Stevens*[2]

When a new client comes into a lawyer's office, the lawyer usually knows nothing about the facts of the client's situation. The lawyer needs to know the legally relevant facts, and it is up to the client to give the lawyer the basic picture. Do not, however, assume this means that it is the client's job to make sure the lawyer is adequately informed. On the contrary, as every good lawyer is well aware, clients are very apt to provide only a mass (or mess) of facts, and to make little distinction between

---

[1] The honorific "Esq." has come to common use when writing the full name of lawyers, both male and female. When referring to a lawyer by last name only, the use of "Mr.," "Ms.," etc. is usual.

[2] Nix v. Whiteside, 475 U.S. 157, 190 (1986) (Stevens, J., concurring).

the legally relevant, the totally irrelevant, the crucial, the incon-
sequential, and so on. Clients are not noted for their ability to
recall and communicate the legally important facts. Memories
must be dredged up, typically from the fairly distant past, about
events whose legal aspects the client probably never noticed in
the first place. The farther back the events go, the more tricks the
clients' memories are likely to play — either innocently or inten-
tionally. Like all human beings, clients tend to recall the more
favorable facts with great vividness while the unfavorable bits
and pieces seem to slip away.

In most cases, even the client does not have direct knowledge of many relevant parts of the transactions or events that are
the basis of a dispute. For instance, when Mrs. Baldinger first
consulted Mr. Sills, she probably did not have the faintest idea
what basis Mrs. DeWeerth might have for claiming to own the
painting. She probably had no idea there were some dark deal-
ings in the painting's past and, indeed, was most certainly
unaware that the painting had ever been unlawfully taken
from *anybody*. Yet, information concerning various details of
these matters might easily have been crucial facts in this case.
(For example, Mrs. Baldinger could hardly be required to turn
over the painting to Mrs. DeWeerth if Mrs. DeWeerth never had a
legal right to it in the first place.) To supplement what the client
supplies, therefore, a lawyer preparing a case must normally
perform an independent investigation, interview people other
than the client, and sift through bits of potential evidence
until, very soon, the lawyer knows more about the facts of
case than the client does.

Even a client who knows most of the facts is usually unable
to provide the potentially relevant facts in a neat bundle. After
all, the ability to recognize which facts are likely to have legal
relevance is one of the primary professional skills of the lawyer.
It is a skill that lawyers begin to acquire in law school and, you
will find, picking out legally relevant facts in the cases you read is
an important part of your job as a law *student*. When you read
decisions of courts for your classes, you will find that the judges
very often set out the "facts of the case" without a careful

separation between those facts that are pivotal in the court's legal thinking and those that are merely marginal, or even totally beside the point. When you are asked to recite "the facts" in class, however, your professor will be normally be interested in hearing only the *legally relevant* facts. The time is now to begin honing your skills at fact discernment.

Okay, you might say, but what does it mean for a fact to be "legally relevant"? Basically, from the lawyer's standpoint, a fact is relevant if there is a substantial likelihood that the fact's existence will influence some decision by the court, either by bearing directly on the final judgment or by affecting one of the many lesser rulings that the judge will make along the way. From the court's standpoint, a fact is legally relevant if a decision in the case would actually be affected by it — if the court would incline toward one side when the fact is present, and toward the other side if it is absent. Since a court's decisions are made according to law's standards and rules, legal relevance depends on the legal standards and rules that are applicable to the lawsuit before the court.[3]

Some facts are obviously not relevant. For example, it should not have any legal bearing at all that *Champs de Blé à Vétheuil* was an oil painting rather than a watercolor, or that it depicted wheat instead of barley. Mr. Sills certainly did not have to go to law school to learn that. But the relevancy of other facts may be less easy to determine. It probably should make no difference that Mrs. Baldinger resided on Park Avenue, but it *was* a matter of importance that she lived in New York State. (Actually, it might have been of a matter of crucial importance; do you see why?). The news article quoted earlier stated there were some American soldiers quartered in the house where Mrs. DeWeerth

---

[3] If you have been alert, you might note a bit of a chicken-and-egg thing here: Deciding which facts are legally relevant depends on the applicable legal rules, but, at the same time, the "applicable legal rules" depend on what the legally relevant facts are. As a practical matter, therefore, a lawyer often must determine the "applicable law" and the "relevant facts" in an ongoing and essentially concurrent process of give and take, trial and error. This is just one of the many respects in which *actual* processes of legal thought differ from the "deductive" models of legal reasoning that people frequently (and erroneously) believe that lawyers employ.

had sent the painting for safekeeping, and that the painting's disappearance was noted soon after their departure. Is any of that relevant? The news article also makes note of Mrs. DeWeerth's efforts to locate the painting following its disappearance, efforts that were described by the district judge as "diligent, although fruitless." Is this relevant?

During their on-going investigations to prepare for litigation, Mr. Sills and the other lawyers had to decide whether this fact or that would become legally relevant at some point in the lawsuit. They needed to be ready to deal with the relevant facts, and to avoid spending time on irrelevant ones. For example, if Mrs. DeWeerth's level of effort to find the stolen painting was not legally relevant one way or the other, it would have been a waste of time and money to ascertain and prove what efforts, if any, she actually made.

As you will see, however, the amount of "diligence" that Mrs. DeWeerth used in trying to find her stolen painting turned out to be a central issue in the case. Factual research on this question would have been extremely worthwhile. Indeed, it looks from the record as though some effective advocacy from Mrs. Baldinger's side is what converted the question of Mrs. DeWeerth's efforts from a basically irrelevant point into a central issue. In other words, one way a good advocate can win a case is to look at the facts that are actually available and then persuade the court to regard one of those facts as "legally relevant," even though the legal significance of such a fact may never have been recognized before. A lawsuit is not merely an occasion for "finding the facts and applying the law," but also for extending or contracting the law.

It is not unusual, of course, for lawyers in a case to come up with differing versions of the underlying facts, depending on which side they are on. Indeed, though questions of law frequently arise, most litigated disputes are essentially *factual* disputes (who did what?), not disagreements about the law. In these factual disputes, somebody has to decide which version of the story is closest to the truth and, in most kinds of cases, this task of "finding" the facts can be submitted to a jury (traditionally, twelve citizens from the community) rather than the judge. If the parties waive a jury trial, however, then the fact finding is done by the judge.

When lawyers investigate the facts of the case, it is not enough merely to seek out what happened; they must also keep clearly in mind that the client's cause will prevail only if the lawyer can convince the fact finder. This need to be *persuasive* adds further levels of complexity.

One ever-possible threat is, of course, perjury (intentional lying), but that is perhaps among the least of the lawyer's problems. Far more common than deliberate falsification are sincere disagreements among parties and witnesses as to what actually happened. Take a simple fender-bender at a traffic light. While some onlookers may honestly believe the defendant entered the intersection on red, others may be equally confident that the light was amber or green. Listen to two people going through a divorce as they talk about their reasons for breakup and you may wonder if they are referring to the same marriage. Whenever there is conflicting testimony, somebody has to be getting it wrong, but who?

Self-interest is, of course, one of the factors that leads different people to see the same events differently, but other things are at work, too. In the past several decades, there have been many psychological studies of human perception, memory, and eyewitness identifications, and these give us considerable reason to doubt some of the psychological folk theory that the law has relied on since time immemorial (long before the use of rigorous methods of scientific investigation in these fields). Careful studies show that eyewitness testimony is often fallible and, it turns out, even confessions can be unreliable, due to the intense psychological strain under which most confessions are made. In the light of these studies, it is not surprising that the stories of even the most honest witnesses sometimes are inconsistent, or that numbers of DNA exonerations are as high as they are.

In addition to gathering evidence with a view to fending off false testimony (both intentional and "honest"), a lawyer also has to consider how to put the client's side of the matter in the most favorable light possible. Do not think that all a lawyer does with the facts is to collect them and dispassionately present them. In the process of marshalling the evidence in a case, the lawyer will typically have many opportunities to affect others' *perceptions* of the facts by stressing what is favorable to the client while downplaying valid evidence that is unfavorable, sometimes not even mentioning it. The rules of evidence and procedure offer many possibilities for the well-prepared advocate to keep out material that is deemed "harmful" to his or her client and to introduce material calculated to inflame passions against the other side. Lawyers may thus seek out ways to bend the perceptions of jurors in ways that help their clients' interests, for example, attempting to make over a street-gang client by dressing him up for court so he looks like a businessman, or a choirboy.

There are, however, limits. Outright lies, destruction of evidence, witness tampering, and other such illegal strategies are clearly out of bounds. But how about shading the evidence in the client's favor while staying, nonetheless, within the limits of the law and lawyer ethics? Many would contend that protecting clients' interests to the limits of the law is simply good advocacy. After all, "loyalty to the client" is one of our profession's core values, and some say the duty of loyalty practically *requires* lawyers to do whatever they lawfully can so that jurors will see things to their clients' best advantage. One might even say that the lawyer who does not do so — who does not go the full distance that law and lawyer ethics allow — falls seriously short. Other lawyers (probably a minority) feel that justice is not merely the responsibility of the system as a whole, but rather is also a personal responsibility of each lawyer in it, and no lawyer should obfuscate or distort the facts just so the client can get some advantage. What do you think?

However you may come out on the "client-loyalty vs. personal responsibility" issue, it should now at least be clear to you just how crucial a lawyer's fact-gathering role actually is. A reliable system of justice depends on it. A general proposition of law may be very crisp and clear, but whether it applies to the case at hand typically depends on the facts, and these may initially be very uncertain. A lawyer does not just investigate and present facts; a lawyer *advocates* — marshalling the raw evidence to support the interests of the client. It is the lawyers' advocacy and final sorting out of factual issues, not the questions of "law," that more typically turn out to be crucial in deciding who wins.

This stress on advocacy does not mean that the system we have is not a generally sound vehicle for finding truth and doing justice. Our system is an *adversary* system, which presupposes that truth is most likely to be discovered when competing advocates are set against one another and allowed to do their persuasive best. While the results are not always perfect, our system is the best that our forebears were able to devise, in their times, to search out the truth. Obviously there may still be room for tweaking and, possibly, even for substantial overhauls in the light of modern knowledge. But until some kind of machine is invented to take us back in time to re-enact the facts as they actually happened — a sort of universal instant-replay feature for life itself — we must rely mainly on the testimony of witnesses and discernment of human fact finders. We can and should, however, temper that reliance with a keen alertness to detect and correct for the inevitable inadequacies of human perception and memory.

Given that perfection is unattainable, some have asserted that the true job of the legal system is not really to do perfect "justice" (whatever that may mean), but to settle disputes — to resolve controversies, one by one, with impartiality and as many safeguards as are reasonably possible. In a given case a guilty person may go free, or an innocent one may be called on to pay substantial damages, go to prison, or even pay the ultimate price.[4] Perhaps. Even if this is the reality, however, it should not lead us to resignation. Lawyers (including, soon, you) should

---

[4] *See* Herrera v. Collins, 506 U.S. 390, 400 (1993). In *Herrera*, the U.S. Supreme Court said that evidence of "actual innocence" was not in itself a basis to set aside a state death sentence once the judgment had become final. The Court was concerned about "the very disruptive effect that entertaining claims of actual innocence would have on the need for finality in capital cases." *Id.* at 417.

continually strive to improve the fact-finding system even while we must recognize that perfect justice may never be obtained as long as we have to depend on imperfect human capabilities.

Facts of *DeWeerth v. Baldinger* as Summarized by the Trial Court:

In the first judicial decision that was rendered in *DeWeerth v. Baldinger*, District Judge Vincent L. Broderick summarized the facts as follows:

> Plaintiff Gerda Dorothea DeWeerth seeks the return from defendant Edith Marks Baldinger of a painting by Claude Monet entitled "Champs de Ble a Vetheuil" ("the Monet"). * * *
>
> Mrs. DeWeerth is a citizen of the Federal Republic of Germany, and Mrs. Baldinger is a citizen of the State of New York. The Monet which is the subject of this action . . . is an impressionistic depiction in oil of a wheat field, a village and trees near Vetheuil, France. It measures 65 centimeters by 81 centimeters, and is signed and dated "Claude Monet '79".
>
> Mrs. DeWeerth's father, Karl von der Heydt, purchased the Monet in or about 1908, and he thereafter kept it in his house in Bad Godesberg, West Germany. Plaintiff inherited the Monet from her father after his death on August 9, 1922, in the division of the works and objects of art in his estate. With the exception of the years 1927 to 1929, when the Monet was kept in her mother's house, plaintiff kept the Monet in her residence in Wuppertal-Elberfeld from 1922 until August 1943, where it was on display on a wall next to a sculpture by Auguste Rodin, also inherited from her father. This sculpture is still in plaintiff's possession at her West German residence, and plaintiff has submitted a 1943 photograph showing the Monet and the Rodin displayed together in her residence. From that time until the present, she neither sold nor otherwise disposed of the Monet, nor did she entrust the Monet to anyone else to sell or otherwise dispose of it.
>
> In August 1943, during the Second World War (the "War"), Mrs. DeWeerth sent the Monet, along with the Rodin sculpture and other valuables, by van to her sister Gisela von Palm (now deceased) in Oberbalzheim in Southern Germany, for safekeeping.

Although the van arrived, plaintiff never saw the Monet again. In the fall of 1945, Gisela von Palm informed plaintiff of the disappearance of the Monet from Mrs. von Palm's house in Oberbalzheim. There is no direct evidence as to what caused the disappearance of the Monet. American soldiers were quartered in the house after the close of the War in 1945, and it was after they had left that its disappearance was noted. I infer that either one of those soldiers, or someone else, stole the painting from the von Palm house where it had been sent for safekeeping. * * *

Mrs. DeWeerth was approximately 50 years old when she learned of the Monet's disappearance. Subsequently, she made efforts to locate it. In 1946 she reported the loss of the Monet to the military government then administering the Bonn-Cologne area after the end of the War. In 1948 she solicited the assistance of her lawyer, Dr. Heinz Frowein, in attempting to find and recover it. Plaintiff also made inquiries in 1955 of one Dr. Alfred Stange, known to Mrs. DeWeerth as an art expert. In 1957 she reported the Monet as missing to the *Bundeskriminalamt* (the West German federal bureau of investigation) in Bonn. All of these efforts to find the Monet were unsuccessful.

By December 1956, however, the Monet had found its way to the United States through Switzerland. . . . Wildenstein & Co., Inc. ("Wildenstein"), an art gallery in New York City, appears to have acquired the Monet on consignment from Francois Reichenbach, an art dealer from Geneva, Switzerland, in about December 1956. From December 1956 to June 1957, Wildenstein had possession of the Monet in New York. A Wildenstein record shows a 1962 payment, or credit, to Reichenbach, evidently for the Monet.

In June 1957, Wildenstein delivered the Monet for inspection to Mrs. Baldinger at her residence at 710 Park Avenue, New York, New York. Mrs. Baldinger, after several days, purchased the Monet in good faith and for value from Wildenstein on or about June 17, 1957.

After its purchase by Mrs. Baldinger, the Monet was publicly exhibited only on two occasions. Mrs. Baldinger exhibited the Monet at a benefit held in the Waldorf-Astoria Hotel in New York City, from October 29 to November 1, 1957, and loaned it to Wildenstein for display during a Wildenstein exhibition entitled "One Hundred

Years of Impressionism" held April 2 to May 9, 1970, at its gallery
in New York City. At the close of this exhibition, Wildenstein
returned the Monet to Mrs. Baldinger. Except for those two exhibitions, Mrs. Baldinger maintained the Monet exclusively in her residence at 710 Park Avenue, New York City, from June 1957 to the
present date.

There are only four published references to the Monet in the art
literature: two of them are in catalogues in connection with the
exhibitions already cited, and the other two are in publications
with which Wildenstein was apparently connected:

(1) *Claude Monet: Bibliographie et Catalogue Raisonne, Vol. 1
    1840-1881*. Published by la Bibliotheque des Arts, Lausanne,
    Paris; introduction by Daniel Wildenstein; collaborators Rodolphe
    Walter, Sylvie Crussard, and the Foundation Wildenstein, 1974,
    Geneva; painting no. 595.
(2) The exhibition catalogue *One Hundred Years of Impressionism,
    A Tribute to Durand-Ruel, A Loan Exhibition*, April 2 - May 9,
    1970, Wildenstein Gallery, New York; painting no. 43.
(3) *Monet: Impressions*, Daniel Wildenstein, published in New
    York, 1967, Library of Congress call no. ND553.M76W5313.
(4) The exhibition catalogue *Festival of Art*, October 29 - November 1,
    1957, Waldorf-Astoria Hotel, New York; item 125.

In or soon after July 1981, plaintiff, through the efforts of her
nephew Peter von der Heydt, discovered that the Monet had
been exhibited in 1970 at the aforementioned Wildenstein loan
exhibition. Plaintiff thereafter retained counsel in New York in
1982 to determine whether Wildenstein knew the identity of the
present possessor of the Monet. When Wildenstein refused to
disclose the possessor's identity or the Monet's whereabouts,
plaintiff commenced a proceeding in November 1982 against
Wildenstein in New York State Supreme Court seeking "disclosure
to aid in bringing an action" under N.Y.C.P.L.R. §3102(c).
On December 1, 1982, the State Supreme Court found for the
plaintiff, ordering Wildenstein to reveal the identity of the

possessor. Plaintiff thereafter learned that defendant Baldinger possessed the Monet.

By letter to Baldinger dated December 27, 1982, plaintiff demanded return of the Monet. By letter dated February 1, 1983, Baldinger refused the demand. This action ensued.[5]

* * *

Notice how much longer the judge's statement of facts is compared with the news story on page 4. Obviously, Judge Broderick provides many more facts, but does he provide more *legally relevant* facts — or does he merely provide more of the supporting facts? It is too early for you to say, but note for now that the news story might touch on all of the legally relevant facts even though it is much shorter. Which version is "best"? It depends on the purposes at hand, of course, but in legal writing as elsewhere shorter is often better. If you are asked to state the facts of a case in class, something as long as the news story would probably be just about the *outer limit* of what would be tolerated; shorter would be better. You must learn to speak and write concisely. They are important legal skills.

STUDY QUESTIONS

1. How and when did Mrs. DeWeerth come to be the owner of the Monet painting?
2. What proof did Mrs. DeWeerth have that she ever had possession of the painting?
3. How and when did Mrs. DeWeerth lose possession of the painting?
4. How old was Mrs. DeWeerth when she learned of the painting's disappearance?

---

[5] Editor's note: Judge Broderick found the foregoing facts after a "bench" trial (*i.e.*, without a jury). See Introductory Note, page xi.

5. What efforts did Mrs. DeWeerth make to locate the painting?
6. When and how did Mrs. Baldinger acquire the painting?
7. When and how did Wildenstein & Co. get possession of the painting?

Final note: You might want to take a quick glance ahead at the facts as summarized by the Court of Appeals, on pages 193-195. The appeals court *reversed* the judgment issued by Judge Broderick and, in doing do, it described the facts slightly differently.

THE LAW

Lawyers are not expected to have memorized all of the laws of these United States. In fact, it is a pretty safe bet that no one has even come close. Because of this, lawyers frequently encounter the need to do *legal research*. Through legal research, a good lawyer learns law constantly, for the entire duration of his or her career. A word of caution, however. Do not believe (as some occasionally say) that all you need to do is learn to "think like a lawyer" and then, after law school, look up whatever law you need. That will not work either. Without a firm grounding in the basic vocabulary and conceptual structure of the law — the more the better — it would be hard for a lawyer to have the skills and insights necessary to do an intelligent and efficient job of research and then apply what is found. Indeed, without some knowledge of the law that will probably apply in a case, it may be nearly impossible for the lawyer even to understand the "facts," to separate the relevant from the irrelevant and to shape the issues in a way that is beneficial to the client and conducive to justice. In short, the more law you know, the more likely it is that you will know *what* to look up.

For example, suppose Mrs. Baldinger had come to see you last June and asked your advice regarding the demand she received from Mrs. DeWeerth. Would you have known that one of the key legal provisions is the New York *statute of limitations* referred to in the news story, which says a person has three years to bring a lawsuit to recover a chattel?[6] Would you have had a clue where in the vast law library to look for such a law? Mr. Sills had to know these things before he could even begin efficient research into the details and actual applicability of this crucial statute.

But then, who says that New York's law should even apply? After all, the theft occurred in Germany, and Mrs. DeWeerth herself was still living there. Maybe the law of Germany applies. Would it have occurred to you, before law school, that there are special "choice-of-law" rules to guide the courts when more than one legal system is involved? Would you have known where to look for those? One of your primary goals in law school should be to acquire the needed background so you can efficiently learn the specifics in later research.

Once Mrs. Baldinger had received Mrs. DeWeerth's demand, a legal action to recover the painting itself was likely to follow. The time was ripe for Mr. Sills to do some detailed research into the law. From the facts already then available to the defense side, Mr. Sills could see that he probably should focus his initial legal research in two areas:

(1) **Legislation:** the statute of limitations that requires lawsuits to recover chattels be brought within three years of the date the cause of action accrues; and

(2) **Common law:** prior court decisions ("precedents") on the questions of "choice of law" and interpreting the legislation referred to above.

---

[6] Do you know what a "chattel" is? As you read these materials and your later assignments you will likely run into many words or usages you are not familiar with. You should look these words up in your law dictionary (or, until you get one, in a good regular dictionary). You should *not* simply pass them by. For the remainder of law school and of your entire legal career, you will well serve yourself and your eventual clients only if you take the time to learn what is meant by the legal words you do not know.

Later on in these materials, you will read full chapters on each of these two main sources of American law: legislation and the common law. (The third basic source of legal norms, the regulations and rulings of administrative agencies, will also be briefly described.) In the meantime, we will focus on getting the DeWeerth-Baldinger lawsuit underway, limiting our initial observations here to a few important introductory points.

In this case the pivotal statutory provision, referred to in the news article above, is a section of the New York Civil Practice Law and Rules (the "CPLR"). It is part of a larger "statute of limitations" and, in relevant part, it reads as follows:

> §214. **Actions to be commenced within three years;**
> ∗ ∗ ∗ The following actions must be commenced within three
> years: ∗ ∗ ∗
>
>   3. An action to recover a chattel or damages for the taking or detaining of a chattel; ∗ ∗ ∗[7]

One look at this statute, CPLR §214, and you might think that Mr. Sills could breathe a sigh of relief. He could phone up Mrs. Baldinger and tell her she doesn't have a worry in the world. After all, doesn't the statute say clearly as can be that an "action to recover a chattel" must commenced within three years? In this case it has been 37 or 38 years. Surely that's too long. No?

Well, perhaps, but three years from *when?* Look very carefully at the words of CPLR §214. Do they say when the three-year period starts? If not, is the starting point at least logically implied? Perhaps it is to some extent implied. After all, it would not make much sense to say that Mrs. DeWeerth's time to sue began running out before she was even legally able to bring her lawsuit — or, to put it in the usual technical terminology, a statute of limitations does not begin to run until the "cause

---

[7] The "∗ ∗ ∗" means something has been omitted from the quotation because it is not relevant for present purposes. The ordinary ellipsis (. . .) is also a common device to show that something has been omitted when quoting legal materials. You should become alert for the various signals and devices that lawyers use for quotations and citations in legal writing. They are, in a way, part of the law's specialized vocabulary.

of action" has "accrued." But when in this case did the cause of action (right to sue) "accrue"? Could it have accrued—and perhaps even have run out—before Mrs. DeWeerth even knew who had her painting, before she even knew whom she should sue? Maybe, or maybe not. The problem here is that CPLR §214 simply does not say. And this raises a general point about statutes, administrative regulations, and any other general statements of law: They are *never* complete on their face. There is always the possibility of interpretive questions, and statutes do not interpret themselves.

To supply what is missing when specific cases arise, courts must *interpret* statutes. The interpretive "gloss" that a court puts on a statute may be as much "law" as the words of the statute itself. That is to say, a court's interpretation of a statute gives the statute additional meaning because the court's interpretation establishes a *precedent*, which must generally be taken into account in later applications of the statute.[8]

As we will later see in greater detail, the New York courts have interpreted CPLR §214 in such a way that, in cases like this one, the three-year period does not even *begin* to run until the owner makes a "demand" and it is refused. In other words, even though the Monet had been out of Mrs. DeWeerth's hands for 37 or 38 years, including the nearly three decades with Mrs. Baldinger, it looked very likely that the three-year statute of limitations had not even *begun* to run. On the contrary, it looked as though the three-year period would start only after the refusal by Mrs. Baldinger to comply with Mrs. DeWeerth's demand to turn over the painting. Since Mrs. DeWeerth had only just made her demand, it looked like Mrs. DeWeerth would be easily able to commence her action within the statutory three-year period.

---

[8] As we shall discuss further in Chapter VII, judicial precedents may be "mandatory" authorities or, merely, "persuasive" authorities. A court is required to follow an interpretation by a hierarchically superior court in the same jurisdiction; it is "mandatory" or "binding" authority. Decisions of out-of-jurisdiction courts or courts that do not have higher rank in the jurisdiction are generally considered "persuasive" authority; they do not have to be followed, but they deserve consideration and, when not followed, a later court often feels compelled to give reasons for not doing so.

So much for any quick sighs of relief. It looks like more legal research is going to be needed; something else will have to be found if Mrs. Baldinger is to keep the Monet. Specifically, it will be necessary to research the *case law* — both the cases interpreting the statute quoted above as well as cases on legal topics that have no legislative basis whatever. Most of the law of property is in this latter category, having no legislative basis and consisting largely of judicial cases. Another such topic, which holds some promise in this case, is the "choice of law" question, mentioned earlier. Maybe the court will not apply New York law at all; maybe it will apply German law. Mr. Sills would not be able to find any statute to provide guidance on this question. He would only find prior cases, prior judicial decisions in which the courts announced various rules and standards for deciding "choice of law" questions. This judge-made law is the essence of the "common law" and, as we will see in Chapter VII, the common law makes up a considerable piece of American law.

Let us however assume that, before Mr. Sills gets very deeply into either of these research projects, he receives word that a *summons and complaint* have been served on Mrs. Baldinger. It looks as though the lawsuit has been commenced. Let's take a look at what the plaintiff, Mrs. DeWeerth, and her counsel have been doing.

*f*or 35 years Mrs. DeWeerth had no leads at all on the whereabouts of her lost Monet. Then, finally, in the summer of 1981, she got a break. Her nephew, living in New York, learned that the Monet had been loaned out ten years earlier, for display at an exhibition. The exhibition, *One Hundred Years of Impressionism*, had been presented at the Wildenstein Gallery in New York City. With something to go on at last, Mrs. DeWeerth sought and retained a New York attorney to follow up on this lead. The attorney she retained was John R. Horan, Esq., of a firm then known as Fox, Glynn, and Melamed.

Initially, the Wildenstein Gallery would not tell Mrs. DeWeerth who had *Champs de Blé à Vétheuil*. In order to compel disclosure, Mr. Horan brought the state-court proceeding that was mentioned by Judge Broderick in his statement of facts, which we saw in Chapter II. The state court issued a ruling ordering disclosure. Once Mrs. DeWeerth knew who had the painting, she was finally in a position to make a demand for its return and then to sue to get it back. After her demand had

27

been made and (predictably) refused, Mrs. DeWeerth had some decisions to make. She had to decide *whether* to sue and *where* to sue.

Getting involved in a lawsuit can be one of the most time-consuming and expensive things a person ever does. Therefore, advising an aggrieved client whether to sue, or not, is a very important part of the lawyer's job. In advising Mrs. DeWeerth *whether* to sue, Mr. Horan, was faced with questions and challenges very similar to those already encountered by Mr. Sills, counsel for Mrs. Baldinger: Mr. Horan had to ascertain the relevant facts, and he had to determine the applicable law. Specifically, Mr. Horan had to familiarize himself with the facts surrounding Mrs. DeWeerth's acquisition of the painting and the circumstances of its loss, as well as with both the applicable statutes and case law. Only after he had done all this was he prepared to advise his client as to the probable outcome of a lawsuit.

In discussing with Mrs. DeWeerth the prospects for a successful outcome, Mr. Horan might well have begun his legal opinion something like this: "Based on the applicable statute and the prior decisions interpreting it and on the choice of law principles that are most likely to apply, it is my opinion that . . . ." (Actually, this level of formality would have been more normal for a written "opinion letter," and Mr. Horan would probably have spoken more conversationally when advising Mrs. DeWeerth in person. The essential message would, however, have been the same.)

In advising Mrs. DeWeerth whether she should sue for the painting, Mr. Horan had to make a prediction as to what a court would probably do. In making such a prediction, he was required, in effect, to employ the same kind of reasoning that courts use in their *adjudicative* functioning. That is, he would determine which legal rules appear to be applicable to this general type of situation (some found in statutes and others in cases), and then he would apply these general rules to the specific facts of Mrs. DeWeerth's situation. He would employ this reasoning in order to decide — in effect, to *judge* — what would be the likely result in court when the judge later applied those same rules to the facts of Mrs. DeWeerth's case.[9]

Sometimes a lawyer will have to tell the client that the lawyer believes there is little or no chance of successful litigation. In that event, no lawsuit is brought, and the client must bear her own loss; there is no one else who is legally responsible for that loss. In Mrs. DeWeerth's case, however, Mr. Horan reached the opposite conclusion, deciding there was a good chance of a successful litigation.

Notice that, unlike Mrs. DeWeerth, the defendant Mrs. Baldinger did not have the option to decide whether a suit was brought or not. That is a choice that is, in the final analysis, left entirely to plaintiffs. Nevertheless, just like a plaintiff's lawyer, a defense lawyer must likewise evaluate the prospects for success, the prospects for mounting a credible defense. If the defense lawyer concludes that the defendant has little or no chance of defending successfully, the defendant may offer to *settle* with the plaintiff instead of wasting time and money to stave off the inevitable. Few cases, however, look utterly hopeless, and a defense is usually initiated in hopes of gaining, at very least, more favorable terms of settlement.

A case may be settled at any time before trial, during the trial, and even after trial and judgment.[10] In most cases the lawyers will do at least some probing with one another to see if there might be mutually agreeable terms for a settlement. Often the lawyers get into active negotiations for settlement, discussing possible terms of a settlement with one another and, with their clients, the advisability of accepting such terms. The law favors and encourages settlements between the parties. The

---

[9] Is predicting what a court will do the same thing as saying what the law is? The great American jurist and legal thinker Oliver Wendell Holmes, Jr. thought so. In a famous passage, he wrote: "The prophecies of what the courts will do in fact, and nothing more pretentious, are what I mean by the law." Oliver Wendell Holmes, *The Path of the Law*, 10 HARV. L. REV. 457, 461 (1897). Would you agree?

[10] Note the spelling of this word. Why do you suppose a party who wins a judgment in court would ever be interested in settling the case for less than the amount of the judgment?

judge does not in any sense resent a private settlement and often will exert considerable pressure to encourage one.

It should be already obvious that the function of applying law to facts, *adjudication*, is not entirely left to the courts but is a key component of a litigating lawyer's normal functions. When a lawyer advises the client that there is no chance of recovery, the lawyer is in a very real sense "adjudicating" the claim, often with as much effectiveness as though a judge had decided the case. When a case is settled after suit has been commenced, each of the lawyers is once again acting, in effect, as a "judge" in relation to that claim.

As we already can guess, Mr. Horan's advice to Mrs. DeWeerth was that her chances of a successful litigation were good, that she had a good chance at law of recovering her painting. Mrs. DeWeerth's decision was to commence the lawsuit. As it might typically happen, Mrs. DeWeerth would have been sitting across the desk from Mr. Horan and, after discussing various aspects of the case, the lawyer fees and the court costs, she would have said, at a certain point, something like: "Okay, let's sue!" For Mr. Horan this meant that the next step was to decide which court to sue in.

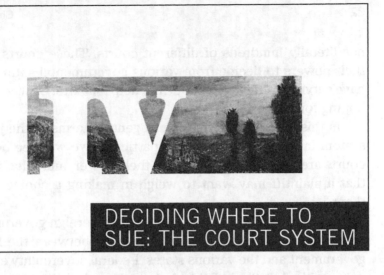

IV

DECIDING WHERE TO
SUE: THE COURT SYSTEM

*O*nce it became obvious that Mrs. Baldinger was not going to return the Monet painting voluntarily, Mrs. DeWeerth had only one lawful recourse — to persuade a court to lend its power (ultimately, its *physical* power) to help her get it back. But which court?

The power to make law and to enforce the rule of law is held by governments. Within their own territories, governments exercise "sovereignty" — the supreme right to rule, decide, and judge. While Mrs. DeWeerth might have preferred to bring her lawsuit in a court near her home in Germany, the painting was in the United States. A German court would eventually have to seek the assistance of American authorities anyway. Besides, as we shall see,[11] it would not likely have been possible, as a practical matter, for a German court to obtain jurisdiction (authority to render judgment) over Mrs. Baldinger. But even though it was clear that Mrs. DeWeerth could realistically sue only in the United States, she still had choices to make. The United States

[11] In Chapter V.

has literally hundreds of different courts. These courts derive their powers to decide from various governmental sources and have varying abilities to provide the help that Mrs. DeWeerth was hoping for.

In this chapter we will look in general terms at the judicial system in the United States. In particular we will see how the courts are set up, where they get their power, and what factors that a plaintiff may want to weigh in making a choice among them.

As you probably already know, the sovereign governmental power in the United States is divided up between the federal government and the various states. Federal sovereignty extends nationwide, but the individual states have jurisdictional power only within their individual territories.[12] The federal government maintains and administers its own system of laws, which are separate and distinct from the various states' laws. Still, the power of Congress to make federal laws is limited, in theory, to areas specifically mentioned in the U.S. Constitution, the so-called "enumerated powers." In actual practice, the individual states provide most of the law that applies to ordinary disputes between private persons, such as the law of contracts, tort law (injury compensation), and property law, as well as the basic criminal law. Federal law is primarily directed toward areas of particularly nationwide, interstate, or international concern.

One of the consequences of this dual-sovereignty system is that there are, in every state, two separate systems of courts — the federal courts and the state courts. The federal courts are a branch of the federal government, while the state courts are created by and part of the individual state's government. Some might argue this is at least one court system too many and, indeed, the drafters of the U.S. Constitution had some doubt about the question, sufficient doubt that they left it to Congress to decide whether a separate system of federal courts should be

---

[12] As we will see in a bit, individual states use various forms of "long arm" jurisdiction to launch and entertain proceedings against persons outside their territories, but they may not lawfully apply direct coercive effects inside the territories of other jurisdictions without the cooperation of the authorities there.

created.[13] Congress decided "yes," and it established the federal court system. In the first years, the federal court system existed primarily for the purpose of handling disputes between citizens of different states, or between American citizens and those of foreign nations. Nowadays, however, the federal courts are primarily concerned with criminal and civil cases arising under federal law.

You should already be starting to see where the DeWeerth-Baldinger dispute fits into this picture. Mrs. Baldinger was a U.S. citizen and Mrs. DeWeerth was a citizen of Germany, meaning that their dispute involved precisely the "diversity of citizenship" that the federal courts were meant to handle. Before going further into these specifics, however, let us pause for a moment and consider where law comes from, the *constitutional* bases for the creation of laws and for the courts' powers to impose laws on persons.

FEDERAL COURT SYSTEM

Ultimately, the source of all legal power in the United States lies in *constitutions* — the U.S. Constitution for the federal government and, in each of the states, a separate state constitution for the government of that state. All lawmaking power emanates from these fundamental laws. You will have a course in Constitutional Law where you will examine the U.S. Constitution in some detail. For now, however, a few general ideas are important.

The U.S. Constitution represents the effort of our nation's founders to reduce to writing their agreement on three fundamental issues:

A. *Creation and Allocation of Federal Power.* Initially, following independence from Great Britain, all government power lay with the

---

[13] The exception here is the U.S. Supreme Court, which the Constitution established expressly.

states. An attempt was made to run a national government on this basis under the Articles of Confederation, and it failed. A decision was reached that some of the states' power had to be transferred to a federal government. This transfer was made by adopting the U.S. Constitution, in 1789.

B. *Limitations on Governmental Powers.* Certain portions of the Constitution were designed to limit governmental powers in order to protect individual rights and private property. For example, the Constitution states that no person shall be "deprived of life, liberty, or property, without due process of law; nor shall private property be taken for public use without just compensation."[14] Initially, most of these protections were contained in the first ten amendments to the Constitution (known as the Bill of Rights), but additional amendments and protections have been added since 1789.

C. *Separation of Powers.* The U.S. Constitution contains separate articles establishing the executive, legislative, and judicial branches of the federal government, and allocates certain (limited) powers to each of these branches. The executive power is in the President, the legislative (or lawmaking) power is conferred on Congress, while the judicial power is vested in the courts. You will see that this "separation of powers" is not airtight. Courts, for example, engage in a narrow form of lawmaking when they rule on specific cases. Nevertheless, one most valuable effect of this separation is our nation's *independent* judiciary, in which the judges are free to interpret and apply the law without interference from the executive or legislative branches.

The U.S. Constitution is the highest law of the land.[15] It is superior to all state constitutions and to all acts or laws of Congress, of state legislatures, and of any other lawmaking bodies in the nation (for example, city councils, county boards, and other

---

[14] U.S. CONST. amend V. If the Constitution says this, how did it possibly happen that a federal court in DeWeerth v. Baldinger cancelled a woman's property rights in a painting and then declared the owner to be somebody else, as mentioned in Chapter I? We shall see.

[15] *See* U.S. CONST. art. VI, §2.

state-created municipal bodies). If the courts find any such acts or laws to conflict with the terms of the Constitution, they are said to be *unconstitutional* and are void.

Theoretically, the Constitution cannot be changed except by a cumbersome amending process. However, the Supreme Court has from time to time "interpreted" the Constitution in ways that have wrought some pretty radical modifications of the prevailing constitutional rules, even without any formal amendments. This power of the courts to re-interpret the Constitution and declare laws void places the courts in a very formidable position — especially when coupled with our nation's deeply rooted tradition of an independent judiciary. The willingness of courts to review and strike down legislative enactments has grown over the past two centuries, and many have criticized this growth as anti-democratic. This charge has been made with particular force when legislators elected by the people make laws that are then struck down by federal judges, who are appointed for life, and are answerable essentially only to themselves. (Why should courts have this power to overturn choices made by the elected representatives of the people?[16])

The system of federal courts was created by Congress acting under the authority of Article III of the U.S. Constitution. Read it carefully:

Section 1. The judicial Power of the United States, shall be vested in one supreme Court, and in such inferior Courts as the Congress may from time to time ordain and establish. . . .

---

[16] How one feels about this issue often depends on the specific facts of the case. For instance, Justice Scalia, an articulate conservative on the Supreme Court, once wrote an opinion in which he seethed about the "Imperial Judiciary" of "unelected, life-tenured" judges, which "succumbs" to the "temptation [of] systematically eliminating checks on its own power," and he quoted the fear that soon "the people will have ceased to be their own rulers." What he was objecting to was the Supreme Court majority's decision to strike down a state law that would have limited abortions. Planned Parenthood v. Casey, 505 U.S. 833, 981, 996-97 (1992). On the very same day, however, the same Justice Scalia issued a strong majority opinion by which the Court struck down an environmental protection law that had been adopted by the elected legislators of another state. Lucas v. South Carolina Coastal Council, 505 U.S. 1003 (1992).

Section 2. The judicial Power shall extend to all Cases in Law and Equity, arising under this Constitution, the Laws of the United States, and Treaties made, or which shall be made, under their Authority; — to all Cases affecting Ambassadors, other public Ministers and Consuls; — to all Cases of admiralty and maritime Jurisdiction; — to Controversies to which the United States shall be a Party; — to Controversies between two or more States; — between a State and Citizens of another State; — between Citizens of different States, — between Citizens of the same State claiming Lands under Grants of different States, and between a State, or the Citizens thereof, and foreign States, Citizens or Subjects.

In all Cases affecting Ambassadors, other public Ministers and Consuls, and those in which a State shall be Party, the supreme Court shall have original Jurisdiction. In all other Cases before mentioned, the supreme Court shall have appellate Jurisdiction, both as to Law and Fact, with such Exceptions, and under such Regulations as the Congress shall make.

The Trial of all Crimes, except in Cases of Impeachment, shall be by Jury; and such Trial shall be held in the State were the said Crimes shall have been committed; but when not committed within any State, the Trial shall be at such Place or Places as the Congress may by Law have directed.

It is going to be necessary to pass over several questions that these sections raise. For example, you will notice that in Section 2 the federal courts have "power" (often called jurisdiction) over cases and controversies. What is a "case"? What is a "controversy"? What is the distinction between "law" and "equity"? Who is a "citizen" of a state? Consideration of these questions will have to wait until later in law school. For now we shall direct our attention to the primary purpose of this segment: the organization of the federal system of courts.

Carefully reread Section 1 (just quoted above). What does it mean? It says that it *vests* judicial power in a group of courts — the federal courts. Is *all* of the judicial power vested in the federal courts? Certainly not, or there would be no state courts. The phrase "of the United States" gives us a clue to the answer and to what is coming in Section 2.

What is the purpose of the first paragraph of Section 2? Does a federal court have judicial power over:

- All automobile collision cases?
- All lawsuits for broken contracts?
- All criminal cases?

The answer is, obviously from Section 2, "no," in each case. The federal judicial power, though extensive, is a limited rather than a "general" jurisdiction. Essentially it is limited, as is the legislative power of Congress itself, to matters of national, inter-state, or international concern. However, the category of "national, interstate, or international concern" is plenty broad, and a huge quantity of federal litigation, both civil and criminal, occurs every year.

A Note on "Civil" and "Criminal" Cases: Before we look at the particular federal courts, this might be a good time to say something about the distinction between "civil" cases and "criminal" cases. Our case is about a stolen painting, and theft is of course a crime; yet, our case is a civil case, not a criminal one. Why?

As you proceed through your study of law, you will see it is not always easy to tell the difference between criminal and civil proceedings, but in their extremes the distinction is clear. A *civil action* is a lawsuit commenced in order to recover damages for injuries suffered or, less commonly, to obtain some specific per-formance, such as the return of a painting.[17] When private per-sons sue other private persons, the proceeding is a "civil" case, though government entities can also be (and frequently are)

---

[17] That statement will suffice for now. But just tuck away in the back of your legal thinking the idea that a civil action may also be brought for the sole purpose of obtaining a "declaratory judgment," stating what the law on some disputed point actually is.

Historically, a proceeding to compel a person to do (or refrain from doing) an act was usually considered a suit in "equity," while most actions for damages were said to be at "law." Nevertheless, for historical reasons an action in *replevin* to compel return of a chattel is also considered to be at "law."

parties in civil lawsuits. The *plaintiff* commences a civil action for the purpose of obtaining a legal remedy for some wrong committed (allegedly) by the *defendant*. The alleged wrong may take the form of injury to the plaintiff's person or property, a breach of contract, or some other form of harm to a legal interest that the plaintiff claims to have.

By contrast, in a criminal *prosecution* the government (state or federal[18]) proceeds on behalf of the *public generally* against a defendant who allegedly violated some rule of conduct for which the legislature[19] has prescribed a punishment. In theory, the government's primary role in criminal prosecution is not to vindicate the crime victim's private rights but to make the defendant answer for a "wrong against the state."[20] What the government seeks in a criminal case is some form of *punishment* of the defendant, which may be imprisonment or a fine or both (or worse).

When people do things to wrong other people, they often commit a wrong against the state as well. As a result, for many cases two kinds of legal proceedings are possible, both civil and criminal, and sometimes both kinds are brought. When both are brought, the results may not necessarily be the same. You probably remember, for example, that O.J. Simpson was acquitted *criminally* but found responsible *civilly* in the death of his former wife, Nicole. The verdict of "not guilty" in the criminal prosecution, brought by the state of California, did not prevent an opposite result in the subsequent private *civil* action, for "wrongful death," brought by Nicole's family members. One reason that these sorts of

---

[18] The federal government prosecutes for crimes under federal law.

[19] Originally, the criminal law was almost entirely a matter of judge-made common law. Nowadays, by contrast, the prohibitions of the criminal law are almost entirely codified in penal statutes. One recent attempt to punish for a purely *common-law crime* occurred when a prosecutor in Michigan proceeded without a statute against Dr. Kevorkian for the common-law crime of assisting suicide; the attempt ended in acquittal. (Dr. Kevorkian was later convicted under a statute.) *See* Jack Lessenberry, *Jury Acquits Kevorkian in Common-Law Case*, N.Y. TIMES, May 15, 1998, A14.

[20] In medieval England crimes were originally considered to be mainly private affairs, and they were privately prosecuted. The victim went out and got a lawyer to institute the criminal proceedings. The notion of "wrong against the state" and public prosecution came later. Today, the right of private citizens to bring criminal prosecutions has been drastically cut back (for example, to minor crimes called "misdemeanors") or eliminated.

inconsistencies can occur is that there are different *standards of proof* for the two types of proceedings: A criminal conviction requires proof "beyond a reasonable doubt," while liability in civil actions normally requires only a mere "preponderance of the evidence." Another reason for potential inconsistencies is that jury trials are not perfect as fact-finding tools. Even when the same standards of proof apply, such as in separate trials of criminal accomplices, inconsistent verdicts can occur and, in general, the courts are willing to allow inconsistent verdicts to stand.[21]

* * *

Acting under Article III of the Constitution, Congress has established two main levels of courts inferior to the Supreme Court of the United States: the United States District Courts and the United States Courts of Appeals.

1. District Courts: It is in the United States District Court that most of the federal actions are commenced. It is in this court that Mrs. DeWeerth must commence her action *if* she chooses to sue in the federal system. Of all the federal courts, the district courts are the ones most similar to the courts you have probably seen portrayed in legal dramatizations on television and in movies, with one judge presiding over a courtroom, a jury sitting in a jury box, separate tables in front of the judge's "bench" for each of the opposing sides, and, near the judge, a witness stand. It is in these courts that most of the important federal trials, civil and criminal, take place.

There is at least one federal judicial district in each state. New York has four:

- Eastern District (Long Island and Staten Island)
- Southern District (Manhattan, Bronx, Westchester, and near-north counties)

---

[21] *See* Eric L. Muller, *The Hobgoblin of Little Minds? Our Foolish Law of Inconsistent Verdicts*, 111 Harv. L. Rev. 771, 812 (1998) (arguing that the courts' general tolerance of inconsistent verdicts reflects a deep "pro-government bias masquerading as equity").

- Northern District (Greene-Columbia and north, west to Cayuga Lake)
- Western District (roughly, west of Cayuga Lake)

When a plaintiff brings a lawsuit in federal court against a defendant residing in New York City (as Mrs. Baldinger did), the plaintiff may well choose the Southern District of New York as the *venue* for the case.[22] In general, individual federal district courts do not have nationwide jurisdiction. Much like the state courts, they generally can exercise jurisdiction only over cases that have an appropriate jurisdictional (geographical) connection to the district.

Take another look at the portions of Article III of the U.S. Constitution that were set out earlier. As you reread these sections, consider this question: Does an attorney have an option to bring *any* case or controversy in a federal district court, or must certain special facts exist in order to give the federal courts power over the action? Suppose, for example, that Mr. A negligently drives his automobile into one belonging to Ms. B. Both persons are lifelong residents of Westchester County, New York. Can B sue A in the United States District Court for the Southern District of New York? Would your answer be different if A was a lifelong resident of New York and B was a lifelong resident of Connecticut? In this connection, consider the following statute, 28 U.S.C. §1332(a) (2001):[23]

(a) The district courts shall have original jurisdiction of all civil actions where the matter in controversy exceeds the sum

---

[22] Do not confuse "venue" with jurisdiction. As used here, venue simply means the place (court) where the lawsuit is litigated. You will learn in your civil procedure course that there are different rules for determining when a court has "jurisdiction" and when it is a proper "venue" for litigating a case.

[23] What do the various elements of this citation mean? The abbreviation "U.S.C." stands for "United States Code," the official government publication that contains the codified statutory law of the federal government. The first number, 28, tells us the *article* in the United States Code where the statute is found, and the "§1332(a)" tells us the specific section and subsection of the quoted wording. Finally, the parenthetical contains the date in which the particular volume of "U.S.C." was published.

or value of $75,000 exclusive of interest and costs, and is between—

(1) citizens of different States;

(2) citizens of a State and citizens or subjects of a foreign state; * * *

Congress enacted this statute for the purpose of conferring jurisdiction on the federal district courts in so-called "diversity cases," (*i.e.*, in which there is "diversity of citizenship" between the parties).

Would an action by Mrs. DeWeerth against Mrs. Baldinger be a "diversity case" falling within this section? Why? Notice that this statute gives the *option* of going to federal court, but does not mandate it. Plaintiffs in diversity cases generally remain free to bring their actions in state courts if they wish.

Notice, too, that diversity of citizenship alone is not enough to get you into federal court. When considering whether to bring Mrs. DeWeerth's action in federal court, her lawyer, Mr. Horan, had another thing to consider: whether the amount in controversy exceeded the so-called "jurisdictional amount" specified in this statute.[24] But where does the Congress find the constitutional power to require the amount in controversy to exceed $75,000? Look hard at Article III of the Constitution, quoted above. Do you see the basis for this authority? Do we conclude that 28 U.S.C. §1332(a), quoted above, is "unconstitutional"? Don't be too quick: This statute is today being applied by every United States District Court. How?

The district courts are the primary trial courts in the federal system. It is here that the parties have an opportunity to present evidence to support their claims and it is here that the factual issues are resolved. The basic division of labor is that the jury, selected from citizens of the community, decides the questions of fact (who did what, etc.?) and the judge decides the questions of law (what is the legal consequence of the various events

---

[24] At the time, the amount was only $10,000, not $75,000, and the Monet had an estimated value of half a million or more. Still, this "jurisdictional amount" had to be satisfied.

and acts of the people in the case?). The judge also acts as a kind of "referee," making sure the lawyers, in their advocacy zealousness, stay within the procedural bounds.

The decisions of all federal district courts are published in a series of books known as the "Federal Supplement," which is abbreviated "F. Supp." The district court's opinion in *DeWeerth v. Baldinger* can be found in the Federal Supplement at 658 F. Supp. 688 (S.D.N.Y. 1987).[25]

2. United States Courts of Appeals: Ranking immediately above the federal district courts are the United States Courts of Appeals. Whereas many states have two or more federal district courts, there are only 13 courts of appeals for the whole country, one for each of the 13 federal "circuits." Eleven of the federal circuits are numbered, and these numbered circuits each cover a geographical area of at least three states. New York is in the Second Circuit, along with Connecticut and Vermont.[26] The geographically largest circuit is the Ninth, which includes most of the western portion of the county. It is based in San Francisco. The highly populous Fifth Circuit got so many cases that it was divided, a few years ago, into two circuits—the new smaller Fifth Circuit, based in New Orleans, and the Eleventh Circuit, based in Atlanta. Finally, there is a District of Columbia Circuit and a so-called "Federal Circuit," which handles specialized cases—such as patent cases—from around the entire country.

If one of the parties in a federal case believes the district court has made a mistake, the court's action may be appealed to the United States Court of Appeals for the circuit in which the district

---

[25] What do the various elements of this *citation* mean? You know that "F. Supp." refers to the "Federal Supplement." The first number, 658, tells us the volume of the Federal Supplement that contains the case, and the second number, 688, tells us the page number. The specific district court that decided the case is indicated in the parentheses—the "S.D.N.Y."—along with the year of decision. You should by now be able to make a good educated guess as what the abbreviation "S.D.N.Y." stands for. Hint: What would be the abbreviation if the case had been decided in the *Northern* District of New York?

[26] The courthouse for the Second Circuit is at Foley Square, in lower Manhattan, in the courthouse complex that includes the Southern District and the New York County (Manhattan) state courts.

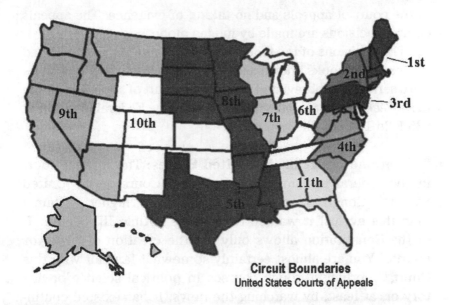

Circuit Boundaries
United States Courts of Appeals

court is located. The court of appeals reviews the legality of what the district court has done and then can *affirm, reverse,* or *modify* the district court's action. This power to review is called "appellate jurisdiction." The decisions of law issued by a court of appeals are binding on all of the district courts within its circuit, but they are not binding on the courts in the other circuits. As a result, "conflicts among the circuits" are not at all uncommon.

While a court of appeals may have a dozen or more active judges at any given time, the work of the court is usually performed by three-judge *panels* who read the parties' *briefs*, listen to their oral arguments, and then decide, by majority vote, the correctness of the lower court's decision. Occasionally, a court of appeals will meet and decide a case *en banc* — with all of the judges participating, but this is relatively rare.[27] There is no jury

---

[27] "[E]n banc procedures are seldom used merely to correct the errors of individual panels: "* * * We take cases en banc to answer questions of general importance likely to recur, or to resolve intracircuit conflicts, or to address issues of transcendent public significance — perhaps even to curb a 'runaway' panel — but not just to review a panel opinion for error, even in cases that particularly agitate judges. . . ." Hart v. Massanari, 266 F.3d 1155, 1172 (9th Cir. 2001), *quoting* EEOC v. Ind. Bell Tel. Co., 256 F.3d 516 (7th Cir. 2001) *(en banc)* (Posner, J., concurring).

in the court of appeals and no taking of evidence. The appeals courts' decisions are made by judges alone.

The decisions of the federal courts of appeals are published in a series of books known as the "Federal Reporter," now in its third series and abbreviated "F.3d". The court of appeals' opinion in *DeWeerth v. Baldinger* can be found in the Federal Reporter at 836 F.2d 103 (2d Cir. 1987).[28]

3. Supreme Court of the United States: The highest court in the federal system is the Supreme Court of the United States.[29] Congress could not establish a "higher" tribunal than this even if it wanted to because Article III, Section 1, of the Constitution allows only for the creation of *"inferior* courts." You are almost certainly somewhat familiar with this Court,[30] perhaps through courses in political science or history or, at least, by watching the news. It has existed continuously since the first appointments were made by President Washington. It is now composed of the Chief Justice and eight Associate Justices. Its sessions are held in the Supreme Court Building in Washington, D.C.[31]

Basically, the Supreme Court is an appellate tribunal. That means its principal function is to listen to and to decide cases that have come to it from inferior federal courts and, sometimes, from the various states' courts. One of the Court's most important functions is to resolve conflicts (or "splits") that arise among the circuits. Technically, litigants usually get their cases before this Court not by an "appeal" but by submitting a document called a "petition for a writ of

---

[28] In which circuit was this appeal decided? When? Is this case in the third series of the Federal Reporter?

[29] *See* U.S. Const. art. III, §1. Can you figure out what this citation means? The provision that is cited was reproduced in these materials a few pages earlier.

[30] Note that the word "Court" is never capitalized in legal writing *except* (1) when referring to the U.S. Supreme Court, (2) when writing out a court's name in full, or (3) when referring in litigation papers to the court that will be receiving the papers.

[31] On the top floor of this building there is a basketball gymnasium, popular among Supreme Court law clerks (recent law grads who work for the justices). They call this facility "the highest court in the land."

certiorari."[32] Only a tiny proportion of these petitions are granted, and the Court renders full decisions in fewer than 100 cases per year. In most cases "certiorari is denied." (Mrs. DeWeerth petitioned twice for certiorari in *DeWeerth v. Baldinger* and both petitions were rejected.)[33]

4. Other Federal Courts: The federal court system also includes a number of courts for various special purposes (such as for tax law disputes, bankruptcy, military justice, eminent domain claims, etc.) plus various "local" courts in U.S. overseas territories, possessions, and the like. These courts may be both courts of first instance (trial courts) as well as some special purpose appellate courts. You do not need to concern yourself about these other courts now, but be aware that they exist.

STATE COURT SYSTEMS

Each state has its own judicial system, which has been created under the state's own constitution and statutes. In general, a state judicial system has direct power ("jurisdiction") only over persons and things within the boundaries of the state. A state court cannot, for example, issue enforceable orders (such as arrest warrants and property seizures) directly to the officers and agents of other states or of the federal government. Likewise, if a state court were to issue a judgment concerning matters having no connection to its territorial jurisdiction, the courts of other states would not have to recognize it. Thus, as a rule of thumb, the state court system has the power to act inside the state's boundaries, except against federal agents and officials. While modern procedure provides various bases for "long-arm" jurisdiction,[34] the effectuation of a court's will

---

[32] Historically, a "writ of certiorari" was an order issued by a higher court directing a lower court to send up the certified record of a case for review. Today, the term is used almost solely to refer to reviews by the U.S. Supreme Court.

[33] 486 U.S. 1056 (1988) and 513 U.S. 1001 (1994).

[34] *See* Chapter V.

outside its territory requires the cooperation of other states' courts and authorities.

Every state court system is different, but they are broadly similar in their general outlines. Many state court systems have, like the federal system, three principal levels of courts:

1. trial courts
2. intermediate appellate courts
3. a court of last resort (typically called the "supreme court")

These three levels of courts are arranged in pyramidal structure depicted in Figure 1, and this arrangement is typical of the court systems found in the more populous states. The main variation among state court systems is that some states do not have the intermediate level of appellate courts. In those states, appeals from the trial courts go directly to the highest court of the state. Another notable variation among the states is in the *names* of the courts at the different levels, especially at the trial level. As described further below, the courts' names vary considerably from state to state.

FIGURE 1

Typical Pyramidal Court System
Trial Courts, Courts of Appeals, Supreme Court

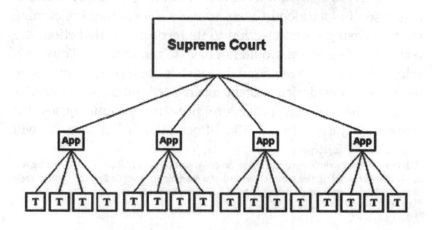

1. Trial Courts: Every state has one or more sets of courts to hear cases in the first instance, taking evidence and rendering judgment. Most cases not only start but also end at the trial-court level, usually by settlement or, in the case of criminal prosecutions, by a plea of guilty to an agreed charge or charges (a so-called plea bargain). In most states there is at least one trial court that has *general jurisdiction*, for cases in both law and equity.[35] In New York, this court of general jurisdiction is called the "Supreme Court of New York" (New York court names are, from the national perspective, particularly idiosyncratic). More commonly, trial level courts of general jurisdictions have such names as "district court," "circuit court," "superior court," and "court of common pleas." In addition, most states have, in addition to their courts of general jurisdiction, a welter of other trial-level courts, including municipal courts (*e.g.*, "city courts") and often various special purpose courts, such as the "Probate Courts" and "Family Courts."[36]

To say that a court has "general" jurisdiction means that, at least in theory, *any* kind of case (almost) can be commenced there. As a practical matter, however, when a municipal or specialized court also has jurisdiction to handle a case, there typically are significant procedural deterrents to discourage litigants from using the court of general jurisdiction instead. Therefore, trial litigation in the courts of general jurisdiction is, at least in the more populous states, more or less confined to higher-value civil matters and the more serious criminal cases.

Although the territorial jurisdiction of state trial courts is generally statewide, that does not mean that any case can be brought in any of the courts that happen deal with the particular subject matter involved. Typically there are rules concerning proper *venue*, which require that a legal action be commenced in a court having an appropriate geographical connection to the facts or parties in the case — a kind of rough protector against

---

[35] *See supra* note 16.
[36] In case you're curious, what makes the New York Supreme Court "supreme" is that it is higher than the other trial-level courts.

being forced to defend at a pointlessly distant location. In New York, for example, for most practical purposes the proper choice of venue for a case is determined on a county-by-county basis. However, the rules for proper venue vary from state to state, and you will learn more about them in your courses on civil procedure.

In their overall function the state trial courts are comparable to the federal district courts. The state trial courts of general jurisdiction are typically the ones most similar to the courts portrayed in legal dramatizations, with a presiding judge, a jury in its jury box, tables in front of the judge's bench for the opposing sides, and a witness stand near the judge. The lesser trial courts are similar in their overall look and feel but often are streamlined in various respects. For example, some of them rarely or never have juries, and often they run through dockets of dozens of cases per day.

One last terminological note: The judges who staff the United States Supreme Court are officially known as "justices" (just as, but the way, are the judges of the New York "Supreme Court," which handles trials). The judges of most other trial and appellate courts are called "judges," as are the judges of federal district courts and courts of appeal.

2. State Courts of Appeals: In most states, but not all, there is a level of appellate courts lying between the trial courts and the state's highest court. Typically these mid-level courts are referred to as "courts of appeal," though here again there are some variations. (The intermediate appellate courts in New York, for example, are known officially as the "Appellate Division of the Supreme Court of New York." That is to say, New York's intermediate appellate courts are, in form, a special subdivision of the same institution that contains the trial courts.) The primary job of the state's appellate courts is to hear and decide cases in which one of the parties is claiming that the lower court made some mistake of law.

Typically the state courts of appeal operate within defined appellate districts, similar to the "circuits" of the courts of appeal at the federal level. Thus, a state court of appeals normally receives appeals only from the trial courts within its own designated portion of the state. This raises the question, which occasionally comes up, of what happens if a state's intermediate appellate courts reach different conclusions (in different but similar cases) on a particular point of law?

You will recall that at the federal level a legal decision issued by a court of appeals is not legally binding on the courts (district or appellate) in the other federal circuits. As a result, "conflicts among the circuits" often occur. Within the state systems, however, there is some variation. In California, for instance, "an opinion by one of the [intermediate] courts of appeal is binding on all trial courts in the state, not merely those in the same district. . . . However, court of appeal panels are not bound by the opinions of other panels, even those within the same district."[37] In New York, by contrast, the courts take the federal approach. The four departments of the appellate division have equal judicial rank and do not have to follow one another's legal interpretations. The trial courts must follow the decisions of their own department's appellate-division court. The law of New York may therefore be one thing in part of the state and something else in another. Until the state's highest court resolves the discrepancy, both conflicting versions of the law can be said to be "New York State law."

Terminological note: In New York, however, the "Court of Appeals" is not an intermediate appellate court but the highest court of the state. As previously stated, the "Supreme Court of New York" is a trial court.

3. State Supreme Courts: These are the courts that are at the very top of the state court structures. They are the courts "of last resort" to which persons can appeal when they are dissatisfied by the results obtained in the lower courts. If the state does not have any intermediate appellate courts, a dissatisfied trial litigant can appeal to the state's supreme court directly from

---

[37] Hart v. Massanari, 266 F.3d 1155, 1174 n. 30 (9th Cir. 2001).

the trial court. In the more populous states, however, persons dissatisfied at trial have to go to an intermediate appellate court first.

A state's supreme court has final authority in deciding questions of state law. There is no higher court to go to on state law questions. Only in a case where there is a question involving the meaning of a federal statute or the U.S. Constitution can the case be further appealed from the state supreme court to the Supreme Court of the United States. Appeals to the United State Supreme Court are allowed in these latter cases because the Constitution makes federal law the "supreme law of the land," and it is the United States Supreme Court that has the final word on the questions of federal law. If, however, there is no federal law issue in the case, the supreme court of the state has the final word.

We have not mentioned any federal law issues in *DeWeerth v. Baldinger* and, seemingly, none was litigated. Therefore, if the case had been brought in one of New York's state courts, it would never have been eligible for appeal to the United States Supreme Court; the New York Court of Appeals is where the case would stop (if it even got *that* far). The remote possibility of an appeal to the United State Supreme Court is not, however, much of a consideration in choosing where to sue. The likelihood of a case being accepted by the United States Supreme Court is so minuscule anyway. (As noted earlier, the two petitions for Supreme Court review made in *DeWeerth v. Baldinger* were both rejected.)

4. Other State Courts: As already mentioned, in addition to the main three (or two) levels of courts, states also have a number of other courts or relatively freestanding court divisions for various special purposes (probate, juvenile and family matters, condemnation claims against state, etc.), plus a range of municipal courts, such as township courts, village courts, city courts, county courts, criminal courts, and so on. These are invariably courts of first instance, *i.e.*, not appellate courts. A few states also have limited jurisdiction appeals courts. You do not need to learn any details about them now, but just be aware they exist and may be mentioned in your readings.

THE BEST COURT FOR MRS. DeWEERTH?

Having decided to sue in New York, Mrs. DeWeerth had the option of bringing her action either in the federal court system or in the Supreme Court of New York. Her civil action was of a type that fell within the jurisdictional power of either of these courts. It was therefore up to Mr. Horan to advise her which way to go.

Which forum would you have advised, state court or federal? There are a number of considerations. One court system may have a lighter docket than the other, promising a potentially speedier resolution. The judges in one court system may reputedly be better informed in the particular area of law, or possibly be more likely to lean one way or another. (Why do you think "diversity" jurisdiction was conceived for federal courts in the first place?) In addition, if a jury trial is expected, the pool from which jurors are drawn may be very different in the two court systems. For example, the state court in Manhattan (New York County) draws jurors only from Manhattan Island whereas the district court for the federal Southern District draws jurors from the entire southern region of the state (except Long Island and Staten Island). In the mind of an advocate, depending on the type of case, this *might* make a difference.

Perhaps a more important consideration in forum selection is the rules of procedure that will apply. The procedural rules in the federal courts are not the same as those in state courts. All federal courts use the Federal Rules of Civil Procedure while the state courts each follow the civil practice rules adopted by their own state. In New York the civil procedure rule are contained in the CPLR (the usual abbreviation for the "Civil Practice Law and Rules"). The CPLR differs from the federal rules in many particulars. On the whole, it takes longer to reach final judgment in New York's state courts than it does in the New York-based federal courts. Even in the many states where local procedures are modeled on the federal rules, there are variations in content and implementation, and these may significantly affect the course and duration of litigation in particular cases.

Finally, Mrs. DeWeerth may well want to consider the fact that she would come to court as a foreigner, a person whose claim arose out of the post-war occupation of her country by American soldiers, whom she now accuses of making off with a precious work of art. She would be asserting this claim, moreover, against a respectable American citizen, a woman who purchased the painting in complete good faith. Elements of this factual situation bristle with intangibles that should give Mr. Horan pause. It is not that Mrs. DeWeerth would not receive a fair trial in New York's state courts. No one could say that. On the other hand, the federal district court for the southern district is perhaps especially renowned for the quality and objectivity of its judges, and for the relatively small influence that politics has in their selection. A lawyer in Mr. Horan's position might easily have felt that, for what it was worth, Mrs. DeWeerth might have gained at least a *little* edge for herself if he brought her case in federal court rather than New York Supreme Court.[38]

There is one factor you might think enters into the choice of courts but, at least in theory, does not make a difference at all. That factor is the choice of the applicable *substantive* law. ("Substantive law" refers to the legal rules and standards that define rights and wrongs and, accordingly, who should win the lawsuit, as distinguished from the *procedural* law, which structures the legal proceedings in which the determinations of right and wrong are made.)

We noted earlier that the federal government has its own separate system of laws but that most ordinary private law (including stolen-property law) is traditionally left to the states. In line with this basic division of governmental power, when cases are brought in federal court, that court is supposed to use state law unless a valid federal law, regulation or constitutional provision applies. Thus, if a case is in federal court due solely to "diversity of citizenship" (so there are no

---

[38] For a report of a recent empirical study showing a substantial degree of prejudice against non-American parties litigating in American courts, *see* Kimberly A. Pace Moore, *Xenophobia*, George Mason Law & Economics Research Paper No. 02-05, George Mason University School of Law (2002).

issues of federal law), the federal court is supposed to apply exactly the same substantive law as the local state court would have used to decide the case. Litigants are not supposed to have any incentive to engage in "forum-shopping," looking for a court that will apply a more "favorable" rule of law.

Some degree of "forum shopping" still occurs, of course, because litigants are still able to seek specially favorable *procedural* rules (as described earlier) and other unique advantages that one court system might offer over the other in particular situations. However, the Supreme Court closed off the option of suing in federal court for the purpose of *substantive* law forum-shopping in the landmark case of *Erie RR. v. Tompkins*,[40] decided in 1938. You will no doubt read the *Erie* case later this year in your civil procedure course. Meanwhile, it is enough for you to know that for the *DeWeerth-Baldinger* case the meaning of *Erie* was crystal clear: No matter which court, state or federal, decided their case, the substantive rules and standards were supposed to be exactly the same. There should have been no substantive-law advantage for either party in having the case litigated in this court or that. Such, at least, is the theory.

---

[40] 304 U.S. 64 (1938).

*O*nce Mr. Sills received word that a *summons and complaint* had been served on Mrs. Baldinger, the choice of courts had been made. As the document below indicates, Mrs. DeWeerth had filed a complaint with the federal District Court for the Southern District of New York, at its courthouse in lower Manhattan. According to Rule 3 of the Federal Rules of Civil Procedure: "A civil action is commenced by filing a complaint with the court." A lawsuit has been commenced.

Let's start by taking a look at the summons and complaint. First, here's the summons:

𝔘nited 𝔖tates 𝔇istrict 𝔠ourt
FOR THE
SOUTHERN DISTRICT OF NEW YORK

```
- - - - - - - - - - - - - - - - - - - - -X
                                         :
GERDA DOROTHEA DE WEERTH,                 :        83 Civ. 1233
        Plaintiff,                        :
                                         :
                                         :
              v.                          :        SUMMONS
                                         :
                                         :
EDITH MARX BALDINGER,                     :
        Defendant                         :
                                         :
- - - - - - - - - - - - - - - - - - - - -X
```

To the above named Defendant:

You are hereby summoned and required to serve upon FOX GLYNN & MELAMED,

plaintiff's attorneys, whose address is One Broadway, New York, New York 10004,

an answer to the complaint which is herewith served upon you, within 20 days after service of this summons upon you, exclusive of the day of service. If you fail to do so, judgment will be taken against you for the relief demanded in the complaint.

Signed: *Raymond F Burghardt, Clerk*

Clerk of Court

Dated: February 16, 1983

[Seal of Court]

This summons is issued pursuant to Rule 4 of the Federal Rules of Civil Procedure.

Carefully examine the summons and notice:

- the person that this summons is *issued by*.
- the person that this summons is addressed *to*.
- the legal document that is *served with* the summons.
- what the addressee of the summons is required to do.
- what happens if she does not do it.

The *summons* can, of course, be an exceptionally conse-quential piece of paper. If the recipient does not answer in a timely way, "judgment will be taken against [her] for the relief demanded in the complaint." What makes this little piece of paper so special? By what specific authority does it carry such dire possibilities for Mrs. Baldinger, forcing her to do things she'd rather not do, to spend her money on big legal fees she'd rather not have to pay, and to change the course of her life, her plans, in many ways, large and small? The answer is, of course, visible right at the bottom of the summons, where it was signed and sealed by an agent of the government, the Clerk of Court, who has issued it. Specifically, it has been issued and *served* pursuant to Rule 4 of the Federal Rules of Civil Procedure, which reads in part:

> **(b) Issuance.** Upon or after filing the complaint, the plain-tiff may present a summons to the clerk for signature and seal. If the summons is in proper form, the clerk shall sign, seal, and issue it to the plaintiff for service on the defendant. * * *
> **(c) Service with Complaint; by Whom Made.**
> (1) A summons shall be served together with a copy of the complaint. The plaintiff is responsible for service of the summons and complaint within the time allowed[40] . . . and

---

[40] In general, the summons and complaint must be served within 120 days after the complaint is filed. If it is not (except for good cause shown), the court shall either (1) order service within a specified time or (2) dismiss the action "without prejudice." FED. R. CIV. P. 4(m). The words "without prejudice" mean the plaintiff can re-file the complaint and start over again — provided, of course, the statute of limitations has not run out in the meantime.

shall furnish the person effecting service with the necessary copies of the summons and complaint.

(2) Service may be effected by any person who is not a party and is at least 18 years of age. At the request of the plaintiff, however, the court may direct that service be effected by a United States marshal, deputy United States marshal, or other person or officer appointed by the court for that purpose. * * *

(*l*) **Proof of Service.** [T]he person effecting service shall make proof thereof to the court. . . . [If service is not by U.S. marshal], the person shall make an affidavit thereof. * * *

According to Rule 4 (just quoted), answer the following:

- Who physically prepares the summons?
- How does the summons get signed and sealed, so that it is "official"?
- Does the clerk have *discretion* as to whether to sign, seal, and issue the summons?
- How does the summons get into the hands of the defendant?
- How does the court know that the summons actually got into the defendant's hands?

Obviously, a main function of the summons is to *notify* the defendant that a civil action has been filed against her, and that an "answer" must be provided to the plaintiff's counsel by a definite date. Merely filing the complaint in the courthouse would not provide this notice and, without some sort of notification mechanism, people would have no way of knowing they had been sued and were at risk of a default judgment.

Yes, you might be thinking, but couldn't the complaint alone serve the exact same purpose as the "summons and complaint"? The complaint has to be served anyway, along with the summons. Why the added piece of paper for the summons itself, instead of just adding a few words to the complaint? Perhaps the ultimate answer is just "tradition." There is, however, at least a superficial rationale for continuing the tradition, and that is this:

Although the complaint is the plaintiff's document, prepared *and issued* by the plaintiff, the summons is the *court's* document by which the court officially subjects the defendant to the court's jurisdiction. It is, moreover, the court's certification to the defendant that a lawsuit has in fact been commenced, *viz.* that the complaint has actually been filed.

Okay, you may say, but that still does not explain the "service" requirements. Why not just mail the defendant a letter — or a registered letter — or give him a ring on the phone, or send an email? Why the ritualistic mumbo jumbo about service, proof of service, affidavits, and all that? The answer is that the requirement of "service of process" had (and to a lesser extent, still has) a significant *jurisdictional* function.

Under historically rooted notions of justice and jurisdiction, a court could not attach personal control over a defendant who was totally *in absentia.* Courts were able to reach only those persons who could be found, for at least a crucial moment, within their territories. Traditionally, this meant that a court official had to "catch" and serve a defendant while the latter was physically present within the court's jurisdictional boundaries before the court could obtain the legal *power* to bind the defendant, personally, by its judgments.[41]

While this historical approach of jurisdiction by presence-plus-service is still one of the ways of subjecting a person to a court's power, it is no longer the exclusive way of doing so. During your law studies you will learn about many other techniques and theories (such as "long-arm" jurisdiction), and today it is probably more accurate to say that the former general rule, sometimes dubbed the "tag" rule, has been totally replaced by a different general rule, a constitutional rule, of "minimum contacts." A person cannot be subjected to a court's power unless

---

[41] By way of contrast, in some European civil law systems, a defendant can be held to answer for a personal judgment in virtually any amount if, merely, an item of his property is found in the territorial jurisdiction of the court. In a much-noted case, for example, a world famous Olympic skier was held personally liable for a large paternity judgment in a country he had once visited even though his only jurisdictional "contact" with the court consisted of an article of underwear, inadvertently left behind.

the person has at least "minimum contacts" with the jurisdiction. Consider, for example, the following cases:

Case 1. Silvia Gorman was traveling on business between Boston and Washington, D.C. While her train was passing through Pennsylvania, she was served with a Pennsylvania summons and complaint. She has no other connection with the state of Pennsylvania. Do you think it would be in accordance with justice and due process of law for the Pennsylvania courts to have the power to render a binding judgment against her merely because she was successfully "nabbed" in Pennsylvania? How about if she was served while flying over Pennsylvania in an airplane?

Case 2. Raymond Selmer drove his automobile through North Carolina on his way from Florida, his home, to a friend's house in Boston. While in North Carolina, his car was involved in a rear-end collision caused by the sole fault of the other driver. Now the other driver is suing Selmer for damages, alleging that Selmer was the one at fault. Do you think it would be in accordance with justice and due process of law to compel the other driver to go to Florida to bring her lawsuit against Selmer, or should the North Carolina courts have the power to compel Selmer to return to the state to defend himself against the allegations?

Case 3. William Dover lives in Michigan and has no contacts with Oregon except that he once used an Internet auction site to sell an electric saw to a buyer who lives in Oregon. Dover negligently failed to inform the buyer that the saw has an intermittent short-circuit inside, which can cause it unexpectedly to become "hot" with 120-volt current. The first time the buyer used the saw, it shorted out, causing the buyer serious injury — nearly electrocuting him. Should the buyer be compelled to go to Michigan to bring his lawsuit for the injuries suffered? Suppose the seller was a manufacturer who sells thousands of power saws, via channels of distribution, into Oregon but has no direct contacts with the state?

These cases are meant to illustrate why no cut and dried geographical rule of jurisdictional reach seems quite appropriate, even though our sense of justice suggests there should be at least some limits on the geographical power of courts. We may wish to allow "long-arm" jurisdiction and alternative service-of-process in a variety of cases but, at the same time, not wish to be vulnerable to lawsuits and huge judgments in places we've never been, thousands of miles from home.

Consider:

- What if Mrs. DeWeerth had sued Mrs. Baldinger in Germany, where the theft occurred; would that seem "just"?
- Why, on the other hand, should Mrs. DeWeerth be forced to sue in the United States when it was not her fault in any way that somebody had unlawfully transported her painting here?
- Suppose Mrs. DeWeerth had lived in Alaska at the time the painting had been stolen from her possession. Would you feel any better about forcing Mrs. Baldinger, a resident of New York, to go and defend in Alaska?

In any event, even though the old geographic "nabbing" principle of personal jurisdiction has effectively been supplanted as the *general* principle, it still remains as a special case; it still suffices to give a court personal jurisdiction if the defendant can be served with process inside the court's territorial jurisdiction. Personal service of process gives the court judicial power over the defendant's person, and it gives the defendant notice. When Mrs. Baldinger received the summons in our case, she learned both that an action had been commenced against her and that the United States District Court for the Southern District of New York had asserted its judicial power over her person.

Mr. Horan had pushed the button and the judicial machinery was rolling. It was up to Mr. Sills to take the next step.

His next step would almost certainly be to read the complaint.

THE COMPLAINT

*t*he civil action known as *DeWeerth v. Baldinger* was commenced when Mr. Horan filed the complaint on the next page, on behalf of Mrs. DeWeerth, at the federal courthouse.

Notice in reading the complaint that, unlike the standard "boilerplate" of the summons we saw in the last chapter, the wording of the complaint is tailored closely to the specific facts of the case. Carefully consider the words and allegations chosen by Mr. Horan in light of what you already know about the law that appears to apply.

UNITED STATES DISTRICT COURT
SOUTHERN DISTRICT OF NEW YORK

- -X
                                      :
       GERDA DOROTHEA DE WEERTH,   :
                         Plaintiff,   :   83 Civ. 1233
                                      :
             -against-   :   COMPLAINT
                                      :
       EDITH MARX BALDINGER,   :
                         Defendant.   :
                                      :
- -X

     Plaintiff, Gerda Dorothea De Weerth, by her attorneys,
Fox Glynn & Melamed, complaining of the defendant, Edith Marx
Baldinger, alleges as follows:

     1. Plaintiff is a citizen of the Federal Republic of Germany,
residing at Kurfurstenallee 1a, Bonn-Bad Godesberg.

     2. Defendant is a citizen of State of New York, residing at
710 Park Avenue, New York, New York 10016.

     3. The matter in controversy, exclusive of interest and costs,
exceeds the sum of $10,000.

     4. The jurisdiction of the court over the subject matter is
based on diversity of citizenship, 28 U.S.C. Sec. 1332 (a)(2).

     5. Plaintiff is the owner of a unique painting by Claude Monet
known as "Champs de Blé à Vetheuil", having the dimensions
25-$^1/_2$ × 31-$^3/_4$ inches, signed and dated "Claude Monet '79"
(the "Painting"). The Painting has a value of approximately
$500,000.

     6. On August 31, 1943, during World War II, plaintiff stored the
Painting for safekeeping in the family castle at Oberbalzheim,
Germany. During the occupation of said castle by American troops
in the period April–July, 1945, the Painting was stolen or
otherwise removed from said castle.

     7. In December, 1982, plaintiff learned that defendant is the
possessor of the Painting, and on December 27, 1982, plaintiff made
written demand upon defendant for return of the Painting.

     8. On February 1, 1983, by written reply to the demand of
plaintiff, defendant refused to return the Painting to plaintiff.

9. Plaintiff is entitled to the Painting, and defendant is a converter and in wrongful possession thereof.

WHEREFORE, plaintiff demands judgment against defendant awarding the return of the Painting and the costs and disbursements of this action, and such other and further relief as the Court may deem just.

Dated: New York, New York
       February 9, 1983

                              FOX GLYNN & MELAMED
                              Attorneys for Plaintiff

                              By: _____
                                        A Partner

                              One Broadway
                              New York, New York 10004
                              (212) 555-1234

THE CONTENT OF PLEADINGS

A complaint is a kind of document known as a *pleading*. Pleadings are the papers that the parties exchange in order to let each other know the basic nature of the legal and factual positions they intend to assert in the lawsuit. In earlier times, there were many kinds of "pleadings" but in modern civil practice most of them have been abolished. Other than the complaint, the most important pleading still in use today is the *answer*. The defendant serves the answer in response to the complaint. Although there are also a number of other pleadings for use in special situations, let us for now focus on the main pleadings used in virtually every civil action, first the complaint, then the answer.

According to Rule 8 of the of the Federal Rules of Civil Procedure, a complaint must contain:

"(1) a short and plain statement of the grounds upon which the court's jurisdiction depends . . . ,

(2) a short and plain statement of the claim showing that the pleader is entitled to relief, and

(3) a demand for judgment for the relief the pleader seeks. * * * "

Do you see where and how each of these three "essentials" is contained in the complaint that Mr. Horan prepared on behalf of Mrs. DeWeerth? It should now be very clear why it was so important for Mr. Horan to determine all the relevant facts *before* he commenced the action. In his very first paper, the complaint, he had to tell the essential core of Mrs. DeWeerth's story to the court and to the defendant.

Neither statements of law nor recitations of evidence are necessary or, in theory, even proper in a pleading (though lawyers frequently include them and opponents rarely move to strike them). Notice that the complaint in this case sets out none of the *law* applicable to the facts it alleges, nor does it say why any of the facts are legally important. Neither does it recite any of the *evidence* that will be presented in support of the factual contentions alleged. The reason for this approach is largely historical. Prior to the middle of the nineteenth century, pleadings were highly artificial and formalistic documents. Actually, they provided only broad generalities of what really happened, often leaving the defendant and his attorney in the dark as to the real nature of the cause of action. The reforms made in the last half of the nineteenth century required pleadings to state facts, leaving the arguments of law and production of evidence to later stages of the trial.

Even without assertions of law or recitations of evidence, however, Mr. Sills should have had no difficulty seeing what Mrs. DeWeerth was after or the intended legal basis for her claims. The legal principles on which the plaintiff is relying are thickly implicit in the facts that are alleged. Each of these alleged facts (most of them, anyway) is legally significant — they are the kinds of facts that, if proved, will make a legal difference and, taken together, will be the basis for deciding who is entitled to the painting.

THE COMPLAINT'S LEGAL SUFFICIENCY — A MOTION TO DISMISS

Now it is time for Mr. Sills to begin preparing a response to the complaint, to review the results of his research to date and, perhaps, do a little more. Remember, the summons says, in accordance with the Federal Rules, that Mr. Sills has 20 days to answer. In actuality, however, he probably has more time than that: *Extensions* of time to file papers are very commonly requested from, and granted by, opposing counsel. Such courtesies are common among busy members of the bar. A lawyer might, of course, decide to play "hardball" and insist on strict compliance with one of the time limits, and possibly achieve a temporary advantage as a result. In doing so, however, the lawyer incurs a distinct risk of getting back some hardballs in return. Most lawyers agree that, on the whole, practicing with "civility" works to everybody's advantage, even in the most hotly contested litigation. But isn't it "disloyal" to your client not to grab every advantage you can? What would you do if asked for an extension?

Mr. Sills probably concluded that, on its face, Mrs. DeWeerth's complaint looked legally sufficient. Filed complaints usually do, as long as the drafter was halfway competent (and Mr. Horan was certainly far more than that). Here, all the key *elements* of plaintiff's cause of action seem to be in place: that Mrs. DeWeerth owned the Monet, that it was taken from her, that Mrs. Baldinger now has it, and that a demand has been made and refused. This definitely seems to state a "claim showing that the pleader is entitled to relief" under the New York law that we looked at briefly in Chapter II. But wait, Mr. Sills might well have asked himself. Who says New York law should apply to this case at all? What about German law?

As with any international (or interstate) set of facts, this one presents the threshold legal question: Whose law should apply? A valuable art object has been stolen in a foreign country, and then it winds up here in the United States. Whose law determines the ownership, the law of the foreign country in which the object was stolen or the law of the state where the object is now? Note, too, an added complication: Because this case involves property that has been transported across international boundaries, the situation might even be the subject of federal legislation, enacted by Congress.[42] (The Constitution gives Congress the power to regulate interstate and international commerce.) Mr. Horan and Mr. Sills certainly needed to check for such a statute but, as of the date of *DeWeerth v. Baldinger*, no applicable federal legislation had been enacted. In the absence of a congressional statute, therefore, the federal court should (as you will recall) apply the same law that the state courts would apply. That still leaves the question, though, of which law would New York state courts apply to determine the question of ownership — German law or the law of New York State?

This choice-of-law question is not just an arid technical issue. The final outcome of the case may well turn on whose laws of ownership the court decides to use, those of Mrs. Baldinger's jurisdiction or those of Mrs. DeWeerth's. This question, on which all the rest may ultimately depend, is determined using rules and standards found in a legal subject area known as "conflict of laws." (In your later years of law study you will be offered a course called Conflict of Laws, and you will find that very similar considerations apply whether the conflict is international, as here, or interstate.) Before we go further, however, let's look at some "policy" considerations that bear on the choice of law.

Suppose somebody broke into your home, here in the United States, and stole something you value very much. Then, later, the thief is somehow discovered in his own country in Europe, Africa, or Asia. He still has your property. You try to get your

---

[42] If you are interested in this issue, you might want to take a look, sometime later, at the federal statute known as the Convention on Cultural Property Implementation Act, 19 U.S.C. §2610 et seq. (1983), which gives the force of U.S. law to pieces of *international law* (treaties), namely, the 1954 Convention on the Protection of Cultural Property in the Event of Armed Conflict (the "1954 Hague Convention"), 249 U.N.T.S. 215 and the UNESCO Convention on the Means of Prohibiting and Preventing the Illicit Transport, Export and Transfer of Ownership of Cultural Property (the "UNESCO Convention"), 823 U.N.T.S. 231 (1972).

property back but are told that, due to some technicality of law in the thief's home country, you cannot have it — maybe you had to file a police report within a certain time or else there would be a presumption of a "gift" under the foreign law. Seem fair? Whatever you may think of the foreign law's intrinsic fairness (or lack), does it seem right to you that you should be subject to it at all? Why should you, the victim of a theft here in the United States, be subjected to foreign law? Basically, this is what Mrs. DeWeerth was facing.

On the other hand, suppose you buy a classy wristwatch in the town where you live (a Rolex, or something) and you pay lots of your hard-earned money for it. You are then sued in your local state court by some guy who claims the watch was stolen from him, in a country you have barely heard of. Does it seem fair that you might lose the watch because your local court decides to apply some rule of *foreign* law? Why on earth should Mrs. Baldinger have her rights decided by German law? These considerations (among others) are part of what make choice-of-law questions sometimes difficult.

Before going too far worrying about choice of law, however, Mr. Sills would probably want to get a fairly good idea of how the German law on ownership would apply in this case. It might turn out to be favorable to his client, or it might be extremely unfavorable. Either way Mr. Sills needs to know. Most American lawyers have little or no knowledge of European legal systems, so a consultation with an expert on German law would probably be in order. Let's assume that Mr. Sills made an inquiry and received an opinion letter that included the following:

Law Offices of Gustaf Keinmann

Dear Mr. Sills:

   We have reviewed the facts you provided us and examined the
applicable portions of the German Civil Code. Here are our
conclusions:

                            * * *

   Under the German Civil Code, Mrs. DeWeerth's claim would be
subject to the doctrine of "Ersitzung," which roughly means the
same thing as "prescription" in American law. Specifically, under
§937 of the Code:

      "(1) A person who possesses a movable thing for ten years
      acquires the ownership (prescription).

         "(2) The prescription is precluded if the possessor does
      not acquire the possession in good faith or if he later learns
      that he does not have the ownership."[43]

                                         Very truly yours, etc.

                                         Gustaf Keinmann
                                         Rechtsanwalt

From the standpoint of Mrs. Baldinger, this letter looks very
good indeed. Mr. Sills should be delighted. Do you see why?
   Consider:

---

[43] Translation by author: In this day of burgeoning globalization, American lawyers
still depend on foreign counsel not merely to help them interpret foreign laws but even
to read them. This is not ideal. If you can read some German, you might want to take
a look at the original, in German:

Bürgerliches Gesetzbuch §937:

(1) Wer eine bewegliche Sache zehn Jahre im Eigenbesitz hat, erwirbt das Eigentum
     (Ersitzung).
(2) Die Ersitzung ist ausgeschlossen, wenn der Erwerber bei dem Erwerb des Eigenbesitzes
     nicht in gutem Glauben ist oder wenn er später erfährt, dass ihm das Eigentum nicht
     zusteht.

   As the district court opinion summarized this law: "title to movable property may
be obtained by good faith acquisition of the property plus possession of it in good
faith, and without notice of a defect in title, for . . . ten years from the time the rightful
owner loses possession." DeWeerth v. Baldinger, 658 F. Supp. 688, 692 n.3 (S.D.N.Y.
1987). Do you see the possibly important discrepancy between this translation and the
translation in the letter quoted above?

- How long has Mrs. Baldinger possessed the painting?
- Did she acquire possession of the painting in good faith?
- How long did she possess it before learning that her ownership was defective? Therefore . . .

In short, it looks like Mrs. DeWeerth would not have a very good case at all under the German law of ownership, assuming it applies. On the contrary, it is *Mrs. Baldinger* who would have the better case under German law, because she possessed the painting for over 25 years and during that time she never had notice of any adverse claim. Indeed, it appears almost certain that Mrs. Baldinger would now be considered the painting's owner under the German Civil Code. For Mrs. DeWeerth, by contrast, getting the federal court to use New York law, and not the law of her own country, may be her only chance of recovering the painting.

Suddenly it looks as though the choice-of-law rules might control the outcome of the case. If Mr. Sills can persuade the court to apply German ownership law, and not New York's, then the complaint filed by Mrs. DeWeerth is not legally sufficient, and his client gets to keep the Monet. Specifically, he needs to convince the court that New York's own choice-of-law rules would call for the law of Germany to apply in this kind of a case. If he can convince the court of this right away, he can save Mrs. Baldinger the risk of a trial as well as a huge amount of litigation expense. A quick look at the Federal Rules would have shown Mr. Sills that Mrs. Baldinger legally may not even *have* to answer the summons and complaint served by Mrs. DeWeerth. For Rule 12(b)(6) of the Federal Rules of Civil Procedure states:

> [T]he following defenses may at the option of the pleader be made by motion: ∗ ∗ ∗
>
> (6) failure to state a claim upon which relief can be granted. . . .

Pursuant to this Rule 12(b)(6), Mr. Sills might have made a so-called "12(b)(6)" motion such as the one that follows:

UNITED STATES DISTRICT COURT
SOUTHERN DISTRICT OF NEW YORK

- X
                                                    :
            GERDA DOROTHEA DE WEERTH,   :
                              Plaintiff,   :   83 Civ. 1233
                                                    :
                    -against-   :   *Notice of Motion*
                                                    :
            EDITH MARKS BALDINGER,   :
                     Defendant.   :
                                                    :
- X

   Please take notice that upon the annexed affidavits of Edward
M. Sills, sworn to the 9th of April, 1983, and of Gustaf Keinmann,
sworn to the 9th of April, 1983, and upon Defendant's Memorandum of
Law submitted herewith, and upon all the papers and proceedings
heretofore had herein, the undersigned will move this Court, at a
motion term thereof to be held at the Courthouse, Foley Square,
New York, New York, on the 30th of April, 1983, at 10:00 o'clock
in the forenoon of that day or as soon thereafter as counsel may be
heard, for an order pursuant to Fed. R. Civ. P. 12(b)(6) dismissing
the action because the complaint fails to state a claim against
defendant upon which relief can be granted.

   Dated: New York, New York
           April 9, 1983

                                    _____

                                    EDWARD M. SILLS
                                    Attorney for Defendant
                                    225 Broadway
                                    New York, New York 10007
                                    Tel. No.: (212) 555-6789

   To: John R. Horan, Esq.
        Attorney for Plaintiff
        One Broadway
        New York, New York 10004

   Do you see the specific basis on which Mr. Sills might make a
motion such as this? Observe that the motion document asserts
that the complaint fails to state "a claim . . . upon which relief
can be granted," but it does not say *why* it fails. This is not,

however, something Mr. Sills should leave for the court to speculate about. Normally, a motion like this one would be accompanied by supporting documents, including a "memorandum of law" and one or more affidavits.[44] The opposing party is then given the opportunity to oppose the motion, with her own memorandum of law and affidavits. Often a hearing is held, where the parties' attorneys can present the judge with legal arguments in support of and opposed to the motion.

The major legal question presented by this motion is, of course, the "conflict of laws" question. Specifically, it is this: Under the New York law on "conflict of laws," and given all the allegations of Mrs. DeWeerth's complaint, should the court apply the New York law of ownership, or should it instead apply the German Civil Code provision on "Ersitzung" (prescription) and immediately dismiss the lawsuit against Mrs. Baldinger?

Where do Mr. Sills and Mr. Horan go to find the New York law on "conflict of laws," so they can write their respective memoranda of law? How do they find out which body of ownership law a New York state court (and, hence, the federal court) would apply in this case? Where does the judge go to find out? The answer is not fixed by any statute. To find the applicable choice-of-law rule, the lawyers and judge will look to see what courts have done in similar situations in the past. They will look to see what the precedents are. In short, the question of which ownership should apply in this case is a question of *common law*.

In the next chapter we will take an extended look at the common law and how it works. First, however, let's take a look at how Judge Broderick responded to the "choice of law" issues that were raised in *DeWeerth v. Baldinger*.

---

[44] Affidavits are sworn written statements given under penalty of perjury. Ordinarily, questions of foreign law are treated as matters of "fact" by American courts, and an expert's affidavit would be used to inform the court as to the effect of the foreign law on the facts of the case at hand.

DECISION ON MOTION TO DISMISS

After the district judge has considered the parties' motion papers, memoranda of law, affidavits (if any) and other supporting documents, a ruling would be issued. Here is Judge Broderick's opinion on the choice of law question. As you read it, be especially on the lookout for the *basis* on which Judge Broderick decides the way he does: What *legal authority* does he rely on? What are the *reasons* for the decision, as expressed by Judge Broderick and the authority he cites?

DeWeerth v. Baldinger
658 F. Supp. 688 (S.D.N.Y. 1987)

BRODERICK, District Judge

[For the judge's recitation of the facts, *see* Chapter II.]

Under *Klaxon Co. v. Stentor Electric Manufacturing Co.*, 313 U.S. 487, 85 L. Ed. 1477, 61 S. Ct. 1020 (1941), in this diversity action I must apply the same substantive law that New York would apply, including New York's choice of law rules. The question [presented by this motion to dismiss] is whether, under New York choice of law theory, German or New York law is applicable to determine who owns the Monet.

In resolving this issue, I am guided by *Kunstsammlungen Zu Weimar v. Elicofon*, 536 F. Supp. 829, 845 (E.D.N.Y. 1981), *aff'd*, 678 F.2d 1150, 1160 (2d Cir. 1982) ("*Elicofon*"), a case upon which both parties rely. In *Elicofon*, a diversity action brought by a German government art museum . . . the court was required to determine the ownership of two Albrecht Duerer portraits executed around 1499. These portraits had been stolen in 1945 from a castle in what is now East Germany and discovered in 1966 at the New York residence of Elicofon, an American citizen, who alleged that he had purchased them in good faith 20 years earlier from an American ex-serviceman who appeared at his Brooklyn home and represented that he had bought them while in Germany. On cross-motions for summary judgment, the district court held for the German government art museum and against Elicofon, finding that the art museum had sufficient ownership interest in the paintings to pursue the action. In doing so, the district court ruled that German law [of *Ersitzung* or "prescription"] was not applicable to determine whether Elicofon acquired title to the paintings. It found that "New York's choice of law dictates that questions relating to the validity of a transfer of personal property are governed by the law of the state where the property is located at the time of the alleged transfer." 536 F. Supp. at 846[, *citing* Wyatt v. Fulrath, 16 N.Y.2d 169, 264 N.Y.S.2d 233, 211 N.E.2d 637 (1965); Zendman v. Harry Winston, Inc., 305 N.Y. 180, 111 N.E.2d 871 (1953); Hutchison v. Ross, 262 N.Y. 381, 187 N.E. 65 (1933); Goetschius v. Brightman, 245 N.Y. 186, 156 N.E. 660 (1927); Restatement (Second) of Conflict of Laws §246 (1971)]. Moreover, it noted that the same result would obtain if it applied the "significant relationship" analysis . . . to the facts of the case, that is, if it determined which state had the most significant relationship to the chattel and to the parties. *Id.*

Applying either analysis dictated the same result in *Elicofon*: New York law applied. The court ruled that "Germany's connection with the controversy [was] not sufficient to justify displacing the rule of *lex loci delictus*." *Id. citing Neumeier v. Kuehner,* 31 N.Y.2d 121, 335 N.Y.S.2d 64, 71, 286 N.E.2d 454 (Ct. App. 1972). It found the fact that the theft of the paintings occurred in Germany was "totally irrelevant to the policy of [German law] to protect bona fide purchasers so as to promote the security of transactions." *Id.* Instead, it found significant contacts with New York:

[T]he contacts of the case with New York, i.e., Elicofon purchased and holds the paintings here, are indeed relevant to effecting [New York's] interest in regulating the transfer of title in personal property in a manner which best promotes its policy. The fact that the theft of the paintings did not occur in New York is of no relevance. In applying the New York rule that a purchaser cannot acquire good title from a thief, New York courts do not concern themselves with the question of where the theft took place, but simply whether one took place.

Similarly, the residence of the true owner is not significant for the New York policy is not to protect resident owners, but to protect owners generally as a means to preserve the integrity of transactions and prevent the state from becoming a marketplace for stolen goods.

* * *

Id. at 846. [On appeal, the Second Circuit affirmed.]

Under *Elicofon*, I find that the law of New York governs all issues in this case, including the question of which party has the superior right to possession of the Monet. New York is the place where the sale of the painting to Mrs. Baldinger occurred and where the Monet is and has been located. The fact, as in *Elicofon*, that the theft of the Monet took place in Germany and not New York is irrelevant, as is the fact that Mrs. DeWeerth is a resident of Germany and inherited the painting while in Germany. New York policy, as described in *Elicofon*, is to protect owners generally "as a means to preserve the integrity of transactions and prevent the state from becoming a market place for stolen goods." This policy warrants the application of New York law in the case before me.

[Motion to dismiss denied.]

STUDY QUESTIONS

The foregoing opinion is presented as an example of how courts reason their way to a conclusion in common-law decision making. In order to be sure you were able to follow the court's reasoning, answer the following (and be ready to do so in class):

1. What was the question presented and decided in Judge Broderick's opinion?
2. What was the primary legal authority (prior case) on which the judge relied?

3. What are "cross-motions for summary judgment" referred to in the second paragraph? (Look up "cross-motions" and "summary judgment" in your law dictionary.)
4. According to the district court in *Elicofon*, when there is a question "relating to the validity of transfer of personal property" which state's law would the New York courts use to decide the question?
5. How did the district court in *Elicofon* know which law (New York's or Germany's) the New York courts would use to decide such questions? What cases did the *Elicofon* judge cite to "prove" this point?
6. The *Elicofon* court mentioned a second test or "analysis" often invoked by New York courts to decide which state's law should apply to a transaction. What was this second test?
7. According to the *Elicofon* case, would this second test have given a different result in that case?
8. What is "*lex loci delictus*"? (Look it up in your law dictionary.) What was the "delictus" (apparently) in *Elicofon*? In what legal jurisdiction did it occur?

> Hint: There are at least two *potential* "wrongs" in this case, each with a different location:
> - The theft of the painting (occurred in Germany)
> - The refusal to return the painting (occurred in New York)

Which of these two wrongs is directly at issue in Mrs. DeWeerth's lawsuit? In which legal jurisdiction did *it* occur? Ergo, you should see, New York law = "*lex loci delictus.*"

9. The court also discussed a second test or "analysis" used by New York courts to decide choice-of-law questions: the "significant relationship" analysis. What are the relevant policy concerns of New York, to protect good faith purchasers or to protect owners?
10. According to Judge Broderick, the *Elicofon* court seemed to think that the German law of *Ersitzung* reflected a "policy of [German law] to protect bona fide purchasers so as to promote the security of transactions." How would the law of

Ersitzing (quoted above in the letter from the German legal expert) tend to do this?

11. In light of the policy goals referred to in the preceding question, why would "the fact that the theft of the paintings occurred in Germany" be "totally irrelevant" to those goals? Why did this irrelevance matter so much in deciding the choice of law issue?

   > Hint: The German law of *Ersitzung* might have been concerned with protecting bona fide purchasers worldwide, but the *Elicofon* case assumed it was not: "Such a concern does not extend to transactions which take place beyond [Germany's] borders," the court explained.

12. Now, the decisive question: Why, specifically, did the court pick New York law as the applicable law? Here, again, are the relevant competing policies:

   German law policy: To protect people who buy in good faith in Germany.

   New York law policy: To protect the true owners of property, wherever they reside.

   ■ Do the facts of this case have "contacts" with Germany relevant to carrying out the German policy? (No; there's no innocent buyer making a purchase in Germany.)

   ■ Do the facts of this case have "contacts" with New York relevant to carrying out the New York policy? (Yes; the stolen item is in New York, which is committed to seeing it get back into the true owner's hands.)

   So, which jurisdiction has the contacts that are most "significant" to carrying out the policies of its law, Germany or New York?

* * *

One last thing before going on: Let's quickly take another look at the *caption*, which appears at the first page of court's opinion in the case. Always pay attention to these captions.

The information they contain can be very important. Here it is again:

DeWeerth v. Baldinger
658 F. Supp. 688 (S.D.N.Y. 1987)

First you see the name of the case, which is taken from the names of the parties. Notice, however, that unlike the official caption you saw in the notice of complaint and motion papers shown earlier, this caption does not include the parties' full names. Instead, a sort of distillation or shorthand is used, and these abbreviated versions of case names are what lawyers normally use when they refer to cases.

Many years ago an elaborate set of rules for citing court opinions and other legal materials was developed by the editors of several prestigious law reviews, and these rules (in their current incarnation) are contained in a special book known as the "Bluebook" (its full name: A UNIFORM SYSTEM FOR CITATION). There is also a more recent and competing citation guide that is called the ALWD Citation Manual. Your choice between these two citation systems will generally be made for you, by your legal writing professor, by your law review editor, and eventually by the rules of the courts in which you practice. Although you don't have to begin learning these rules immediately, now is a good time to start paying attention to the citations in the documents you read. Try to get as much useful information you can out of them and notice their formats — most of which follow the Blue-book, more or less.

Beneath the case name in the box above you see the *citation* of the case, the volume and page of the "Federal Supplement" where you can find the case, along with an indication of the deciding court and the date of the case. *See* footnote 23 on page 40.

A Note on "Briefing" Cases: One of the perennial mysteries for entering law students is the process known as "briefing" cases.

You may find that different professors have different expectations about what case briefs should contain, and these differences may add to the mystery. There are, however, some points of general agreement. Most importantly, just about everyone agrees that students should carefully brief the cases they read and that the briefs should be adequate to prepare the student to recite on and discuss those cases in class.

In terms of content and detail, my own leaning is toward briefs that are brief. I still remember the student who sat next to me during most of my first year. He came to class with briefs that were much longer than mine, sometimes longer than the cases themselves. I genuinely worried I wasn't doing enough. But the following year the poor guy was no longer there. When it comes to briefing, more is definitely not always better.

The work that you do in briefing cases has several different functions, all of which are better served by shorter length: First, and most mundanely, briefing is note taking, the task of jotting down and condensing key ideas so that you can quickly refresh your recollection later. Similar to any other note taking, good briefing will greatly ease the way when you need to look at the case again — or find yourself called on to talk about it in class. Second, briefing is a process of absorbing the important points of the reading into your mind and then putting those ideas into words again as concise expressions of your own, as your own personal understanding of what the case is about. Finally, briefing cases can give you an efficient study tool for use later on, such as when the time comes to get ready for your final examinations. At semester's end, a thousand pages of unprocessed stenography are a very poor study aid, but 50 or so pages of briefs and class notes, carefully distilled to trigger larger recollections in your mind — and short enough to be read through three or four times before the exam — can be a valuable tool indeed.

This is, at any rate, my take on briefing. If some of your own professors want you to do something different, you should of course try to meet their expectations. Meanwhile, here is a sample brief, complete with my favored abbreviations, of the case we have just read and its statement of facts reproduced earlier, in Chapter II.

DeWeerth v. Baldinger —

Facts: A painting belonging to P was stolen in Germany and later purchased in New York by D, a BFP who has held it in New York for many years. P demanded it but D refused to give it back.

Issue: Which S/L should apply, Germany's (where the painting was stolen) or New York's (where painting was purchased and held, and is being detained)?

Held: New York's S/L applies.

Reasoning: Following a precedent on all fours, *Elicofon* the ct ruled that New York law would apply under either
    (a) *lex loci delictus rule*, or
    (b) "*significant Rship*" analysis:
        • *lex loci*: NY was the place of both the wrongful
          transfer to D & of D's refusal to return.
        • "*Signf Rship*": the NY contacts were relevant to
          promoting policy of NY's S/L, *BUT*
          Germany's contacts were irrelevant to
          promoting Germany's policy of its S/L.

(German S/L policy: to protect people who buy in GF in Germany
NY S/L policy: to protect true owners, wherever they reside)

With its abbreviations both of words and ideas, this brief admittedly may not have a lot of meaning to somebody who was not already fairly familiar with case. But for the person who wrote it, the brief should suffice to bring back just about everything, with as little "additional" reading as possible. The point is not comprehensiveness but comprehension, not stenography but distillation — to derive and put down the essence from which the brief's writer can readily reconstitute all else of importance in his or her own mind.

> [T]he most general point of law, if it has one at all, is to establish a justifying connection between past . . . decisions and present coercion. —*Ronald Dworkin*[45]

*M*any non-lawyers believe the way you find the law is to pull down a set of statutes (or find them on a computer), look through them, and pick out the ones that are applicable. You may have noticed, however, that Judge Broderick's decision in the previous chapter did not mention any statutes at all. It was based entirely on case *precedent*, primarily the *Elicofon* case. Obviously, statutes are not the whole of "the law" — far from it. The Anglo-American system of jurisprudence just did not grow that way.

---

[45] RONALD DWORKIN, LAW'S EMPIRE 98 (1986).

In every state but one, the legal system is based on the "common law," which originated in England. The lone exception is Louisiana, whose laws are based on the so-called "civil law." The *common law* and the *civil law* are the two main legal systems that grew up in the Western world. The civil law, which is derived from the old Roman law, came to predominate on the European continent, while the common law ruled in England. Today, both of these legal systems have a reach far beyond their original homelands, as countries throughout Africa, Asia, the Americas, and Oceania borrowed one or the other as the basis for their own national systems of laws. Former English-colonized areas have tended to remain within the common law tradition while areas formerly colonized by France, Spain, Portugal, and the Netherlands tend be civil-law countries. Today roughly two billion people live in common law jurisdictions.[46]

There are, of course, many similarities between these two legal systems, but there are many differences in the detail. Among the more striking differences:

1. Trials in civil law countries are typically conducted as investigative (or "inquisitorial") proceedings in which the search for truth is actively managed by the judge. In turn, the judge's actions are closely monitored and scrutinized by the attorneys who represent the parties. By

---

[46] A terminological note: The term "civil law" has more than one meaning, which makes things a little confusing. In Anglo-American jurisprudence, the term "civil law" usually is used to refer to those areas of our law that apply primarily in disputes between private persons (*e.g.* contracts, torts (injury-compensation) and the details of property ownership), as distinguished from the criminal law, administrative regulatory law, constitutional law, and other legal areas that primarily concern governmental powers and the relationship between government and citizen. At the same time, "civil law" is also the name for a whole legal system, such as Louisiana's.

The term "common law' is also sometimes confusing. Originally it referred to those laws that applied throughout the entire English nation and, accordingly, were "common" to all people of the realm. The common law was thus distinguished from early England's various local laws, which it gradually supplanted. Nowadays, when lawyers speak of the "common law" they generally mean that portion of the law that is found in judicial precedents (*i.e.*, judicial opinions) as opposed to the law that is found in statutes (legislation), administrative regulations, or other similar textual sources.

contrast, the trials in the common law system are normally conducted as so-called "adversary" proceedings, and the parties' attorneys control the production of proof. The judge acts more like an umpire than a manager, refereeing between the zealously contending lawyers.

2. In the civil law system, the main body of the law is embodied in a set of structured and comprehensive legislative enactments, or "codes" (for example, the famous French "Code Civil," adopted under Napoleon). By contrast, in common law jurisdictions much of the law's traditional core has been left in the form of individual case precedents — in opinions issued by courts — and statutory codifications remain a relatively recent and far-from-complete supplement to the case law.

The common law arose during the Middle Ages and, "at its core, was a reflection of custom, [which] had a built-in flexibility that allowed it to change with circumstance."[47] It was not thought necessary to have written laws or statutes in order to reach just solutions to legal problems. Instead, people tended to believe that right and wrong existed as essentially "objective" categories, like north and south, or hot and cold. The normal expectation was that judges could use their powers of reason to determine what is right and what is wrong, as these values were reflected in the customs and mores of the society. The belief that legal decisions should reflect "objective" right and wrong, discoverable through the use of reason, is referred to as the jurisprudence of *Natural Law*. People from the Middle Ages right up till relatively recent times have tended to take Natural Law for granted — either as something ordained by God or simply as something that is inherent in the nature of the world.

At any rate, since early times the reasoned decisions (or "opinions") issued by courts in specific disputes have been regarded as being, at the very least, instructive guidelines for

---

[47] Hart v. Massanari, 266 F.3d 1155, 1167 (9th Cir. 2001).

deciding later cases. As the permanent records of judicial precedents accumulated over the centuries, there was an ever growing stock of prior decisions to look to and an increasing tendency to treat them as binding, and they eventually came to be the basis of the modern legal system that we now refer to as the "common law." Even to this day there are many disputes brought before the courts in which there is no controlling *legislation* on the main substantive points, so the rights and duties of the parties have to be determined *solely* by reference to the common law. People can be required to pay damages, perform various actions and, even, to spend time in jail for violations of these court-recognized rules and standards of conduct, despite the fact that they have violated no written statute whatsoever.[48]

We have already seen how the "choice of law" rules important to *DeWeerth v. Baldinger* continue to exist as an area of common law. Another largely common-law field important to that case is the law of ownership, or *property* law. Consider, for example, the question of who should be recognized as the owner of an object that has been stolen and then purchased later by a totally innocent purchaser. In such a case, one of two innocent persons must suffer (assuming we can't find the thief). Which one? As analyzed under the common law, this question breaks down into two parts.

The first part is easy—who should be entitled to a stolen object as between the original holder and the thief? The correct answer is obvious. The point is, though, that in our legal system the answer was given to us, not by any statute, but as a rule of common law. It is one that goes back, no doubt, to time immemorial.

The second part of the question is closer to our actual case, but presents us with a greater moral quandary: Suppose a thief sells stolen property to a "good faith" purchaser—that is, not to a "fence," but to somebody who pays fair value, honestly

---

[48] As previously noted in Chapter IV, the prohibitions of the criminal law have been almost entirely codified in American jurisdictions, which severely limits the possibility of "time in jail" for violating purely common law.

and without any reason at all to suspect something amiss. Here the law often has no choice but to cause a serious loss to fall on an innocent person, either the original owner (such as Mrs. DeWeerth) or the good faith buyer (such as Mrs. Baldinger). Here again, the applicable law originates in judicial opinions, without the help of a statute. Under the common law of property, as the courts have held for centuries, "[n]o one can transfer to another a better title than he has himself"[49]; since a thief has no title (or, as we sometimes say, has a *void* title), a thief can confer no valid title at all. A buyer from a thief receives only such title as the thief had, namely, a void title. This is the rule that applies even if the buyer was innocent and acted in complete good faith.[50]

Today, of course, legislatures have created vast new areas of law by statute in an effort to deal with new kinds of problems and challenges that were barely known to the earlier common law (for example, environmental and securities law). Also, substantial portions of the common law, such as the criminal law, have now been put into statutory form. Despite these statutory inroads, however, the common-law tradition still ties together the various states' laws into an American legal system and sets our system apart from those in much of the rest of the world. The American legal system (perhaps even including Louisiana) is deeply infused with a consciousness of common-law method and common-law habits of thought.

For instance, a common-law court's interpretation of a statute is not just "one person's opinion" as it would normally be in civil law countries. Rather, in common law jurisdictions, a court's interpretation of a statute is *precedent* and can be binding

---

[49] The phraseology of this maxim is Chancellor Kent's, quoted in Saltus v. Everett, 20 Wend. 267, 275 (N.Y. Ct. Err. 1838). The word "title" is a commonly used synonym for ownership.

[50] In a somewhat odd twist, when a person obtains another's property by *fraud*, as a "con man" does, the defrauder *can* transfer "good" title to a buyer in good faith. Much of this common law has been partially codified in the UNIFORM COMMERCIAL CODE §2-403, a statute that has been adopted in all common-law states. The "UCC" did not apply in DeWeerth v. Baldinger because Mrs. Baldinger purchased the painting before its effective date in New York. *See* 658 F. Supp. at 696 n.13.

legal authority just as any other common-law precedent. Lawyers do not usually refer to the cases interpreting statutes as "common law" (that term being usually reserved for the traditional common-law subject areas). Nonetheless, the judicial decisions that interpret statutes are analyzed, synthesized, and utilized by lawyers and judges in much the same way as the holdings of cases in the traditional common-law fields. The approach and methodology are essentially the same.

The nature of the common-law system means that when Mr. Sills, Mr. Horan, and Judge Broderick researched the law, they could not confine themselves to statutes. They also had to try to find precedent *cases* and that, as you might guess, is a considerably more daunting task than looking up a section or two in a well-structured civil code. For this reason, the legal research job that faced Mr. Horan, Mr. Sills, and the judge was a good deal more complicated than would have been faced by a lawyer or judge in a civil-law country. After they found the statute of limitations ("CPLR §214. Actions to be commenced within three years"), they had to research the cases interpreting it because the bare language of the statute left potentially important questions open.

Here, the advocates Sills and Horan would have encountered a distinctly common-law phenomenon in statutory interpretation: Sometimes, the interpretive "gloss" that courts place on legislative materials goes far beyond the statutory text itself, considerably embellishing or restricting the basic meaning of the words. For example, the simple phrase "due process of law" in the U.S. Constitution has spawned a huge body of constitutional case law, brimming with rules, principles, exceptions, exceptions-to-exceptions, and so on, a legal area that is, in structural complexity, comparable to many areas of purely common law.

As we already saw briefly in Chapter II, the courts in New York have glommed a rather substantial judicial embellishment on the three-year statute of limitations involved in *DeWeerth v. Baldinger*. Namely, they have said that a *demand and refusal* must occur before the three-year period actually starts to run. But take a look back at the statute itself: Do you see there anything about "demand" or "refusal"? You have only part of the statute, of course, but even if you go to the statute book itself you still won't find any statutory requirement of demand and refusal. It's not there. At some point along the way, it appears that some court or another just made up the requirement.[51] Or, more precisely, a very clever lawyer *persuaded* a court to impose the rule of "demand and refusal" so the lawyer's clients, who waited more than three years to sue, could still have a shot at recovering their property. The lawyer's argument might have gone something like this:

> [A]n innocent purchaser of stolen goods becomes a wrongdoer only after refusing the owner's demand for their return. Until the refusal the purchaser is considered to be in lawful possession. ... [Therefore,] the statute of limitations begins to run only upon the purchaser's refusal to return the property.[52]

Get it? Because the court does not want to treat an innocent buyer as a wrongdoer, it denies her the legal protection of the statute of limitations. So no matter how long the innocent buyer "honestly" holds possession, she will probably never become the owner! Who *can* claim the valuable protection of the statute of limitations? Why, a *thief*, of course, since thieves indubitably are wrongdoers from the moment they get their hands on the loot. Steal it, and it's yours in three years; buy it in good faith and, well, you'll probably never own it. In short, New York's three-year statute of limitations has been interpreted to give more protection to thieves than to good faith buyers.[53]

Naturally it is not a New York policy to favor thieves and, in fact, the apparent advantage given to light-fingered gentry is

---

[51] The first New York case to clearly hold that a demand and refusal are necessary to commence the statute of limitations is Menzel v. List, 253 N.Y.S. 43, 44 (1st Dept. 1964).
[52] *Quoted from* Kunstsammlungen Zu Weimar v. Elicofon, 678 F.2d 1150, 1061 (2d Cir. 1982).
[53] This last point was specifically acknowledged by the New York Court of Appeals in the case of Solomon R. Guggenheim Found. v. Lubell, 569 N.E.2d 426, 429 (N.Y. 1991).

really only an illusion. As a practical matter thieves rarely appear in civil lawsuits to assert their rights as thieves. The real concern in the New York cases is to protect *owners*, and New York's demand-and-refusal rule does this (at the expense of innocent buyers) by effectively extending the time in which owners are allowed to sue. Thus, it is the owners of stolen valuables who get the real protection in those factual settings that are actually likely to come to court. In fact, the New York courts have given owners an immense advantage by adopting the demand-and-refusal rule because in doing so they have, in practical effect, virtually "repealed" the statute of limitations for chattels enacted by the legislature. (Is it okay for a court to do that?)

Whatever may be the wisdom of the court created demand-and-refusal rule, however, the point here is that the rule is now a part of the New York statute of limitations as a matter of law — not a mere "interpretation," but law. Once an appellate court placed its imprimatur on this interpretation, no lower court could say "Gee, those appeals judges got it wrong, but we can fix that. We can read the legislature's words just as well as they can, and we don't find 'demand and refusal' in the statute."

We will see some further twists placed on these issues in *DeWeerth v. Baldinger* a little later on, as we look at how the Second Circuit added some ideas of its own to the statute. First, though, let us take a closer look at this "common law" that ties the various state laws together and sets our American legal system apart.

THE EMERGENCE OF AMERICAN COMMON LAW

The common law had its birthplace in England, and it was there that it spent its formative years. At the beginning of the modern age, English settlers colonized the lands that became the early United States, and our predominant national culture, especially our political and legal culture, was heavily influenced by that of England, both before and after the War of

Independence.[54] While many early settlers came here from other parts of the Old World, including from other culturally distinct portions of the British Isles (Scotland, Ireland, and Wales), the colonial governance and lawmaking power emanated from England's capital, London, the seat of the common law.[55]

From the Magna Charta (1215) forward, the English common law developed a growing authority and the courts an increasing independence so that, at the time of the American colonies, the common law had become a kind of force unto itself. By the 1600's, the common law already operated as a check on the monarch's royal power (which was at the time generally regarded as the most "dangerous" aspect of government). In a famous interchange, King James I suggested that he should be above the law, and the Lord Chief Justice Coke responded with a head-threatening riposte that still resonates in American constitutional law: *Rex non debet esse sub homine, sed sub Deo et lege* ("the King is subject to no man, but is subject to God and the law").[56]

Two very important features of colonial-era English political consciousness were the so-called "the rights of an Englishman," conferred by the common law, and the Magna Charta's principle that no one's liberty or property could be taken without "due

---

[54] The French rationalist philosophers, such as Montesquieu and Voltaire, were another major influence on the Framers who created our nation's system of government. However, the French *legal* influence, as distinguished from its philosophical influence, has generally been minimal. One notable exception is the Civil Law notion of "community property," applicable in Louisiana and eight other states (all bordering on or west of the Mississippi), which presumes that most property of married persons is owned 50-50 by both spouses. In most states, by contrast, marital property is governed by the common-law rule, in which each spouse presumptively owns his or her property separately from the other spouse.

[55] Note that "England" and "Great Britain" are not the same thing. England and Scotland (and, historically, Wales) were all separate nations. Notably, Scotland is traditionally a *Civil Law* jurisdiction, not a common law one. Our American law is derived from *English* common law, not from "British" law.

[56] Quoted in the case of Paula Corbin Jones v. William Jefferson Clinton, 869 F. Supp. 690, 693 n.1 (E.D. Ark. 1994). Have you heard of this case? By the way, Lord Edward Coke's name is pronounced "Cook," and he was one of the leading expositors of the early modern common law. He was also chief justice of both the Common Pleas Court and the Court of King's Bench in the early seventeenth century.

process of law."[57] While the rights of an Englishman were not airtight protections, they were, for the time, pretty unusual, and "even the humblest Englishman seems to have been certain of his superior 'birthright' to liberty and justice under the common law."[58] Indeed, one of the causes of the American Revolution was a widespread perception that the English Parliament was unwilling to respect these rights in its colonial subjects.

As a check on governmental power, the common law served much the same general role that *constitutional law* serves in the United States today, helping to make the English people (at least in their own eyes) "the Envy of all around us."[59] But rights against the state were not the only kind of common-law rights that the people of England regarded as important. During the common-law's heyday in the sixteenth and early seventeenth centuries, English men and women were very litigious, making ample use of the courts in order to obtain redress for private grievances. Their propensity to sue helped fill out the rules of the common law and make it, to a considerable extent, a thing of the people.

American courts borrowed heavily from the early English decisions in shaping our own common law. As a result, our legal system owes a great debt to such English courts as the Court of King's Bench, Court of Common Pleas, Court of Exchequer, the Privy Council, and the House of Lords. You will still see occasional cases from these courts in your law school assignments and, even, occasional citations to their cases in modern American decisions. The basic common law principles that tie together the common law of our states also continues to link us, to a lesser degree, with England and the other common-law jurisdictions around the world. However, as the specific policies within the various jurisdictions have diverged over time, the guidance that is sought from non-U.S. cases dwindles. Nevertheless, in some

---

[57] *See* Pacific Mut. Life Ins. Co. v. Haslet, 499 U.S. 1, 28 (1991) (the Magna Charta itself said "law of the land," rather than "due process of law," but the two were regarded as meaning essentially the same thing, and the latter phrase became the basis of much of our American constitutional liberty today.

[58] DAVID LEMMING, PROFESSORS OF THE LAW 9 (2000).

[59] *Id.*

fields, such as property law, legal stability is considered a great virtue (do you see why?), and longstanding English common-law conceptions are still very much alive here, even some that have long been superseded in England itself.[60]

The adoption of English common law on the American continent was, however, far from direct and straightforward. The original colonists were often not educated people and they did not in any case bring along many law books. In most colonies, direct governance from England was initially weak or non-existent. As a consequence, the earliest colonial law was a kind of "popular" law having only a fairly vague imprint of the common law as practiced in London. As learning and sophistication grew, however, the legal systems of the American colonies evolved until, "during the decade immediately preceding independence, the English common law was generally praised and apparently most readily received by the larger part of the American courts."[61] At the same time, though, "the marks of the old popular law remain[ed] strong and most of the original features of American jurisprudence can be traced back to the earliest times."[62]

Because England acquired the Province of New York by "conquest" (from the Dutch), direct royal authority was applied

---

[60] As a British law teacher once said to me, "For us, American property law is such a marvelous *museum*!"

[61] Paul Samuel Reinsch, *The English Common Law in the Early American Colonies*, in I SELECT ESSAYS IN ANGLO-AMERICAN LEGAL HISTORY 367, 371 (1907).

[62] *Id.* Sometimes people ask about Native American tribal law, which already held sway across the American continent at the time of the European's arrival. The short answer is that the laws of the indigenous peoples had little or no influence on the early lawmaking in the American colonies or states. In contrast to most modern immigrants, those who arrived from Europe in colonial times did not come to this continent with any intention of becoming a part of the societies that were already here. Instead, they established and lived almost entirely within their own expanding enclaves, in societies they kept carefully separate from those of the Native Americans. When the English settlers made laws, they were primarily concerned with preserving the peace and justice within in their own societies, and their legal systems therefore reflected the background customs and arrangements of their own ethnicity. It probably hardly even occurred to them to look to Native American law as a source of legal principles or norms of conduct to apply among themselves.

That was long ago, however, and things have changed quite a bit. Nowadays, Native American law, jurisdiction, and tribal sovereignty are recognized as applicable within some fairly extensive geographic areas, especially in the western United States. Modern Indian law has become of sufficient importance that it is included as a subject on the bar examination of at least one state.

in the colony almost from the beginning, and the colony's "rulers soon accustomed it to the principles of the English common law."[63] Following independence, New York, like many states, adopted specific *reception statutes* pursuant to which the English common law was "received" (*i.e.*, adopted) as the law of the state, except where inconsistent with express local laws or conditions. New York's reception statute (actually, a part of the state constitution) reads as follows:

> Such parts of the common law, and of the acts of the legislature of the colony of New York, as together did form the law of the said colony, on the nineteenth day of April, one thousand seven hundred seventy-five, . . . which have not since expired, or been repealed or altered; and such acts of the legislature of this state as are now in force, shall be and continue the law of this state, subject to such alterations as the legislature shall make concerning the same. But all such parts of the common law, and such of the said acts, or parts thereof, as are repugnant to this constitution, are hereby abrogated.[64]

With or without a local reception statute, lawyers made extensive reference to English precedents during the early years of our Republic, and the courts frequently relied on English cases as authority. As the new nation expanded westward across the continent, the American settlers took the common law with them. In many ways, however, American customs were different from those prevailing in England. Here there was a vast and undeveloped country, bursting with energy to expand. England was, by contrast, a mostly settled little island, without frontiers to be explored, whose prospects for expansion lay overseas. Accordingly, as stated by Justice Story, another of the important early scholar-judges of the American common law:

> The common law of England is not to be taken in all respects to be that of America. Our ancestors brought with them its general

---

[63] Reinsch, *supra*, at 390.
[64] N.Y. Const. art. I, §14, derived from the original New York State Constitution of 1777.

principles and claimed it as their birthright; but they brought with them and adopted only that portion which was applicable to their situation.[65]

Thus, the courts in early America were constantly alert to the differences in local conditions that might make a particular English rule inapplicable and, when they thought it necessary, they would fashion an "American rule" to take the place of the original English rule. For instance, in cases of personal self-defense the English common law had long imposed a "duty to retreat," meaning that people had no right to use deadly force against assailants if they could make a safe escape instead. In America, however, many courts rejected this "duty to retreat" requirement saying, for example, that it ran against "the tendency of the American mind"[66] and that a "true man"[67] does not flee when he is attacked.[68] Notably, perhaps, these statements were made in cases decided during the "gunsmoke" era of high-noon showdowns and the O.K. Corral; you would not have to be a member of the Feminist Legal Theory school to observe, with some justification, that they bear a distinct mark of the hyper-patriarchic attitudes of those times. However, American law efforts to expand the definition of justifiable "self-defense" beyond its narrow English common-law bounds have not been limited to those who are anxious about the plight of assailed "true men." Feminist concerns have motivated calls for some expansion as well, to consider, for example, the situation of a victimized woman who strikes back lethally at her domestic tormentor.

---

[65] Van Ness v. Packard, 27 U.S. 144 (1829). Notice, this is an early U.S. Supreme Court case. Justice Joseph Story was a justice of the U.S. Supreme Court and a legal scholar who contributed greatly to creation of American Law.

[66] Runyan v. State, 57 Ind. 80, 84 (1877).

[67] Erwin v. State, 29 Ohio St. 186, 199 (1876), *citing* a much earlier rejection of the "duty to retreat" requirement by the Supreme Judicial Court of Massachusetts, in 1806, *viz.* Commonwealth v. Selfridge, 2 Am. St. Trials 544 (Mass. 1806) [check]. *See also* Joseph H. Beale, *Retreat From Murderous Assault*, 16 Harv L. Rev. 567 (1902).

[68] *See generally* RICHARD MAXWELL BROWN, NO DUTY TO RETREAT: VIOLENCE AND VALUES IN AMERICAN HISTORY AND SOCIETY (1991).

As frequently occurred, some of the states adopted a new "American rule" but others stayed with the traditional English rule (as happened with the rule on the duty to retreat, which remains the *minority* rule). In other words, just because something is called the "English rule" does not necessarily mean it is not also American law; it may be just as much a part of the American law as its newer American counterpart, with some states adhering to one and others to the other. In any event, balancing stability with fluidity was the basic challenge in the formation of the American common law, especially in the nineteenth century. Here's an example of the sort of reasoning used:

Kerwhacker v. Cleveland, Columbus & Cincinnati RR.
3 Ohio St. 172 (1854)

BARTLEY, J.

[Hogs belonging to Mr. Kerwhacker strayed on to railroad tracks next to his property. A passing train hit and killed six of the hogs. Kerwhacker sued the railroad. According to Kerwhacker, the railroad had negligently operated its locomotive "whereby six hogs, the property of the plaintiff, were killed." The railroad responded that the fault was all Kerwhacker's, citing the com-mon-law duty of animal owners to keep their animals fenced. Therefore, argued the railroad, it was not liable for the value of the hogs.]

The doctrine that the owner of cattle, hogs, horses, &c., is bound to keep them on his own lands . . . is said to be derived from the common law of England, and to be in force in this State. . . . [H]aving been adopted in the original States of the Union, and introduced into Ohio, at an early period, the common law has continued to be recognized as the rule of decision in our courts . . . so far as its rules and principles appeared to be based on sound reason, and applicable to our condition and circumstances. [However,] the common law . . . has no force in Ohio, except so far as it derives authority from judicial recognition in the practice and course of adjudication in our courts; and this extends no farther than it illustrates and explains the rules of right and justice as applicable to the circumstances and institutions of the people of the State. . . .

Admitting the rule of the common law of England in relation to cattle and other live stock running at large to be such as stated, the question arises whether it is applicable to the condition and circumstances of the people of this State, and in accordance with their habits, understanding and necessities. . . . What has been the actual situation of affairs, and the habits, understandings and necessities of the peoples of this State from its first settlement up to the present period, in this respect? Cattle, hogs and all other kinds of live stock not known to be breachy and unruly, or dangerous have been allowed at all times, and in all parts of the State, to run at large, and graze on the range of uncultivated and uninclosed lands. And this prevails not only throughout the country, but also in the villages and cities. . . . For many years, in the early settled parts of the State, the people were unable, and at the present time, in some parts of the State, they are yet unable to clear and inclose more ground than that actually needed for cultivation. And there is not at this time inclosed pasture lands sufficient to confine the one-half of the livestock in the State. Even a statutory enactment, imposing the severest criminal punishment for permitting these animals to run at large, could not be enforced without either slaughtering or driving a large portion of them from the State. . . . And it has been only within a few years, and that only in the better improved parts of the State, that uncultivated pasture grounds have been inclosed. And this has not been done because the owners considered themselves required by law to confine their stock within inclosures, but for their own convenience and advantage. . . . The existence or inforcement of such a law would have greatly retarded the settlement of the country, and have been against the policy of both the general and the State governments.

[Held for Kerwhacker.]

STUDY QUESTIONS

The court recognized the general authority of the common law, but then deviated from it in the particular case because it had definite and articulable reasons for doing so.

1. Can you articulate the court's reasons in a sentence or so?
2. Do you think it likely the court would have come to the same conclusion if this case had arisen today?
3. Now what? Can the courts of the state return to the original common law? Should they?

THE FLUIDITY OF THE COMMON LAW

It is revolting to have no better reason for a rule of law than that so it was laid down in the time of Henry IV. It is still more revolting if the grounds upon which it was laid down have vanished long since, and the rule simply persists from blind imitation of the past.   —*Oliver Wendell Holmes*[69]

The early common law was a reflection of custom and, as "unwritten law," it had the built-in flexibility to adjust to changing circumstances. Over the centuries, however, precedents were established to resolve many of the main kinds of disputes that came to the courts, and the practice of generally following these precedents brought much stability (some might say, stultification) to the common law. Even so, it often occurs that a dispute is brought before the courts and there is no precedent or statute that seems quite on point, or the dispute contains certain "distinguishing" factors so the precedents or statutes nearest on point would lead to unappealing results. It is in these areas of

---

[69] Oliver Wendell Holmes, *The Path of the Law*, 10 HARV. L. REV. 457, 469 (1897).

"open texture"[70] that the essential fluidity of the common law can still be seen.

Perhaps a "hypothetical" case[71] may make that last sentence a bit clearer. Let us imagine that Mrs. Anna Jones owns a dog that has been known to snap at guests. Her landlord, Mr. Errol Brown, knows of the dog and its tendencies, but he has done nothing about the situation. One day, little Sarah Gardner, age five, was visiting Mrs. Jones and the dog bit Sarah. The resulting wound required several stitches. Sarah's parents consulted their lawyer, Ellen Dodson, Esq., and she advised them to take the case to court. Since Mrs. Jones has no money (what we call "judgment-proof"), lawyer Dodson also advised the Gardners to sue only the "deep pocket" in the case, landlord Brown. They instructed her to do so, on Sarah's behalf.

Assume there is no statute that says whether a landlord can be held liable for injuries caused by a tenant's dog. Ms. Dodson (as well as Brown's lawyer and, eventually, the court) must look to the common law. Where do they find this? The answer would be relatively straightforward if they needed to concern themselves only with standards of conduct that had been judicially recognized in the past. They could find their answer in the law library, or via one of the computer-assisted legal research services, such as LEXIS and Westlaw. But suppose there is no such

---

[70] The term "open texture" is, I think, originally due to H.L.A. Hart in his masterful treatment of the jurisprudence of Legal Positivism, THE CONCEPT OF LAW 121-132 (1960). *See* footnote 89, *infra*.

[71] You will find that the use of "hypothetical" cases (or "hypos") to be an extremely common method of illustrating points in law school and law practice, even in judicial opinions. While hypos have proven themselves over and over as valuable rhetorical devices, there are at least two things to beware of: First, it is not uncommon to "load" up a hypothetical set of facts with features that are meant to pump our intuitions in particular directions—for example, by depicting the parties in ways that are especially sympathetic or unsympathetic, so the listener has extraneous reasons to *want* to favor one particular legal analysis over another. (Be sure to note how the hypo that follows in the text has been loaded). Second, when courts opine with respect to the proper legal analysis of a purely hypothetical situation in a case, they may make statements that *sound* like rulings of law but which are, in fact, what lawyers call "obiter dictum"—or just plain "dicta." These statements by courts are technically not "precedent," and should be treated as having considerably less authority then the actual legal outcomes (or "holdings") of cases. *See* pages 108-110.

case, and that no court in the state has *ever* held a landlord liable for injuries by a tenant's dog. In other words, suppose Sarah's lawsuit against Brown is what lawyers call a case of "first impression."

First of all, do you see any ethical problem with Ms. Dodson's bringing a legal action against Mr. Brown even though she cannot cite any specific law that makes him liable? Most lawyers probably would not see a problem.[72] Even if no landlord has ever previously been held for injuries caused by a tenant's dog, the court in this case might still decide to impose liability on Brown. After all, there was a time when landlords were not liable for *any* dangerous conditions on the leased premises, and that changed only gradually over the centuries. The new rules and standards of conduct accreted, case by case, but still there had to be a first time for everything.[73] As described by Judge Jerome Frank, a judge on the United States Court of Appeals for the Second Circuit, courts gradually develop new legal rules something like this:

> A court decides a law-suit. The court sometimes gives its reasons for its decision. It says that, with the facts as it finds them, certain legal consequences follow. It states the consequences of those facts in terms of a generalization, that is, a rule. Then another law-suit occurs. The facts, as there found, are much like but not exactly the same as, those in the previous suit. Nevertheless, the court applies the same generalization or rule. In a third suit, the facts seem sufficiently different to require a different generalization, or an exception to the former rule. Thus, by case-by-case decisions, the courts evolve the legal rules."[74]

---

[72] The lawyers' ethical rules specifically permit advocates to make good faith arguments for an extension of existing law. *See* ABA's MODEL RULES OF PROFESSIONAL CONDUCT 3.1, comment [2].

[73] As John Chipman Gray once quipped, in response to the assertion that judges do not "make" law: "What was the law at the time of Richard Coeur de Leon on the liability of a telegraph company to person to whom a message was sent?" Quoted in JEROME FRANK, COURTS ON TRIAL 264 (1949).

[74] *Id.*

The question of "common law" for Ms. Dodson is: How does she find a persuasive legal basis for the court to hold that landlords may have a duty to remove (if they can) dangerous animals from the premises they lease out to others?

The first time a court is called upon to decide a "new" problem the judge should bear in mind, among other things, which practices, customary behaviors and expectations would best further the community life. These considerations will vary depending on the kind of community in which Mrs. Jones, Mr. Brown, and little Sarah live. It may be we are talking about a state whose population lives mostly in larger urban areas, or we may be talking about a largely rural state containing vast areas where unruly dogs are commonplace and formidable watchdogs give valuable protection to single women living alone. Certainly it is very possible that the keeping of gruff and toothy canines might be viewed entirely differently in one situation than in the other. One of the great merits of this thing we call "common law" is that it does not require us to anticipate and make specific rules, in advance, for all the permutations of reality that we might later encounter. Instead it can be readily shaped and molded, case by case, to reflect differing circumstances and needs, and it can reflect changing social conditions as knowledge, values, and public mores evolve with the times. The common law can provide legal decisions that reflect these changes without waiting for a legislature to detect legal omissions, anachronisms, and antiquated provisions.

Although Sarah's case may be one of first impression, with no rule of law directly in point, the court still has no choice but to make a decision. It cannot tell Sarah to come back in five or six years to see if some new law has come up in the meantime. The court must do the best it can with what it has. The court could of course say: "Since Sarah Gardner's counsel cites no cases that hold a landlord liable on facts like these, we conclude that she has no right to recover." It *can* say this, but such a response may well be highly unsatisfactory. Why?

One reason why a court should not simply reject a claim for lack of exact precedent is that cases virtually never have *exact* precedents. No two cases are ever literally "on all fours" with each other (to use a lawyer phrase); there are always differences. Therefore, the question for the court is not whether there is an exact precedent but whether there is a sufficiently analogous precedent, one whose underlying *principles* are broad enough to cover the case at hand.

Suppose, for example, lawyer Dodson finds some cases in which courts held landlords liable to tenants' guests who were injured by various dangerous *devices* on leased premises. She could then argue that, in light of the holdings in the "device" cases, it would be almost perverse for a court to turn down Sarah's claim merely because she was injured by a dog and not a device. Though the specific cause of injury is different, the principle is the same. In other words, Ms. Dodson can use the prior "device" cases as analogous authority to show that Sarah has a common-law right to win — even without a precedent directly in point. As modern legal theorist Ronald Dworkin describes it:

> [E]ven when no settled rule disposes of the case, one party may nevertheless have a *right* to win. It remains the judge's duty, even in hard cases, to *discover* what the rights of the parties are, not to invent new rights retrospectively.[75]

How does the judge "discover" what the rights of the parties are when there are no prior cases right in point? As Dworkin points out, in actual practice judicial precedents often have an influence on later cases as to which they are not directly on point. A precedent can be

> counted in favor of [a] right to recover, in spite of the fact that the earlier decision contained no language that could plausibly be interpreted to enact that right. [A lawyer or judge] would urge

---

[75] RONALD DWORKIN, TAKING RIGHTS SERIOUSLY 81 (1978) (emphasis added.). We set aside, for the moment, the question of whether judges actually "make" new law in these situations or, as Dworkin says, merely "discover" law that was already there. *See* discussion of Legal Realism, *infra* this chapter.

that the earlier decision exerts a *gravitational force* on later decisions even when these later decision lie outside its particular orbit.[76]

In other words, the legal *principles* that underlay the rules in the previous "device" cases are also part of the law for Sarah's case even though those prior cases did not involve attacks by dogs — and even though the judges in those cases may not have given the least thought to dog bites when rendering their decisions.

Nor would Ms. Dodson necessarily be limited to precedents from her own jurisdiction. The area of injury compensation law ("tort" law) is one in which courts have been particularly willing to take guidance from legal developments in other American states as new factual combinations arise in their own states. Each state has its own separate common law, but across jurisdictional lines the common law nevertheless tends to be grounded on the same or similar underlying legal principles. Therefore, the judicial holdings from any common law jurisdiction will be pretty good evidence of the "right" decision for other common law courts as well.[77]

Suppose, for example, Ms. Dodson discovers California cases that hold landlords liable for bites by tenants' dogs if the landlord could have acted to get rid of a known vicious animal but did not do so.[78] If the tort law in Sarah's state were generally similar to that of California, it would be reasonable for Ms. Dodson to

---

[76] *Id.* at 111 (emphasis added).

[77] Should the text here read *a* "right" decision, rather than *the* "right" decision? It is a matter of debate among modern legal thinkers whether legal problems usually have a single right answer. Ronald Dworkin, just quoted, is a primary advocate for the position that a legal question usually does have a single right answer. *See, id.,* at 286, 290, 331-32. Others disagree. *See, e.g.,* RICHARD A. POSNER, THE PROBLEMS OF JURISPRUDENCE 197-219 (1990). Still others, such as those in the Critical Legal Studies movement, would regard the whole debate as essentially incoherent since law is (in their view) mainly political and not about abstract "right" in the first place. *See* Andrew Altman, *Legal Realism Critical Legal Studies and Dworkin,* in PHILOSOPHY AND PUBLIC AFFAIRS, *reprinted in* JOEL FEINBERG AND HYMAN GROSS, PHILOSOPHY OF LAW 176 (5th ed. 1995). Almost everybody agrees, however, that legal questions definitely can have *wrong* answers.

[78] *See, e.g.,* Uccello v. Laudenslayer, 118 Cal. Rptr. 741 (Cal. Ct. App. 1975) (landlord, who could have evicted tenant with dog, was held liable when the dog bit a five-year-old girl as she and the tenant's daughter played together in tenant's kitchen).

predict that the courts of her state might well adopt the California rule on dog bites as well. To be sure, a state's courts are always free to reject legal rules or decisions from other states. Out-of-state decisions are, however, legal authority nonetheless — evidence of the legal principles that underlie specific rules and standards of conduct, and which are part of the common law. Courts typically regard the decisions from other states as being at least "persuasive" authorities even if they are not "mandatory authorities" (*i.e.*, those that the court is legally compelled to follow — often referred to as "binding precedent").

Even the most persuasive line of cases is, however, only a *part* of the law. No matter how relevant a court may find the indirect precedents (say, on dangerous devices), or the precedents from other states, the court might still be persuaded not to apply any of these. The court might find, instead, that there are still *other* legal principles, ones that are overriding. For example, landlord Brown's lawyer might stress to the court that there are strong privacy concerns that weigh against a ruling for Sarah. A judgment for Sarah, he might argue, could wind up motivating landlords to intrude on their tenants' lifestyle choices, for instance by trying to take away their tenants' pets. Maybe Brown's lawyer can convince the court that, if it holds for Sarah, too many landlords might say to their tenants: "Either the dog goes, or you go." He might, in other words, convince the court that it should *distinguish* the "device" cases on the ground that tenants' ill-behaved dogs are legally distinguishable from other kinds of dangerous things.

A court "distinguishes" a precedent by stressing some factor (in either the precedent or the present case) that causes the precedent to be a legally inapt analogy. Because there is no theoretical limit to the kinds of factors that might be considered relevant to a real-life legal question (analogies are something lawyers must learn to "sense"), precedents involving a very wide range of subjects can be invoked as part of the applicable law in any given case. In deciding whether to extend the "device" cases to dog bites, a court might refer to cases involving falling plaster, guard dogs, scratching cats, kicking horses, and privacy as well as, perhaps, cases that do not necessarily involve landlords or even personal injuries at all. Any of these *may conceivably* show the standards and rules of landlord behavior that should be "judicially recognized" with respect to dog bites by tenants' pets. Lawyer Dodson and the lawyers for Mr. Brown must therefore find these potentially applicable cases and decide how to deal with them.

In addition to distinguishing cases, courts also have other practices that allow them to handle precedents and shape the law in accordance with what are, in their views, preferable public policies. Suppose, for example, Mr. Brown's lawyer finds an 1842 case where the court said a landlord is *not* liable for damage caused by his tenant's horse, which escaped and ate the neighbor's prize camellias. If a precedent case is from five or ten years ago, it will probably be regarded as a stronger authority than one that is over 100 years old. Partly, it depends on the subject area—in a slowly changing field like property, a nineteenth century case might be practically "recent," whereas a labor law or civil rights case from the same era may have no precedent value at all. The 165-year-old "prize camellias" case is still evidence of the law, but its authority may well be questioned, especially if the adversary can point to salient ways in which conditions have changed in the meantime.

THE STABILITY OF THE COMMON LAW—STARE DECISIS

A more alarming doctrine could not be promulgated by any American court, than that it was at liberty to disregard all former rules and decisions, and to decide for itself, without reference to the settled course of antecedent principles.

—*Justice Joseph Story*[79]

---

[79] JOSEPH STORY, COMMENTARIES ON THE CONSTITUTION OF THE UNITED STATES §377 (1833), *quoted in* Hart v. Massanari, 266 F.3d 1155 (9th Cir. 2001). *See supra* note 65 concerning Justice Story.

Essentially, the stability of the common law rests on the doctrine of precedent, but what does that mean precisely? In its simplest conception, to follow a precedent means doing again under the same (or similar) circumstances that which was done in the past. In ordinary life if something works for us once, we are likely to try it again. This use of precedent helps us survive by giving pragmatic value to "learning from experience." The legal doctrine of precedent does this and more. As it was stated by Chancellor Kent, a highly regarded scholar-jurist from the formative years of American common law:

> A solemn decision upon a point of law, arising in any given case, becomes an authority in a like case, because it is the highest evidence which we can have of the law applicable to the subject, and the judges are bound to follow that decision so long as it stands unreversed, unless it can be shown that the law was misunderstood or misapplied in that particular case. If a decision has been made upon solemn argument and mature deliberation, . . . the community have a right to regard it as a just declaration of exposition of the law, and to regulate their actions and contract by it. . . . It is by the notoriety and stability of such rules that professional men can give safe advice to those who consult them; and people in general can venture with confidence to buy and trust, and to deal with each other.[80]

In other words, too much legal fluidity would mean no one could plan for the future. Without a stable framework of legal rules for contracting, tort liabilities, organization governance and the like, business people could not confidently invest money, enter long term arrangements or establish the operations that employ thousands of workers. People might find it difficult or impossible to buy a house or even an automobile. Law students could not get student loans. Concerns like these lead to statements like this: "Law . . . unlike science, is concerned not

---

[80] 1 JAMES KENT, KENT'S COMMENTARIES ON AMERICAN LAW 475 (3d ed. 1838).

only with getting the result right but also with stability, to which it frequently will sacrifice substantive justice."[81]

Sacrifice justice? That seems like a hard price to pay just for stability. However, stability can also be seen as *promoting* justice, by contributing to the internal consistency of the law. Consistency is not merely a matter of neatness (which may have no importance at all). On the theory that justice requires equality under the law, many believe it follows that courts should "[t]reat like cases alike and different cases differently."[82] If, for example, two persons do the same acts under similar circumstances, it would not be justice if the first had to pay ruinous damages and the other was totally let off merely because one case got to court on Tuesday and the other one on Friday, or last year and this year. Conditions may, of course change, and if it becomes obvious that a previous decision is obsolete or wrong, then "equality" may have to yield to other justice concerns. However, it is the general idea of the doctrine of precedent that, absent a reason for making a change, judicial decisions should generally be consistent with the rules and principles that courts have previously applied in earlier judicial decisions. As observed by Justice Antonin Scalia, "the appearance of equal treatment [is] a motivating force of the human spirit, that . . . cannot be overestimated."[83]

Perhaps Justice Scalia is right on this, but you should be aware that not everybody necessarily agrees. In particular, there are some who contend that we fool ourselves if we think the doctrine of precedent can make any such *substantive* consistency possible. If this pessimistic view of precedent is correct, then "equality under the law" has to mean something else. What is often cited is a kind of *procedural* fairness in which "equality under the law" means only that everybody

---

[81] RICHARD A. POSNER, THE PROBLEMS OF JURISPRUDENCE 51 (1990). But how does the lawyer fit in? Would you want to be the lawyer who argues: "Your honor, we all know my client was in the wrong, here. But you still should let him win—for stability's sake, we should 'sacrifice substantive justice' "?

[82] H.L.A. HART, THE CONCEPT OF LAW 155 (1961).

[83] Antonin Scalia, *The Rule of Law as a Law of Rules*, 56 U. Chi. L. Rev. 1175, 1178 (1989).

similarly situated is entitled to receive the same legal *process*, but not necessarily the same legal outcomes.[84] The idea is that, if each case is judged as objectively and impartially as possible, with everyone having a fair opportunity to be heard and present evidence, then there is sufficient equality for purposes of justice or, at any rate, it is the best we can do. Actually, this "procedural" equality is probably a pretty close description of what goes on in private arbitrations, where the decisions do not count as "precedent" and the arbitrators' decisions normally cannot be challenged, as a practical matter, for not following the law. Increasing numbers of disputes are being submitted to these private arbitrations (bypassing the courts), which is at least some evidence of how "justice-without-precedents" is publicly perceived.

The common law is in any event deeply committed to the doctrine of precedent, and the epitome of the doctrine is known as the rule of *stare decisis*, which means literally "to stand decided." Under a rigid rule of stare decisis, a court is compelled to follow the so-called *ratio decidendi* of its own prior decisions as well as, of course, the prior decisions of courts that are superior to it. The "ratio decidendi" refers to that portion of a court's opinion that is logically necessary to support and justify the *holding* or *ruling* in the case, *i.e.*, the decision of who won.[85] Although collateral explanatory matters also commonly appear in judicial opinions (for example, discussions of hypotheticals and illustrations), these digressions, "advisory opinions," and other stray comments about the law are not a part of the ratio decidendi. Therefore, the doctrine of stare decisis does *not* require that they be followed in later cases.

---

[84] *See, e.g.*, Simon H. Rifkind, The Lawyer's Role and Responsibility in a Modern Society, 30 the Record 534 (1975). Probably the leading contemporary exponent of the idea that "justice is fairness" is John Rawls. *See* JOHN RAWLS, A THEORY OF JUSTICE (1977). Although Rawls was writing of justice in the broader sense (of which "legal" justice is only a part), his work has been influential in contemporary jurisprudence, and his basic presupposition, that just results emerge from a just process, is surely the best articulated of the arguments for procedural justice.

[85] The term "ratio decidendi" literally means "reason for deciding."

The non-*ratio* material in a judicial opinion is called "obiter dictum" or sometimes, simply, "dicta." Even though obiter dictum does not have to be followed, it is generally treated with respect, often being cited and used by both advocates and judges as though it were part of the "ratio" itself. On the other hand, if a court is so inclined it can dismiss obiter dictum without much ado at all. When judges toss aside dicta, they rarely show anything like the solemnity and assiduous fastidiousness that is normally displayed when they *overrule* a precedent. As a result, you will find it is one of the great legal sports is to determine precisely which portions of an opinion are part of the ratio and which are only dicta. This is not always easy to divine. One of the "judicial luminaries" once was asked about the distinction by one of his colleagues and he replied:

> The rule is quite simple, if you agree with the other [judge] you say it is part of the *ratio*; if you don't you say it is *obiter dictum*. . . . [86]

At any rate, a rigid rule of stare decisis (forbidding courts to overrule their own decisions) is not observed in the American common law, though it is said to apply in England. Still, as you already have gathered, prior court decisions in American common law definitely exert a kind of "gravitational" pull on later decisions, a force of precedent that varies in strength with such factors as the rank of the court, the age of the case, and the reputation of the judge. The difference between this phenomenon and a strict rule of stare decisis is that the strict rule treats the "ratio decidendi" of a single case as being, in essence, law per se (literally "mandatory" authority) while the more pragmatic American doctrine of precedent treats most case authority as being, in effect (if not name), only "persuasive"

---

[86] RUPERT CROSS, PRECEDENT IN ENGLISH LAW 51 (1977). A relatively high-profile example occurred in Keystone Bituminous Coal Ass'n v. DeBenedictis, 480 U.S.470, 484 (1987). There, the majority opinion of a deeply split Supreme Court declared that the bulk of a great landmark precedent, cherished by the dissenters and many political conservatives, was merely an "advisory opinion." This characterization annoyed the dissenters, *id.* at 507, and in later cases it was essentially ignored.

authority, to a greater or lesser degree. Be aware, however, that much case authority is very *highly* persuasive: the "ratio decidendi" in a case from a hierarchically superior court or a group of related decisions that exhibit great consistency over a fair amount of time are as much "the law" as anything can be.

The modern doctrine of precedent is not, however, without some serious challengers. These contend that prior decisions by courts neither should nor, realistically, even *can* constrain the decisions of judges in later cases. For the position that courts should *not* regard themselves as bound by precedent, at least not too tightly, Oliver Wendell Holmes, Jr. had this to say:

> Learning, my learned brethren, is a very good thing. I should be the last to undervalue it, having done my share of quotation from the Year Books.[87] But it is liable to lead us astray. The law, so far as it depends on learning, is indeed, as it has been called, *the government of the living by the dead*. To a very considerable extent no doubt it is inevitable that the living should be so governed. The past gives us our vocabulary and fixes the limits of our imagination; we cannot get away from it. There is, too, a peculiar logical pleasure in making manifest the continuity between what we are doing and what has been done before. But the present has a right to govern itself so far as it can; and it ought always to be remembered that historic continuity with the past is not a duty; it is only a necessity.[88]

Holmes was not merely an immensely influential member of the Massachusetts Supreme Judicial Court and, later, the U.S. Supreme Court. He was also a common-law commentator and legal laureate extraordinaire. He is among the leading founders of the American "Legal Realist" movement, which began toward

---

[87] Editor's note: The so-called Yearbooks were the reports of English cases from the reign of Edward I through that of Henry VIII. They contain the very earliest common-law precedents, often written in Norman French, an archaic version of the French language that was used in English law courts from the time of the Norman Conquest (Battle of Hastings, 1066) until as late as the sixteenth century. If you read any French or Spanish, you should take a look some time.

[88] Quoted in 3 Collected Works of Justice Holmes 492 (Sheldon M. Novick ed., 1995) (emphasis added).

the end of the nineteenth century and flourished during the twentieth. The view taken by the Legal Realists was, in a nutshell: "Let's be *real* when we talk about law. The common law is not *really* something that truly 'exists' in the sense that, say, the objects in a hardware store exist. It is not a body of rules sitting 'out there' someplace waiting for judges to find them and apply them to particular cases. The common law is not, to quote Holmes himself, 'a brooding omnipresence in the sky.'[89] Rather, the common law is whatever judges say it is, and nothing more than that."[90]

The target of the Legal Realists was what they called legal Formalism, or "mechanical jurisprudence." The key Formalist concept is that judges should never be so presumptuous as to *make* law; their job is to *find* what the law is, and then to apply it. A leading jurisprudential light of the nineteenth century, John Austin, had scoffed at the notion that judges merely "find" law, calling it "a childish fiction" of judges who seem to regard the common law as "a miraculous something made by nobody, existing, I suppose, from eternity and merely declared from time to time" by the courts.[91] According to the Formalists, however, a judge would be a lawless renegade, usurping the power of the legislature, unless the judge adheres rigorously to the legal rules and standards already in existence, as handed down from the past. Although the early Formalists did not call themselves by that name (it was originally a term of abuse), their attitude

---

[89] Southern Pac. Co. v. Jensen, 244 U.S. 205, 222 (1917).

[90] American Legal Realism was an outgrowth of legal Positivism, which asserts that all law is "posited" — *i.e.*, manmade. Most specifically, legal Positivists (and the Realists) deny the existence or, at least, relevance of Natural Law (which insists there is such a thing as "objective" right and wrong, and that a morally wrong law is not law at all). *See supra*, page 85. In opposition to the Natural Law view, the Positivists contend that social practices can be "law" (albeit bad law) even when they go against the standards of morality, however defined. Indeed, the founder of legal Positivism, Jeremy Bentham (1748-1832), described the whole idea of Natural Law as "nonsense on stilts." What the legal Positivists were most eager to assert, however, was that law does not depend on morality for its existence so that, even in a world of moral relativism (no absolute substantive right and wrong), there can still be such a thing as law and justice. This probably reflects the thinking of most lawyers and judges today. (Do you agree?).

[91] Quoted in Jerome Frank, Courts on Trial 264 (1949).

toward the judicial role was clear. What they did not like was a style of judging that we today would call "judicial activism," as opposed to "strict constructionism" or "judicial self-restraint." Among lawyers, in law reviews, and even at Senate confirmation hearings,[92] the debate over the propriety of judicial activism is still very much alive.

The second major Legal Realist challenge to the doctrine of precedent is even more radical. It is the view that it is not even *possible* for courts' decisions in specific cases to be constrained by legal rules. The argument goes something like this: In actual practice judges are ultimately free to decide cases whichever way they please, and no mere legal rules can stop them. After all, realistically, how can anyone imagine that a judge's discretion in a given case can actually be *constrained* by words written down on assorted pieces of paper? For one thing, language and meanings are simply not that airtight, and they never can be. We referred earlier to areas of "open texture" in the law, areas that fall in the cracks between the rules, where judges must exercise choice and *make* law. What the later Legal Realists and their successors in the Critical Legal Studies movement came to assert was an even stronger claim, namely, that the law is *all* open texture; it is all "indeterminate." Why?

> [First,] there is always a *cluster* of rules relevant to the decision in any litigated case. . . . The vagueness of any one of these rules could affect the outcome of the case. In any single case, then, there [are] multiple points of indeterminacy due to rule vagueness.
>
> [Second,] in its actual operation the common-law system treats the distinction [between holding and dicta] as a vague and shifting one. . . . Judges have tremendous leeway in being able to redefine the holding and the dictum in the precedential cases. This leeway enables judges, in effect, to rewrite the rules of law on which earlier cases had been decided.
>
> Depending on how a judge would read the holdings in cases deemed to be precedents, she would extract different rules of law

---

[92] Federal judges are appointed by the President for life, but they must be confirmed by the Senate — a process that is frequently contentious.

capable of generating conflicting outcomes in the case before her. . . . The choice of which rules to apply in the first place is not dictated by the law and . . . competing rules will be available in almost any case which reaches the stage of litigation.[93]

The operative claim in CLS [Critical Legal Studies] analysis is that the law is infused with a irresolvably opposed principles and ideals . . . . Those ideological controversies which play a significant part in the public debate of our political culture are replicated in the argument of judicial decision. . . . Of course, CLS recognizes that in legal argument the controversies will often be masked or hidden by talk of intent of the framers, the requirements of *stare decisis*, and so on. The point is that the same ideological divisions which fragment political discourse are replicated in one form or another in a legal argument. [The law] . . . is a patchwork quilt of irreconcilable ideologies. . . . [94]

Whew! Is this possible? Are stare decisis and the doctrine of precedent merely a "mask" to conceal the political predilections of judges? One of the leading Critical Legal Studies scholars, Duncan Kennedy, once developed a list of techniques that judges can use to escape precedents they find problematic and, while appearing to follow the past, make cases come out whichever way they please.[95] But have the Legal Realists and the "Crits"[96] left something out? Have they, for example given too little credence to the keen motivation most judges feel to do what they believe is expected of a person in their institutional role rather

---

[93] Be sure to watch carefully how the techniques described in this paragraph were exhibited again and again in the appeals and reconsiderations of *DeWeerth v. Baldinger*, as you read the various follow-up opinions in Chapters X, XIV, and XV.

[94] Andrew Altman, *Legal Realism Critical Legal Studies and Dworkin*, in PHILOSOPHY AND PUBLIC AFFAIRS, *reprinted in* JOEL FEINBERG AND HYMAN GROSS, PHILOSOPHY OF LAW 176, 177-78, 180, 182-83 (5th ed. 1995) (emphasis added; some omissions and tense changes not shown).

[95] *See* James Boyle, *The Anatomy of a Torts Class*, 34 Am. Univ. L. Rev. 1003, 1051 (1985), summarizing the techniques from published and unpublished writings of Kennedy's. *See also* Duncan Kennedy, *Form and Substance in Private Law Adjudication*, 89 HARV. L. REV. 1685 (1976). For a critique, *see* RICHARD A. POSNER, THE PROBLEMS OF JURISPRUDENCE 254-59 (1990).

[96] As Critical Legal Studies adherents are sometimes called—not always affectionately.

than indulge their own idiosyncratic will to power and notions of "right"?[97]

Most practicing (and practical) lawyers and judges would probably agree that the Legal Realists and, especially, the Crits have gone overboard. The judges encountered in real life seem very concerned both to know what the prior cases have held and to conform their own decisions to the rules and principles that are found in the precedents — not as a mask for their own predilections but as the law. When a judge sits down and writes an opinion, the judge is most likely to see himself in a thinking process of "finding" the law, not of making it. The judge wants to cite and (absent some really strong reason) to follow any particular prior cases that are in point. Even when a lacuna of open texture requires a judge to make a choice, it is only rarely that the judge will "make" law as a legislature does when it passes a statute. On the contrary, as Ronald Dworkin cogently argues, actual judges dealing with open texture normally do not undertake to "invent" law at all but instead try to discover the principles that are already there, "embedded" or "implicit" in the body of earlier decisions — not just in particular precedents but in, potentially, "all other judicial decisions within his general jurisdiction."[98]

Even the great Holmes, in carrying out his duties as a judge, was not immune to the gravitational tugs of precedent. He cited prior cases very much as any other judge would have, using them both to justify his legal decisions and to show them as conforming to the law. And the dominant modern legal-judicial thinker in Holmes's pragmatic tradition, Judge Richard A. Posner, is explicit:

> [A] decision maker must be concerned not only with doing substantive justice in the case at hand but also with maintaining a legal fabric that includes considerations of precedent. . . . [99]

---

[97] *See, e.g.,* RICHARD A. POSNER, THE PROBLEMS OF JURISPRUDENCE 194-95 (1990); RONALD DWORKIN, LAW'S EMPIRE 258-68 (1986).

[98] DWORKIN, TAKING RIGHTS SERIOUSLY, *supra* at 116.

[99] RICHARD A. POSNER, THE PROBLEMS OF JURISPRUDENCE 156-57 (1990). Judge Posner long has served on the law faculty of the University of Chicago and is the intellectual father of the "law-and-economics" movement, which believes "the implicit logic of much legal reasoning is economic," *id.* at 107, and which tends to identify "substantive justice" with utilitarian solutions.

Nonetheless, Holmes and the other Legal Realists remind us of an important point: The common law cannot be taken for granted as an independent and self-operating system of governance but, rather, it depends every step of the way on the actions and choices of individual human beings — lawyers and judges — to give it specific content so that it can be applied as specific cases arise. It was observed in an earlier footnote that there may or may not always be a single "right" answer to legal questions, but it is always possible to give a wrong answer. A less-than-rigid version of stare decisis will usually show us the authoritatively right answer, will help us avoid the wrong answers, and, at the same time, will still leave flexibility to reach for newer and better resolutions when there are good articulable reasons to believe that an older doctrine has become obsolete.

Finally, you should not lose sight of the fact that, as a practical matter, in many or most factual situations the law and its application are rather clear, and not open to much debate. These are not, however, the situations that command very much of a lawyer's legal-analysis skill, and lawyers frequently find themselves required to operate and solve problems in areas of legal and factual ambiguity. Therefore, despite the considerable fluidity and malleability of the law as seen from the perspective of a practicing lawyer (or of a law student), the operation of the legal system is no doubt a good deal more stable and predicable than it sometimes may seem to those who concentrate on its uncertainties.

* * *

How do actual judges view the evolution of American common law, judicial lawmaking, and the supposed "binding" force that makes precedent into "law"? It turns out that, given the way precedent is actually treated in modern times, the whole debate over "make law" vs. "find law" may be pretty much a tempest in a teapot in most situations of importance. We will close this section with an extended quotation from a recent opinion of the Ninth Circuit Court of Appeals, in which Judge Alex Kozinski presents a mini-treatise on the doctrine of precedent as it has come down to us from the common law and has become our modern legacy.

Hart v. Massanari
266 F.3d 1155 (9th Cir. 2001)

KOZINSKI, Circuit Judge

Common law judges did not make law as we understand that concept; rather, they "found" the law with the help of earlier cases that had considered similar matters. An opinion was evidence of what the law is, but it was not an independent source of law. See THEODORE F.T. PLUCKNETT, A CONCISE HISTORY OF THE COMMON LAW 343-44 (5th ed. 1956).[100] The law was seen as something that had an existence independent of what judges said: "a miraculous something made by nobody . . . and merely declared from time to time by the judges." 2 JOHN AUSTIN, LECTURES ON JURISPRUDENCE OR THE PHILOSOPHY OF POSITIVE LAW 655 (4th ed. 1873) (emphasis omitted). Opinions were merely judges' efforts to ascertain the law, much like scientific experiments were efforts to ascertain natural laws. If an eighteenth-century judge believed that a prior case was wrongly decided, he could say that the prior judge had erred in his attempt to discern the law. See Bole v. Horton, 124 Eng. Rep. 1113, 1124 (C.P. 1673). Neither judges nor lawyers understood precedent to be binding in [a] strict sense.

　　　＊　＊　＊

[A]s late as the middle of the nineteenth century, an English judge might ignore decisions of the House of Lords, and the Exchequer and Queen's Bench held different views on the same point as late as 1842. Common law judges looked to earlier cases only as

---

[100] As [Sir Mathew] Hale described it [in 1739], judicial decisions "do not make a Law properly so-called," but "they have a great Weight and Authority in Expounding, Declaring, and Publishing what the Law of this Kingdom is, [and] are a greater Evidence [of a law] than the Opinion of any private Persons, as such, whatsoever." Sir Matthew Hale, The History of the Common Law of England 68 (London, Nutt & Gosling 1739). In Lord Mansfield's view, "the reason and spirit of cases make law; not the letter of particular precedents." Fisher v. Prince, 97 Eng. Rep. 876, 876 (K. B. 1762). (Footnote in original.)

examples of policy or practice, and a single case was generally not binding authority.

* * *

The idea that judges declared rather than made the law remained firmly entrenched in English jurisprudence until the early nineteenth century. . . . Blackstone, who wrote his Commentaries only two decades before the Constitutional Convention and was greatly respected and followed by the generation of the Framers, noted that "the 'law,' and the 'opinion of the judge' are not . . . one and the same thing; since it sometimes may happen that the judge may mistake the law"; in such cases, the precedent simply "was not law." 1 WILLIAM BLACKSTONE, COMMENTARIES 70-71 (1765).

* * *

The modern concept of binding precedent—where a single opinion sets the course on a particular point of law and must be followed by courts at the same level and lower within a pyramidal judicial hierarchy—came about only gradually over the nineteenth and early twentieth centuries. Lawyers began to believe that judges made, not found, the law. This coincided with monumental improvements in the collection and reporting of case authorities. As the concept of law changed and a more comprehensive reporting system began to take hold, it became possible for judicial decisions to serve as binding authority.

* * *

[Then Judge Kozinski described in some detail the law of precedent in the American federal courts. *Ed.*]

When ruling on a novel issue of law, [a federal court] will generally consider how other courts have ruled on the same issue. This consideration will not be limited to courts at the same or higher level, or even to courts within the same system of sovereignty. Federal courts of appeals will cite decisions of district courts, even those in other circuits; the Supreme Court may cite the decisions of the inferior courts [citations omitted]. It is not unusual to cite the decision of courts in foreign jurisdictions, so long as they speak to a matter relevant to the issue before us [citations omitted]. The process even extends to non-case authorities, such as treatises and law review articles. [citations omitted].

Citing a precedent is, of course, not the same as following it; "respectfully disagree" within five words of "learned colleagues" is almost a cliche. After carefully considering and digesting the views of other courts and commentators — often giving conflicting guidance on a novel legal issue — courts will then proceed to follow one line of authority or another, or sometimes strike out in a completely different direction. While we would consider it bad form to ignore contrary authority by failing even to acknowledge its existence, it is well understood that — in the absence of binding precedent — courts may forge a different path than suggested by prior authorities that have considered the issue. So long as the earlier authority is acknowledged and considered, courts are deemed to have complied with their common law responsibilities.

But precedent also serves a very different function in the federal courts today, one related to the horizontal and vertical organization of those courts. See John Harrison, *The Power of Congress Over The Rules of Precedent*, 50 Duke L.J. 503 (2000). A district judge may not respectfully (or disrespectfully) disagree with his learned colleagues on his own court of appeals who have ruled on a controlling legal issue, or with Supreme Court Justices writing for a majority of the Court.[101] Binding authority within this regime cannot be considered and cast aside; it is not merely evidence of what the law is. Rather, caselaw on point is the law. If a court must decide an issue governed by a prior opinion that constitutes binding authority, the later court is bound to reach the same result, even if it considers the rule unwise or incorrect. Binding authority must be followed unless and until overruled by a body competent to do so.

In determining whether it is bound by an earlier decision, a court considers not merely the "reason and spirit of cases" but also "the letter of particular precedents." *Fisher v. Prince*, 97 Eng. Rep. 876, 876 (K.B. 1762). This includes not only the rule announced, but

---

[101] The same practice is followed in the state courts as well. See, e.g., Auto Equity Sales, Inc. v. Superior Court of Santa Clara County, 57 Cal. 2d 450, 369 P.2d 937, 940, 20 Cal. Rptr. 321 (Cal. 1962) ("Courts exercising inferior jurisdiction must accept the law declared by courts of superior jurisdiction. It is not their function to attempt to overrule decisions of a higher court.") (footnote in original).

also the facts giving rise to the dispute, other rules considered and rejected and the views expressed in response to any dissent or concurrence. Thus, when crafting binding authority, the precise language employed is often crucial to the contours and scope of the rule announced.

* * *

Obviously, binding authority is very powerful medicine. A decision of the Supreme Court will control that corner of the law unless and until the Supreme Court itself overrules or modifies it. Judges of the inferior courts may voice their criticisms, but follow it they must. See, *e.g., Ortega v. United States*, 861 F.2d 600, 603 & n. 4 (9th Cir. 1988) ("This case is squarely controlled by the Supreme Court's recent decision . . . . [We] agree[]with the dissent that [appellant] deserves better treatment from our Government. Unfortunately, legal precedent deprives us of discretion to do equity."). The same is true as to circuit authority, although it usually covers a much smaller geographic area. Circuit law . . . - binds all courts within a particular circuit, including the court of appeals itself. Thus, the first panel to consider an issue sets the law not only for all the inferior courts in the circuit, but also future panels of the court of appeals.

Binding authority is not only "powerful medicine," it is also relatively sparingly applied. As Judge Kozinski explained (266 F.3d at 1163):

> [M]ost decisions of the federal courts are not viewed as binding precedent. No trial court decisions are; almost four-fifths of the merits decisions of courts of appeals are not.

THE ANSWER

*t*he court did not dismiss Mrs. DeWeerth's complaint on motion (*see* decision at pages 74-76). Mr. Sills's next step was to prepare and file an answer.

Like the complaint filed by the plaintiff, the answer is a "pleading," and its purpose is generally to apprise the other side of the legal position that person filing the pleading is going to take, in this case the defendant. Like the complaint, the answer should not set out arguments of law, and it should not contain recitations of evidence, but it simply should be a brief statement of the factual allegations on which the defense will be based.

As you read Mrs. Baldinger's answer below, pay particular attention to the "first defense." As for the many matters raised in the other defenses and *counterclaim*, most of them ultimately went nowhere, and you should not be concerned if you don't yet understand them all. Just try to get the general gist of things, including the fact that, in preparing this answer, Mr. Sills was being diligently comprehensive in his approach.

UNITED STATES DISTRICT COURT
SOUTHERN DISTRICT OF NEW YORK
- X
                                                :
      GERDA DOROTHEA DE WEERTH,   :
                            Plaintiff,   :   83 Civ. 1233
                                                :
            -against-   : ANSWER AND COUNTERCLAIM
                                                :
      EDITH MARKS BALDINGER,   :
                            Defendant.   :
                                                :
- X

     Defendant EDITH MARKS BALDINGER, sued herein as EDITH MARX
BALDINGER, by her attorney EDWARD M. SILLS, for her answer and
defenses to the complaint and her counterclaim against plaintiff
sets forth the following:

FOR ANSWER AND A FIRST DEFENSE
     1. Defendant admits the allegations contained in paragraphs 2
and 3 of the complaint; admits that plaintiff claimed to ownership
of a certain painting by Claude Monet owned and possessed by
defendant and demanded its return, which claim defendant denied
and which demand defendant rejected; alleges that she is without
knowledge or information sufficient to form a belief as to the
truth of the allegations contained in paragraphs 1, 4 and 6 of the
complaint; and denies each and every other allegation contained in
the complaint.

FOR AFFIRMATIVE DEFENSES
SECOND DEFENSE
     2. The complaint fails to state a claim against defendant upon
which relief can be granted.

THIRD DEFENSE
     3. The complaint is barred by the applicable statutes of
limitations.

FOURTH DEFENSE
     4. The complaint is barred by laches.

FIFTH DEFENSE
     5. The complaint is barred by plaintiff's failure to
exercise due diligence in pursuit of her claims, and by
waiver and estoppel.

SIXTH DEFENSE
     6. Plaintiff has no right to the possession she claims of the
painting because she made a gratuitous bailment of said painting.

SEVENTH DEFENSE

7. Plaintiff has no right to the possession she claims of the painting because defendant purchased same for value and in good faith, and has good title thereto under the laws of the State of New York, including, without limitation, Sections 2-312 and 2-403 of the New York State Uniform Commercial Code.

EIGHTH DEFENSE

8. Plaintiff has no right to possession because she abandoned the property.

NINTH DEFENSE

9. The complaint is barred by the doctrine of adverse possession.

WHEREFORE defendant demands judgment against plaintiff dismissing the complaint, together with the costs and disbursements of this action.

COUNTERCLAIM

10. Defendant repeats and realigns the allegations of paragraphs 1 through 9 of her answer and defenses to the complaint as if set forth at length herein.

11. The institution of this suit, and the claims of plaintiff in the complaint filed herein to be the owner of the painting and entitled to possession thereof discredits and casts a cloud on the title which was transferred to BALDINGER by WILDENSTEIN & CO., INC. from whom she purchased the same in good faith for value and without notice of any defect in title, and on the provenance provided upon such purchase. The value of the painting has been adversely affected and diminished thereby, and during the pendency of this litigation, such painting is no longer marketable and saleable by public sale, and has no value for such purpose.

12. The claim made by plaintiff DE WEERTH against BALDINGER that she is a converter and is in wrongful possession of a painting which she purchased in good faith for valuable consideration and has prized and enjoyed for over twenty-five years without disturbance since such purchase, has caused her considerable personal distress and anguish, has generated great anxiety over the soundness of the title she received from WILDENSTEIN, and has resulted in grave concern and apprehension lest she be required to part with a uniquely artistic possession to which she has grown strongly attached.

13. Defendant has suffered injury and damage in consequence of the foregoing.

WHEREFORE defendant demands judgment on her counterclaim against plaintiff for damages, attorney's fees and costs of suit.

```
Dated: New York, New York
       April 5th, 1983

                              EDWARD M. SILLS
                              Attorney for Defendant
                              225 Broadway
                              New York, New York 10007
                              Tel. No.: (212) 555-6789
To: John R. Horan, Esq.
    Attorney for Plaintiff
    One Broadway
    New York, New York 10004
```

STUDY QUESTIONS

1. Which facts alleged in the complaint did the defendant admit? Why do you suppose that the defendant admitted these particular factual points?
2. Which facts did the defendant deny?
3. Do you imagine that the defendant had direct or even indirect personal knowledge of the first fact alleged in paragraph 7 of the complaint? If not, was it legitimate for her to "deny" it, based on no real knowledge one way or the other? Why?
4. Notice the part of the answer called the "Affirmative Defenses." Do you see how these defenses are fundamentally different than the "First Defense"? How?

A defense like the "Second Defense" in this answer is sometimes referred to as an "affirmative defense" (as opposed to a denial). It says, in effect, that even if everything alleged by the plaintiff turns out to be true, the defendant still should win the lawsuit because there is something else, some other legal rule or principle, that applies to the case.

"Being right means nothing unless the case stands
up in court."

—*Anon*

*O*nce an answer has been served, the pleading stage is
normally complete. After that, however, several years
can elapse before there is an actual trial. The case of
DeWeerth v. Baldinger was no exception. During this interval,
Mr. Horan and Mr. Sills engaged in a pre-trial process known as
discovery. In the process of discovery, each side is expected to
divulge all relevant materials, documents, witnesses, and testimony that are requested by the other side (literally, "discover" =
"uncover"). In other words, each side is expected to show its cards,
so to speak — provided that a properly formulated and sufficiently
definite demand has been made by the other side. (Also, the
Federal Rules and some state's procedural rules also specify
that certain kinds of basic information must be supplied even
without a demand.)

One of the obvious purposes of discovery is to minimize the use of "surprise" tactics at trial. Perhaps even more importantly, discovery helps to refine and clarify the legal and factual issues before a trial is held. Because of pre-trial discovery, it is possible in many cases to avoid a trial entirely. Traditionally, discovery takes four main forms:

1. Depositions of Parties and Witnesses — A *deposition* is a question-and-answer interview in which the *deponent* gives answers under oath. Parties as well as non-party witnesses can be compelled to give depositions. A lawyer will "notice a deposition" (*i.e.*, demand a deposition) at a stated time and place, and the person named in the notice is then required to be available at the time and place for a pre-trial grilling. If the person to be deposed (the "deponent") is not a party in the case, then a *subpoena* must also be served in order to compel attendance. Sometimes a lawyer will "notice a deposition" of a witness for his or her own side, for example to preserve testimony. A stenographic or video record is made of depositions.

To give you something of the flavor of a deposition, there is an excerpt at the end of this chapter from the deposition that was taken of the president of the Wildenstein & Co. Inc., concerning the information they had concerning the past history of the Monet when they sold it to Mrs. Baldinger. A lengthier series of excerpts, questioning Mrs. DeWeerth, is presented in Appendix A.

2. Interrogatories — These are formal written questions that one side submits to be answered, in writing and under oath, by the opposing party.

3. Requests for Admissions — Either party can serve the other party with a written request to stipulate or "admit" the truth of certain facts. Admissions relieve the necessity of presenting evidence on the point.

4. Requests for the Production or Inspection of Documents or Other Things, Physical or Mental Examinations of Persons — Rules of civil procedure, including the Federal Rules, authorize various requests of these kinds, which round out the possible elements of discovery.

Obviously, these discovery procedures have a significant potential for abuse, and it is not hard to see how a lawyer might use discovery in an "oppressive" way. It is well known, for example, that an extended discovery process can sometimes slow down and "cost up" litigation to the point where a person with a good claim or solid defense may be forced to accept a bad settlement out of pure desperation. There are, of course, rules against abuse, but the courts leave wide latitudes. Their concern is that they might otherwise cut off legitimate factual investigation in the name of preventing abuse. Nevertheless, by taking advantage of the latitudes, lawyers for well-heeled clients have been known to use discovery demands to exhaust the financial resources of less-well-off opponents.

STUDY QUESTIONS

There is no indication that there was any abusive use of discovery in *DeWeerth v. Baldinger*, but before we leave the topic, consider this: Would a good lawyer ever use legally permitted discovery options with a conscious design to wear down the other side? Suppose the lawyer suspects that the information sought will in fact be "useful," but the lawyer knows all the same that her heavy demands for depositions, document productions, examinations, etc., will wear down the other side — likely forcing it to capitulate because it lacks resources to go on. Should the lawyer go ahead and demand the discovery anyway? Wouldn't it be *disloyal* to the client for the lawyer *not* to try to wear down the other side as long as the rules permit whatever discovery demands are made? What would you advise — serve your client but maybe put a pinch on justice, or promote a just outcome, but at the expense of your own client?

EXCERPT FROM DEPOSITION OF MR. HARRY A. BROOKS

EXAMINATION BY MR. HORAN:

Q: Mr. Brooks, what is your title at Wildenstien?
A: President.
Q: How long have you been president?
A: Since '78.
Q: Do you have another title?
A: No.

* * *

THE WITNESS: I would like to say something that —
MR. HORAN: You can say something.
A: I think it's only fair to say that a dealer respects
very often the desire of various people to be anon-
ymous when they sell a picture. There were various
reasons, particularly people in Europe who don't
want for various reasons, don't want their names
mentioned in the sale of a picture. Particularly
the Swiss, who very often don't wish to involve
themselves.
     If they have a painting, they have every reason to
sell it, and that's the reason you every so often see a
Swiss collection or so.
Q: So anonymity by itself isn't to you a circumstance
that is unusual?
A: No.
     In fact, you'll notice all of the indications in
these books of Mr. Wildenstein, the pictures refer to
as belonging to an ''appropriate anonym.''
     In other words, we didn't involve Mrs. Marks or Mrs.
Baldinger, her name in the books.
Q: But isn't it important when you publish the origin
that you know the origin?
A: Well, it depends on how far it goes back.
     If we buy from another dealer, we can't enforce
that other dealer to give us the name of the collector
that they bought it from.

Q: But isn't that a question of trust between dealers?

A: No, even less so, because very often, a dealer may have a connection with a particular collection, and they may get a painting from that collection, and when they sell it, they don't wish to give out the source of that picture, the name of the collection, because they feel that that's a mine of their own.

Q: How can you be sure you are not passing on a stolen painting?

A: Well, these pictures are—the records from the World War are fairly well documented.

   There was a series of volumes printed after the war after various pictures were stolen.

   We always check those, and we respect the source of the person that we bought them from.

   I'm sure Mr. Wildenstein has known the Reichenbachs since they were children.

Q: That's what I meant by trust a moment ago.

A: Yes, but we can't enforce anyone to give us the name of the person that they bought the picture from.

   I mean, we're not liable to.

Q: So, in a given instance it may or may not occur that you learn the original source of the dealer's ownership or possession of the painting?

A: We can. Sometimes if they choose to give it, but we never make that an issue. We certainly don't give out where we have bought all of the pictures.

*a*s Mr. Sills followed the evidence coming in during the discovery process, he was not encouraged. The bottom line seemed to be shaping up like this. Mrs. DeWeerth had substantial evidence to show that:

(1) she inherited the Monet painting,
(2) she previously had it in her possession,
(3) somebody took it away without her consent,
(4) the Monet is now held by the defendant, Mrs. Baldinger, and
(5) the lawsuit was commenced only a few days after the demand was refused.

Although some aspects of Mrs. DeWeerth's story remained vague (such as exactly how the painting disappeared), there seemed little real basis for contesting the main legally relevant facts. From Mr. Sills's standpoint, as counsel for the defense, this was not a great evidentiary posture for trial, nor was it a very strong position for negotiating a settlement.

Still, maybe a trial could be avoided. After all, the discovery process is not just for the purpose of preparing for trial. Another purpose is to help refine and clarify the factual and legal issues. After discovery is completed it sometimes becomes apparent that no trial is needed because the case presents no real issues of fact.

If the parties' only disagreement is about questions of law, with no genuine issue as to any material fact, the case can be decided by a *summary judgment* — i.e., a judgment without trial. The function of the full trial is to let the parties introduce evidence so the fact-finder (typically, a jury) can sort out contested *facts*. The parties do not need a trial to make their respective arguments on the legal issues, and the judge does not need a trial to resolve the questions of law. All of that can be accomplished on paper (the "memoranda of law" we spoke of on page 73) supplemented, typically, by relatively short oral arguments at a hearing on a *motion for summary judgment*.

Under Rule 56 of the Federal Rules of Civil Procedure, a defendant may move for summary judgment "at any time" and summary judgment

> shall be rendered forthwith if the pleadings, depositions, answers to interrogatories, and admissions on file, together with the affidavits, if any, show that *there is no genuine issue as to any material fact* and that the moving party is entitled to a judgment as a matter of law.[102]

So, as far as timing is concerned, Mr. Sills could now move that the court grant summary judgment, in favor of Mrs. Baldinger. But making the motion is one thing, winning it another. A motion by Mr. Sills would not be granted unless he could come up with something more than he seemed to have so far. On the contrary, at this point it looked like *Mr. Horan* had the stronger case for summary judgment, on behalf of Mrs. DeWeerth. If Mr. Sills was going to have any shot at winning this case — on summary judgment or at trial — he needed to find something further. What?

---

[102] Emphasis added.

One thing that must have struck Mr. Sills is this: Mrs. DeWeerth's case is based on a theft that occurred more than 35 years in the past, but the evidence that came out during discovery did not show she did anything much to find the painting in the meantime. "For all we know," Mr. Sills might have thought to himself, "Mrs. DeWeerth was perfectly content just to let this painting float along on the international art market, appreciating rapidly in value, and then eventually reclaim it when it finally emerged." Now here's the question: Can Mr. Sills persuade the court to look at Mrs. DeWeerth's relatively lean effort to find her painting as a legally *relevant* fact? In other words, even though most of the obviously relevant facts seem to be going against him, can Mr. Sills nonetheless prevail by turning one of the seemingly non-relevant facts into something the court will treat as pivotal? To do that, Mr. Sills would need to invoke some further rule or principle of law, one he hadn't yet really thought of. It's time for some more research.

By now, Mr. Sills had thoroughly canvassed the New York law. He already knew, painfully well, that no New York case had ever said explicitly that owners have to make a diligent search for their stolen property or else lose the benefit of the "demand and refusal" requirement. While the courts had held that a plaintiff may not "unreasonably delay" making a demand, no New York case had ever even considered the question of whether that might also require a diligent search.[103] Sometimes, however, legal developments that occur elsewhere take a while to show up in New York cases, and vice versa. Perhaps another look at a treatise (many of which are regularly updated with supplements) or at a recent law review article might turn up something. Suppose Mr. Sills spent an evening in the law library, or asked an associate to do it for him. He may well have come across the following new development in the law, not a New York case, but really right on point.

---

[103] Although Mrs. Baldinger's answer alleged that Mrs. DeWeerth failed to exercise due diligence in pursuing her *claims* (*see* page 122), it did not allege a failure to use due diligence in pursuit of her *painting*. The two are different, aren't they? Under New York law, as we have seen, until Mrs. DeWeerth located the painting and made a demand (and was refused), she did not even have a "claim" to pursue.

O'Keeffe v. Snyder
83 N.J. 478, 416 A.2d 862 (1980)

POLLOCK, J.

[This was an action for replevin to recover paintings by the twentieth century American artist, Georgia O'Keeffe.] In her complaint, filed in March, 1976, O'Keeffe alleged she was the owner of the paintings and that they were stolen from a New York art gallery in 1946. Snyder asserted he was a purchaser for value of the paintings, he had title by adverse possession, and O'Keeffe's action was barred by the expiration of the six-year period of limitations provided by N.J.S.A. 2A:14-1 pertaining to an action in replevin. [Snyder claimed he had bought the paintings from Ulrich A. Frank in 1975, for $35,000.]

The trial court granted summary judgment for Snyder on the ground that O'Keeffe's action was barred because it was not commenced within six years of the alleged theft. The Appellate Division reversed and entered [summary] judgment for O'Keeffe. *O'Keeffe, supra, 170 N.J. Super. at 92.* A majority of that court concluded that the paintings were stolen, . . . and Snyder had not proved the elements of adverse possession. Consequently, the majority ruled that O'Keeffe could still enforce her right to possession of the paintings. . . . We reverse [the Appellate Division] and remand the matter for a plenary hearing in accordance with this opinion.

I

The record, limited to pleadings, affidavits, answers to interrogatories, and depositions, is fraught with factual conflict. * * *

O'Keeffe contended the paintings were stolen in 1946 from a gallery . . . operated by her late husband, the famous photographer Alfred Stieglitz. . . . In 1946, Stieglitz arranged an exhibit which included an O'Keeffe painting, identified as Cliffs. According to O'Keeffe, one day in March, 1946, she and Stieglitz discovered Cliffs was missing from the wall of the exhibit. O'Keeffe estimates the value of the painting at the time of the alleged theft to have been about $150.

About two weeks later, O'Keeffe noticed that two other paintings, Seaweed and Fragments, were missing from a storage room. . . . She did not tell anyone, even Stieglitz, about the missing paintings, since she did not want to upset him.

Before the date when O'Keeffe discovered the disappearance of Seaweed, she had already sold it (apparently for a string of amber beads) to a Mrs. Weiner, now deceased. . . .

There was no evidence of a break and entry . . . on the dates when O'Keeffe discovered the disappearance of her paintings. Neither Stieglitz nor O'Keeffe reported them missing to the New York Police Department or any other law enforcement agency. Apparently the paintings were uninsured, and O'Keeffe did not seek reimbursement from an insurance company. Similarly, neither O'Keeffe nor Stieglitz advertised the loss of the paintings in Art News or any other publication. Nonetheless, they discussed it with associates in the art world and later O'Keeffe mentioned the loss to the director of the Art Institute of Chicago, but she did not ask him to do anything because "it wouldn't have been my way." O'Keeffe does not contend that Frank or Snyder had actual knowledge of the alleged theft.

Stieglitz died in the summer of 1946, and O'Keeffe explains she did not pursue her efforts to locate the paintings because she was settling his estate. In 1947, she retained the services of Doris Bry to help settle the estate. Bry urged O'Keeffe to report the loss of the paintings, but O'Keeffe declined because "they never got anything back by reporting it." Finally, in 1972, O'Keeffe authorized Bry to report the theft to the Art Dealers Association of America, Inc., which maintains for its members a registry of stolen paintings. The record does not indicate whether such a registry existed at the time the paintings disappeared.

In September 1975, O'Keeffe learned that the paintings were in the Andrew Crispo Gallery in New York on consignment from Bernard Danenberg Galleries. On February 11, 1976, O'Keeffe discovered that Ulrich A. Frank had sold the paintings to Barry Snyder, d/b/a Princeton Gallery of Fine Art. [The sale price was $35,000.] She demanded their return and, following Snyder's refusal, instituted this action for replevin.

Frank traces his possession of the paintings to his father, Dr. Frank, who died in 1968. He claims there is a family relationship by marriage between his family and the Stieglitz family, a contention that O'Keeffe disputes. Frank does not know how his father acquired the paintings, but he recalls seeing them in his father's apartment in New Hampshire as early as 1941-1943, a period that precedes the alleged theft. Consequently, Frank's factual contentions are inconsistent with O'Keeffe's allegation of theft.

Frank claims continuous possession of the paintings through his father for over thirty years and admits selling the paintings to Snyder. Snyder and Frank do not trace their provenance, or history of possession of the paintings, back to O'Keeffe.

Snyder moved for summary judgment on the theory that O'Keeffe's action was barred by the statute of limitations and title had vested in Frank by adverse possession. For purposes of his motion, Snyder conceded that the paintings had been stolen. On her cross motion, O'Keeffe urged that the paintings were stolen, the statute of limitations had not run, and title to the paintings remained in her.

II

* * * The Appellate Division accepted O'Keeffe's contention that the paintings had been stolen. However, in his deposition, Ulrich Frank traces possession of the paintings to his father in the early 1940's, a date that precedes the alleged theft by several years. The factual dispute about the loss of the paintings by O'Keeffe and their acquisition by Frank, as well as the other subsequently described factual issues, warrant a remand for a plenary hearing. . . .

III

On the limited record before us, we cannot determine now who has title to the paintings. That determination will depend on the evidence adduced at trial. Nonetheless, we believe it may aid the trial court and the parties to resolve questions of law that may become relevant at trial.

Our decision begins with the principle that, generally speaking, if the paintings were stolen, the thief acquired no title and could not transfer good title to others regardless of their good faith and ignorance of the theft. *Joseph v. Lesnevich,* 56 N.J. Super. 340, 346 (App. Div. 1959); *Kutner Buick, Inc. v. Strelecki,* 111 N.J. Super. 89, 97 (Ch. Div. 1970); *see* Ashton v. Allen, 70 N.J.L. 117, 119 (Sup. Ct. 1903). Proof of theft would advance O'Keeffe's right to possession of the paintings absent other considerations such as expiration of the statute of limitations.

* * *

On this appeal, the critical legal question is when O'Keeffe's cause of action accrued. The fulcrum on which the outcome turns is the statute of limitations in *N.J.S.A. 2A:14-1,* which provides that an action for replevin of goods or chattels must be commenced within six years after the accrual of the cause of action.

The trial court found that O'Keeffe's cause of action accrued on the date of the alleged theft, March, 1946, and concluded that her action was barred. * * *

Since the alleged theft occurred in New York, a preliminary question is whether the statute of limitations of New York or New Jersey applies. [The court concluded: "On the facts before us, it would appear that the appropriate statute of limitations is the law of the forum, N.J.S.A. 2A:14-1"]

IV

On the assumption that New Jersey law will apply, we shall consider significant questions raised about the interpretation of N.J.S.A. 2A:14-1. The purpose of a statute of limitations is to "stimulate to activity and punish negligence" and "promote repose by giving security and stability to human affairs." *Wood v. Carpenter,* 101 U.S. 135, 139, 25 L. Ed. 807, 808 (1879); *Tevis v. Tevis,* 79 N.J. 422, 430-431 (1979); *Fernandi v. Strully,* 35 N.J. 434, 438 (1961). A statute of limitations achieves those purposes by barring a cause of action after the statutory period. In certain instances, this Court has ruled that the literal language of a statute of limitations should yield to other considerations. *Compare, e.g., Velmohos v.*

Maren Engineering Corp., 83 N.J. 282, 293 (1980) *with Galligan v. Westfield Centre Service, Inc.,* 82 N.J. 188, 192-193 (1980).

To avoid harsh results from the mechanical application of the statute, the courts have developed a concept known as the discovery rule. *Lopez v. Swyer,* 62 N.J. 267, 273-275 (1973); Prosser, The Law of Torts (4 ed. 1971), §30 at 144-145; 51 *Am. Jur.* 2d, *Limitation of Actions,* §146 at 716. **The discovery rule provides that, in an appropriate case, a cause of action will not accrue until the injured party discovers, or by exercise of reasonable diligence and intelligence should have discovered, facts which form the basis of a cause of action.** *Burd v. New Jersey Telephone Company,* 76 N.J. 284, 291-292 (1978). The rule is essentially a principle of equity, the purpose of which is to mitigate unjust results that otherwise might flow from strict adherence to a rule of law. *Lopez, supra,* 62 N.J. at 273-274.

This Court first announced the discovery rule in *Fernandi, supra,* 35 N.J. at 434. In *Fernandi,* a wing nut was left in a patient's abdomen following surgery and was not discovered for three years. *Id.* at 450-451. The majority held that fairness and justice mandated that the statute of limitations should not have commenced running until the plaintiff knew or had reason to know of the presence of the foreign object in her body. The discovery rule has since been extended to other areas of medical malpractice. *See, e.g., Lopez, supra* (alleged negligent radiation therapy following a radical mastectomy for breast cancer); *Yerzy v. Levine,* 108 N.J. Super. 222 (App. Div.), aff'd per curiam as modified, 57 N.J. 234 (1970) (negligent severance by surgeon of bile duct).

Increasing acceptance of the principle of the discovery rule has extended the doctrine to contexts unrelated to medical malpractice. * * * The statute of limitations before us, N.J.S.A. 2A:14-1, has been held subject to the discovery rule in an action for wrongful detention of shares of stock [sent erroneously by a broker to a customer]. *Federal Insurance Co. v. Hausler,* 108 N.J. Super. 421, 426 (App. Div. 1970) . . . .

Similarly, we conclude that the discovery rule applies to an action for replevin of a painting under N.J.S.A. 2A:14-1. **O'Keeffe's cause of action accrued when she first knew, or reasonably should**

have known through the exercise of due diligence, of the cause of action, including the identity of the possessor of the paintings. *See* N. Ward, *Adverse Possession of Loaned or Stolen Objects — Is Possession Still 9/10ths of the Law?*, published in *Legal Problems of Museum Administration* (ALI-ABA 1980) at 89-90.

* * *

In determining whether O'Keeffe is entitled to the benefit of the discovery rule, the trial court should consider, among others, the following issues: (1) whether O'Keeffe used due diligence to recover the paintings at the time of the alleged theft and thereafter; (2) whether at the time of the alleged theft there was an effective method, other than talking to her colleagues, for O'Keeffe to alert the art world; and (3) whether registering paintings with the Art Dealers Association of America, Inc. or any other organization would put a reasonably prudent purchaser of art on constructive notice that someone other than the possessor was the true owner.

V

The acquisition of title to real and personal property by adverse possession is based on the expiration of a statute of limitations. R. Brown, The Law of Personal Property (3d ed. 1975), §4.1 at 33 (Brown). Adverse possession does not create title . . . apart from the statute of limitations. Walsh, *Title by Adverse Possession*, 17 N.Y.U. L.Q. Rev. 44, 82(1939) (Walsh); *see Developments in the Law — Statutes of Limitations*, 63 Harv. L. Rev. 1177 (1950) (Developments).

To establish title by adverse possession to chattels, the rule of law has been that the possession must be hostile, actual, visible, exclusive, and continuous. *Redmond v. New Jersey Historical Society,* 132 N.J. Eq. 464, 474 (E. & A.1942); 54 *C.J.S. Limitations of Actions* §119 at 23. * * * [However,] there is an inherent problem with many kinds of personal property that will raise questions whether their possession has been open, visible, and notorious. * * * [A number of] problems with the requirement of visible, open, and notorious possession readily come to mind. For example, if jewelry is stolen from a municipality in one county in New Jersey, it is unlikely that the owner would learn that someone is openly wearing that jewelry in another county or even in the same municipality. Open and visible possession of personal property, such as jewelry, may not be sufficient to put the original owner on actual or constructive notice of the identity of the possessor.

The problem is even more acute with works of art. Like many kinds of personal property, works of art are readily moved and easily concealed. O'Keeffe argues that nothing short of public display should be sufficient to alert the true owner and start the statute running. Although there is merit in that contention from the perspective of the original owner, the effect is to impose a heavy burden on the purchasers of paintings who wish to enjoy the paintings in the privacy of their homes.

In the present case, the trial court and Appellate Division concluded that the paintings, which allegedly had been kept in the private residences of the Frank family, had not been held visibly, openly, and notoriously. Notwithstanding that conclusion, the trial court ruled that the statute of limitations began to run at the time of the theft and had expired before the commencement of suit. The Appellate Division [reversed]. * * * The divergent conclusions of the lower courts suggest that the doctrine of adverse possession no longer provides a fair and reasonable means of resolving this kind of dispute.

The problem is serious. According to an affidavit submitted in this matter by the president of the International Foundation for Art Research, there has been an "explosion in art thefts" and there is a "worldwide phenomenon of art theft which has reached epidemic proportions."

The limited record before us provides a brief glimpse into the arcane world of sales of art, where paintings worth vast sums of money sometimes are bought without inquiry about their provenance. There does not appear to be a reasonably available method for an owner of art to record the ownership or theft of paintings. Similarly, there are no reasonable means readily available to a purchaser to ascertain the provenance of a painting. It may be time for the art world to establish a means by which a good faith purchaser may reasonably obtain the provenance of a painting. An efficient registry of original works of art might better serve the interests of artists, owners of art, and bona fide purchasers than the law of adverse possession with all of its uncertainties. L. DuBoff, The Deskbook of Art Law at 470-472 (Fed. Pub. Inc. 1977). Although we cannot mandate the initiation of a registration system, we can develop a rule for the commencement and running of the statute of limitations that is more responsive to the needs of the art world than the doctrine of adverse possession.

We are persuaded that the introduction of equitable considerations through the discovery rule provides a more satisfactory response than the doctrine of adverse possession. **The discovery rule shifts the emphasis from the conduct of the possessor to the conduct of the owner. The focus of the inquiry will no longer be whether the possessor has met the tests of adverse possession, but whether the owner has acted with due diligence in pursuing his or her personal property.**

For example, under the discovery rule, if an artist diligently seeks the recovery of a lost or stolen painting, but cannot find it or discover the identity of the possessor, the statute of limitations will not begin to run. The rule permits an artist who uses reasonable efforts to report, investigate, and recover a painting to preserve the rights of title and possession.

* * *

By diligently pursuing their goods, owners may prevent the statute of limitations from running. The meaning of due diligence will vary with the facts of each case, including the nature and value of the personal property. For example, with respect to jewelry of moderate value, it may be sufficient if the owner reports the theft to the police. With respect to art work of greater value, it may be reasonable to expect an owner to do more. In practice, our ruling should contribute to more careful practices concerning the purchase of art.

* * *

VI

Read literally, the effect of the expiration of the statute of limitations under N.J.S.A. 2A:14-1 is to bar an action such as replevin.

The statute does not speak of divesting the original owner of title. By its terms the statute cuts off the remedy, but not the right of title. Nonetheless, the effect of the expiration of the statute of limitations, albeit on the theory of adverse possession, has been not only to bar an action for possession, but also to vest title in the possessor. There is no reason to change that result ＊ ＊ ＊. History, reason, and common sense support the conclusion that the expiration of the statute of limitations bars the remedy to recover possession and also vests title in the possessor.

＊ ＊ ＊

We reverse the judgment of the Appellate Division in favor of O'Keeffe and remand the matter for trial in accordance with this opinion.

STUDY QUESTIONS

You should be able to answer the following questions based on the judge's opinion in *O'Keeffe*.

1. What was the critical legal question on this appeal?
2. Did Snyder concede that the paintings had been stolen?
3. What is the purpose of a statute of limitations, according to the court?
4. What is the so-called "discovery rule"? What does it provide?
5. In what kind of case did the New Jersey Supreme Court first announce the discovery rule?
6. What event was it that made O'Keeffe's cause of action accrue?
7. What is the acquisition of title by "adverse possession" based on?
8. What facts have to be present in order to "establish" title by adverse possession?
9. Does the court seem satisfied or dissatisfied with the traditional requirement that, to get a title by adverse possession,

the holder of a stolen painting must possess it "openly"? Why?

10. Does the court stay with the traditional requirements for getting title by adverse possession, or does it employ another rule instead? Why?

11. Is the portion of the court's opinion beginning at subpart "III" obiter dictum? Look at the first paragraph of subpart "III."

* * *

Do you see how Mr. Sills might have been delighted to find *O'Keeffe v. Snyder*?[104] But wait a minute. What court decided *O'Keeffe*? Look back at the caption at the beginning of the case.[105] If *O'Keeffe* is not a New York case, why should a New York court have to reckon with it at all? Does it matter that *DeWeerth v. Baldinger* is in federal court, not a state court? Remember the federal court is supposed to apply the same law that the state court would apply.[106]

* * *

Because *O'Keeffe v. Snyder* is not a New York case, the number-one question for a federal court applying New York law would be this: Would the New Jersey court's *reasoning* seem so compelling to a New York state court that the latter would be likely to adopt it? A New York court would not literally

---

[104] To help make certain that you do see, certain portions of the above opinion have been placed in **boldface** type. In the future, of course, there will be no editorial boldfacing of the saliently important portions of judicial opinions. An important element of legal education is learning, by experience, to separate the crucial from the rest.

[105] Here, you see "83 N.J. 473." This tells you that the case is reported in New Jersey Reports, which is the official reporter of the Supreme Court of New Jersey. This reporter contains *only* cases from that court. Therefore, the "83 N.J. 473" also tells you that this case was decided by the New Jersey Supreme Court. The other number-letter combination (416 A.2d 862) is called a "parallel" citation; it tells you the case is also reported in the "second series" of a set of books called the "Atlantic Reporter," at vol. 416, p. 862. Lastly, the parenthetical number tells us that the case was decided in 1980. Since we already know the identity of the court (from the "N.J." citation), it is not indicated in the parentheses.

[106] If you have any trouble with any of the last three questions, you may want to make a quick review of Chapter VII: The Common Law.

"follow" *O'Keeffe* as the "law" of New York state — that is, a New York court would not just cite it, describe it, and flatly say it "controls." However, a court in New York might well follow the reasoning of *O'Keeffe*.

What does all this mean for Mr. Sills? For one thing, it means that it would not be a good strategy for him simply to cite *O'Keeffe*, point out the similarity to his case, and then assert: "Therefore, judgment should be rendered for the defendant." He must instead argue for the soundness of the *O'Keeffe*'s reasoning, try to find echoes of that reasoning in prior New York decisions, and then argue that the trend of New York law, like New Jersey's, is to require replevin plaintiffs to prove "diligence" before they can get relief from the rigid three-year statute of limitations. While Mr. Sills's argument would almost surely cite *O'Keeffe*, his stress would be on its reasoning, perhaps leaving the case itself in the background — as a mere "example."

If Mr. Sills were to pursue such a strategy, there is still, of course, no guarantee that it would prevail. In fact, here is what District Judge Broderick had to say on the statute of limitations issue, along with some other issues that would simultaneously arise on a summary judgment motion:

DeWeerth v. Baldinger
(DeWeerth v. Baldinger II)
658 F. Supp. 688 (S.D.N.Y. (1987))

BRODERICK, District Judge

Defendant Baldinger has made a motion for summary judgment arguing that the action brought by plaintiff DeWeerth should be barred on timeliness grounds and also because plaintiff has not presented evidence establishing a superior right to possession of the painting. Under Federal Rule 56(c) the motion can be granted only if "there is no genuine issue as to any material fact" and a party "is entitled to a judgment as a matter of law." The court holds that on the present record plaintiff DeWeerth is entitled to summary judgment on the issue of timeliness and, as to the issue of superior right of possession, there are several genuine issues of material fact. Therefore, the defendant's motion for summary judgment is denied, and partial summary judgment is granted for plaintiff, on the issue of timeliness.

The two issues raised by defendant will be discussed in turn.

Timeliness

Defendant has argued initially that plaintiff's action should be barred by the statute of limitations governing actions for recovery of a chattel due to her long delay in asserting her claim, and also because she has not diligently sought to discover the painting's whereabouts until now.

It is not disputed that Mrs. Baldinger acquired the Monet in 1957; that Mrs. DeWeerth upon discovering in December, 1982 that defendant had the painting, demanded return of the Monet on December 27, 1982 and that defendant refused the demand on February 1, 1983; and that on February 16, 1983 plaintiff instituted this action. Mrs. Baldinger asserts that plaintiff's claim is barred by the three year statute of limitations contained in N.Y.C.P.L.R. §214(3).[107]

Under N.Y.C.P.L.R. §214(3) the three year statute of limitations does not commence running until a demand is made to return the property and the demand is refused. *See Kunstsammlungen Zu Weimar v. Elicofon*, 536 F. Supp. 829, 848 (E.D.N.Y. 1981), *aff'd*, 678 F.2d 1150 (2d Cir. 1982) (*citing Frigi-Griffin Inc. v. Leeds*, 52 A.D.2d 805, 383 N.Y.S.2d 339 (1st Dept. 1976)), *aff'd.*, 678 F.2d at 1161. Thus when Mrs. DeWeerth instituted her suit in 1983, it was well within three years of accrual of the cause of action and timely under New York law.

---

[107] N.Y.C.P.L.R. §214 provides:

The following actions must be commenced within three years: . . .

3. an action to recover a chattel or damages for the taking or detaining of a chattel. . . .

It is also true as a matter of New York law that "a party may not unreasonably delay in making a demand which starts the running of the limitations period." *Elicofon,* 536 F. Supp. at 849, *citing Heide v. Glidden Buick Corp.,* 188 Misc. 198, 67 N.Y.S. 2d 905 (1st Dept. 1947).[108] "The question of what constitutes a reasonable time to make a demand depends upon the circumstances of the case." *Elicofon,* 536 F. Supp. at 849, *citing Reid v. Board of Supervisors,* 128 N.Y. 364, 28 N.E. 367 (1891); *Nyhus v. Travel Management Corp.,* 151 U.S. App. D.C. 269, 466 F.2d 440 (D.C.Cir. 1972). Mrs. Baldinger claims that Mrs. DeWeerth did little to locate the Monet and nothing to publicize her loss, and what steps she did take to locate the painting were inadequate. Therefore, Mrs. Baldinger argues that Mrs. DeWeerth's claim is barred by virtue of her lack of diligence in locating and claiming the painting as her own, and by virtue of the unreasonableness of the delay in commencing her suit.

Defendant cites *Elicofon* for the proposition that an initial demand must be made within a reasonable time and that plaintiff has a duty to make genuine and diligent efforts to ascertain who had the painting so as to be able to make her demand. In *Elicofon,* defendant claimed that it was plaintiff's duty to make "genuine and diligent efforts to find the paintings" and because plaintiff failed to make such efforts "any delay in making a demand for the paintings was unreasonable." 536 F. Supp. at 849. Plaintiff in *Elicofon* rejected the contention that it had a duty to look diligently for the paintings, and suggested that "its only duty was to make the demand once it knew of the location of the paintings." *Id.* The court in *Elicofon* did not decide the issue because "the undisputed evidence clearly demonstrate[d] that the [plaintiff] made a diligent although fruitless effort to locate the paintings." *Id.* at 849-50.

The same is true in this case.

After she learned from her sister that the Monet was missing, Mrs. DeWeerth set out on a course to locate and recover it. Her

---

[108] Editor's note: The citation "Misc." refers to New York's "Miscellaneous Reports," the state's official reporter for its *lowest* courts. From this citation we learn, therefore, that the *Elicofon* court based its decision on a case that was from a minimally ranked New York court and was already fairly old. Also noteworthy, the New York lower court's opinion in the case was only about 50 words long and cited no authority.

affidavits credibly aver and defendant does not dispute that (1) in 1946, she reported its loss to the military government then administering the Bonn-Cologne area after the end of the War; (2) in 1948, she solicited the assistance of her lawyer in endeavoring to find it; (3) in 1955, she made inquiries to an art expert she knew of; and (4) in 1957, she reported it as missing to the *Bundeskriminalamt*. Thus, plaintiff made a "diligent although fruitless effort" to find the Monet through 1957. I am further persuaded that, upon the circumstances appearing undisputed on the record, the plaintiff's failure to pursue the Monet after 1957 until her nephew discovered in 1981 that the Monet had been exhibited in New York was reasonable. Mrs. DeWeerth was an elderly woman during that period, and the only published references to the Monet were not generally circulated.

Moreover, any comparison with *Elicofon* is inapposite. There the plaintiff was a government-owned art museum, with resources, knowledge and experience that far exceeded any means an individual such as Mrs. DeWeerth could muster to carry on a credible search for a missing painting.

In sum, "there is no genuine issue as to any material fact" as to what efforts the plaintiff made to find the Monet painting or as to the difficulties she faced in doing so. Accordingly, I find that plaintiff did not unreasonably delay her demand for the return of the Monet and hold that she is therefore "entitled to a judgment as a matter of law" on the issue. I therefore grant summary judgment for plaintiff on the issue of whether her demand for the painting was timely.[109]

---

[109] Even if plaintiff had unreasonably delayed her demand, defendant cannot show that she was prejudiced by the delay. . . .

Defendant could have deposed Reichenbach to attempt to trace the history of the painting's transfers, but she did not. Having failed to exhaust obvious paths of inquiry she cannot sustain her burden of proving that she was prejudiced. [Editor's note: As stated in Judge Broderick's statement of the facts, *supra*, Francois Reichenbach was the Swiss art dealer who had supplied the Monet to Wildenstein, the gallery that then sold it to Mrs. Baldinger. Why do you suppose Mrs. Baldinger skipped the opportunity to take a deposition from Reichenbach, who very possibly could have confirmed exactly where the painting came from?]

Superior Right to Possession

Mrs. Baldinger contends that even if plaintiff's claim to recover the Monet is timely, plaintiff has no evidence that could establish a superior right to possession of the painting because her proof fails to show that she owns the painting, and that the painting was stolen. She argues that Mrs. DeWeerth's evidence is legally insufficient to demonstrate her own prior valid title to the Monet to recover the painting from Mrs. Baldinger, who has possessed it as a good faith purchaser for over 25 years. I disagree.

To establish a cause of action in an action sounding in replevin[110] under New York law, Mrs. DeWeerth must show that she has an immediate and superior right to possession of the Monet. *Wurdeman v. Miller*, 633 F. Supp. 20, 22 (S.D.N.Y. 1986), *citing Honeywell Information Systems, Inc. v. Demographic Systems, Inc.*, 396 F. Supp. 273, 275 (S.D.N.Y. 1975), including proof of ownership. *Elicofon*, 536 F. Supp. at 852 *citing Honeywell Information Systems, Inc., supra.*

Through her testimony and the documentary evidence[111] submitted on this motion, Mrs. DeWeerth has sought to establish that she was the owner of the Monet by inheritance from her father at the time it disappeared from her sister's home, and that she neither sold it nor entrusted it to anyone else to sell. Her testimony with respect to the 1943 photograph further supports that the Monet displayed in 1943 in her residence next to the Rodin sculpture is the same painting as is currently possessed by defendant. I conclude that Mrs. DeWeerth's testimonial and documentary evidence would, if believed by the jury, support an inference that the painting was stolen during the occupation of Frau von Palm's house by American soldiers, after plaintiff had sent the painting to her sister's house for safekeeping with no intention that it be sold.

---

[110] According to the Practice Commentaries to Article 71 of the C.P.L.R., replevin is a term that is no longer used in the C.P.L.R., and is not synonymous with an action to recover a chattel. . . . Whether characterized as an action sounding in replevin or an action to recover a chattel, the burden is still on the plaintiff to establish that she has a superior right to possession.

[111] Mrs. Baldinger admits the authenticity of these exhibits.

Mrs. Baldinger indisputably purchased the Monet in good faith and for value from Wildenstein in 1957. If the jury believes Mrs. DeWeerth's evidence, however, then Mrs. Baldinger would prevail only if she could trace her title back to Mrs. DeWeerth. The trail back from Mrs. Baldinger leads through Wildenstein to Reichenbach, and stops there. There is no evidence before me with respect to how Reichenbach came into possession of the Monet.

Moreover, under New York law not even a bona fide purchaser can acquire valid title of a chattel from a thief, or from one who acquired the property from a thief. *See Elicofon,* 678 F.2d at 1160.

The defendant has . . . sought to shift the burden to plaintiff to prove that the painting was stolen and not sold or consigned by Frau von Palm [DeWeerth's sister]. However, the burden of proof rests with the defendant to show some act by the plaintiff beyond merely entrusting his property to someone who then sells it to an innocent purchaser. *Cf. Hartford Accident & Ind. Co. v. Walston & Co.,* 21 N.Y.2d 219, 287 N.Y.S.2d 58, 68, 234 N.E.2d 230 (Ct. App. 1967) (stockbroker required to establish that it observed reasonable commercial standards in transferring stocks to establish it was bona fide purchaser to avoid liability to owner from whom they were stolen); *United States Fidelity & Guaranty Co. v. Leon,* 165 Misc. 549, 300 N.Y.S. 331, 334 (Municipal Ct. N.Y. Co. 1937) (burden of proof upon defendant if he is asserting title to stolen bond to show he is bona fide holder, and if he is asserting title in his predecessor, that the latter was a bona fide holder).

Based on the record on this motion, I conclude that there is testimonial and documentary evidence sufficient to present genuine issues of material fact as to whether Mrs. DeWeerth was the owner of the Monet, whether it was stolen from her, and whether she therefore has an immediate and superior right to possession of it. ∗ ∗ ∗

Remaining Affirmative Defenses

1. Adverse Possession

Defendant claims as a defense that she has acquired ownership of the painting by "adverse possession," and that the undisputed credible evidence on this motion supports this defense. "Five elements must be established in order to gain title by adverse possession: possession must be hostile and under claim of right, it must be actual, it must be open and notorious, it must be exclusive and it must be continuous." [Citations omitted.] Summary judgment could be granted to defendant on this affirmative defense only if there were no genuine issue of material fact with respect to any of these five elements. The Second Circuit in *Elicofon* observed that "courts and commentators have noted that the mere residential display of paintings may not constitute the type of open and notorious possession sufficient to afford notice to the true owner." 678 F.2d at 1164 n. 25 (citations omitted).

It appears from the record on this motion, however, that except for two brief public exhibitions, one in 1957 for four days and the other in 1970 for a little more than a month, Mrs. Baldinger maintained the Monet exclusively in her home. I hold as a matter of law that such possession is not sufficiently open and notorious to constitute adverse possession, and this defense must fail.

* * *

In summary, plaintiff has produced testimony and documentary evidence which, if believed, would support the conclusion that she owned the Monet, that she did not sell it or authorize anyone to sell it on her behalf, and that defendant Baldinger currently has it in her possession and refuses to return it. This evidence is sufficient to present a genuine issue of material fact as to each of these questions. The affirmative defenses . . . are without merit and are dismissed with prejudice.

Defendant's motion for summary judgment is denied, and partial summary judgment is granted for plaintiff on the issue of timeliness.

STUDY QUESTIONS

You should be able to answer the following questions based on *DeWeerth v. Baldinger II.*

1. Defendant argued that plaintiff's action should be barred on two grounds. What were they?
2. On the timeliness issue, the defendant cited a case to support the proposition that "an initial demand must be made within a reasonable time and that plaintiff has a duty to make genuine and diligent efforts to ascertain who had the painting." Was it a New York state case or a federal case?
3. According to Judge Broderick, did the case cited by defendant actually decide this issue (with respect to either "demand within reasonable time" or "diligent efforts")?
4. Why was Judge Broderick himself not required to decide this legal issue at this time?
5. Based on what evidence did Judge Broderick "find" that Mrs. DeWeerth had made a "diligent although fruitless" effort to locate the painting?
6. What evidence did Judge Broderick mention as supporting the claim that Mrs. DeWeerth's failure to pursue the Monet after 1957 was reasonable?
7. How else did Judge Broderick *distinguish* the facts of the *Elicofon* case?
8. What would Mrs. DeWeerth be required to show in order to "establish a cause of action in an action sounding in replevin under New York law"? What evidence did she have to do this?
9. Based on what particular facts did Mrs. Baldinger assert that *she* was entitled to possession of the painting? What did Judge Broderick have to say about her basis for claiming possession?
10. In what way did Mrs. Baldinger attempt to shift the burden of proof to Mrs. DeWeerth?

11. What did Judge Broderick's opinion have to say about *O'Keeffe v. Snyder*? Were you disappointed? Do you think this was an inappropriate way for the federal court to deal with a New Jersey case given that the court was bound to apply New York law?

* * *

Note: You will see later that, on the appeal of *DeWeerth v. Baldinger*, the Second Circuit Court of Appeals dealt with *O'Keeffe v. Snyder* explicitly, both citing the case and commenting favorably on its reasoning. Judge Broderick was free, however, to handle the case as he did because it was (being out-of-state) only a "persuasive authority" at most and, evidently, it was not very persuasive to him—in particular since he found that Mrs. DeWeerth had used reasonable efforts in any event.

*t*he statute in *DeWeerth v. Baldinger* is very simple, too simple. It says an action to recover a chattel has to be brought within three years, and that's all. It does not say three years "from when," nor does it say what kinds of events would get the three-year period started. Like many of the statutes that roll out of legislatures, this one is incomplete. A court could not apply it at all without doing some "interpretation" to supply crucial omissions. Even when a statute seems complete on its face, however, a court still might decide to add to the statute's literal meaning (or to subtract from it) by judicial interpretation.

As we have seen, Judge Broderick recognized that New York's courts already had read two additional elements into the *DeWeerth v. Baldinger* statute:

(1) a requirement of demand and refusal before the three-year period starts running (when the property is held by a good faith buyer); and

(2) a requirement that the owner not "unreasonably delay" the demand.[112]

Mrs. Baldinger's lawyer, Mr. Sills, invited Judge Broderick to recognize (create?) a third element that was also not in the statute's actual wording. When the owner does not know who has her stolen property, he argued, the law should not consider a delay in making demand to be "reasonable" unless she makes "diligent" efforts to locate the property. As we saw, Judge Broderick declined this invitation. He said that, given the evidence in this case, he did not have to take a position one way or the other on the existence of such a diligence requirement. (In other words, any interpretation he might have declared on this point would have been obiter dictum.) As we will see, however, the Second Circuit later *did* accept the invitation, and it did recognize a (new?) requirement of diligent efforts.

How does this work? Aren't judges supposed to *do* what the law says, not *change* what it says? Here we have a solemn statutory enactment approved by the democratically elected legislature of the state, but then we see that all of the statute's real impact, the very crux of its meaning, is supplied or modified by judges, who blithely go far beyond the Legislature's words. This activity of judges brings up once again the old debate about whether judges "make" law or merely "find" law, but here we see it in a significantly different context. It is one thing to object to the dictatorship of judicial precedent and its "rule of the living by the dead." It is something else again to undermine the rules enacted by a democratically elected legislature. In the civil law tradition such judicial meddling in legislative enactments would be (in theory) unthinkable; in civil law countries the legislature is truly "the" lawmaking body, and courts exist merely to apply the

---

[112] What happens if demand is not made within a reasonable time? There are at least two possibilities: (1) the requirement of demand and refusal is dispensed with and the three-year period commences at the time the good-faith buyer originally took possession; or (2) the three-year period commences at that point in time the time when the owner's delay got to be an unreasonable one. This interpretive question is apparently still an open one.

laws that the legislators make. But the common-law tradition evolved differently. In this chapter we take a look at how. Specifically we will consider what statutes are supposed to do, how they get enacted, and the way in which these first two items are related to what courts should consider when they interpret statutory language. We will also take a quick look at statutes' morphological kin, administrative regulations.

WHAT STATUTES ARE SUPPOSED TO DO

Why do we have to have statutes at all? Why not just leave it to the courts to make the laws we need, case by case, as problems arise, creating new rules or modifying existing ones? The usefulness and desirability of statutes was not always obvious, and legislation got off to a very slow start in the common-law system. All of the statutes adopted during the first four centuries following the Magna Charta (1215) fit nicely into two volumes,[113] comparable in bulk to about one year's work for the legislature of a fair-sized state today. For many centuries the case-by-case method of the common law — of learning from experience — was regarded as far superior to "instant legislation."[114]

> [T]he nations are more happy whose laws have been entered by long custom, wrung out from their debates on particular cases. . . . For thereby the conveniences and inconveniences thereof through a long tract of time are experimentally seen. . . . But in statutes the lawgiver must at once balance the conveniences and inconveniences; wherein he may and often doth fall short. . . . [115]

---

[113] Owen Ruffhead, The Statutes at Large from the Magna Charta to the End of the Last Parliament, 1761 (1763), which you can find in your law school's law library. Since most of the early statutes had to be set out in both English as well as in the original Latin or Norman French, the actual length is somewhat less than two volumes.

[114] Neil MacCormick, Legal Reasoning and Legal Theory 59 (1978).

[115] James, 1st Viscount Stair, Institutions of the Laws of Scotland 1.1.15, *quoted in* Neil MacCormick, *supra* note 113, at 58.

This prejudice against instant legislation was not, however, merely an academic preference about methodology. There were some raw political concerns, as well. Since before the time of Lord Chief Justice Coke[116] the common law courts had considered the common law "to stand between the individual and oppressive action by the state; . . . the [common] law existed to guard "individual interests against the encroachments of state and of society."[117] Thus, legislative interference was viewed with suspicion, as a danger to the ideal of the supremacy of law.[118] You may recall the famous line attributed to the great common-law lawyer, Sir Thomas More, in Robert Bolt's play "A Man for All Seasons":

> "This country's planted thick with laws from coast to coast . . . and if you cut them down . . . d'you really think you could stand upright in the winds that would blow then?"[119]

"Instant statutes" could cut away the trees.

More and more, however, the slowness of common-law change came to be seen as a problem. A relatively static body of law may be just fine in a time of relatively static social arrangements, but the rapid socio-economic developments that accompanied the Industrial Revolution presented new and different kinds of challenges. The common law was increasingly seen as not up to the task of serving society's needs.

Unlike the common law, legislation permits the government to intervene in a comprehensive and coherent way to deal with wide-scale problems. The common law works out new areas of law a piece at a time, based on narrow fact-finding as the cases happen to arise. This approach is the very opposite of comprehensive, and if an early case presents peculiar factual aspects that are not representative, the common law can be led far

---

[116] Remember Lord Coke and his famous riposte that the king is subject to "the law," from Chapter VII. The law that Lord Coke had in mind was first and foremost the common law.

[117] ROSCOE POUND, THE SPIRIT OF THE COMMON LAW 74 (1921).

[118] *See id.* at 45-46, 75, 156-57.

[119] *Quoted in* Tennessee Valley Auth. v. Hill, 437 U.S. 153, 195 (1978).

astray. The legislature, by contrast, is not limited to the particular facts supplied by actual disputants. It can determine that legal changes are needed before an actual dispute even arises, and it can craft its programs after doing wide-ranging studies of large and complex issues. Furthermore, legislatures can adopt whole codes, all in one go, to set up or rewrite entire areas of law when the new conditions, knowledge, or values make such action desirable.

Another problem with the common law method is that new common-law rules become known only after harms (sometimes serious) have already been done and without a fair warning to the persons who are subjected to the new rules. Legislation, by contrast, operates prospectively, anticipating new kinds of mischief and laying down rules for the future conduct of the persons to whom it is addressed.

The perceived advantages of legislative law-making gradually come to outweigh the objections, and the second half of the nineteenth century ushered in what has become a veritable Era of Legislation, with thousands of new statutes being added every year. These new laws both modified and supplemented the common law and, in some cases, they replaced chunks of it outright. By the latter part of the nineteenth century, the Supreme Court enthusiastically intoned: "The great office of statutes is to remedy defects in the common law as they are developed, and to adapt it to the changes of time and circumstances."[120]

This did not mean, however, that the courts immediately embraced the new ascendancy of statutes over the judicial law as the preferred method of keeping the law up-to-date. To the contrary, there was an "attitude of resentment toward legislation on the part of bench and bar,"[121] and courts made it a general policy "to presume that legislators intended no innovations upon the common law and to assume so far as possible that statutes were meant to declare and reassert its principles."[122]

---

[120] Munn v. Illinois, 94 U.S. 113, 134 (1876).
[121] ROSCOE POUND, THE SPIRIT OF THE COMMON LAW 45 (1921).
[122] *Id.* at 156.

"[T]he social reformer and the legal reformer ... had always to face the situation that the legislative act which represented the fruit of their labors would find no sympathy in those who applied it, would be construed strictly and would be made to interfere with the *status quo* as little as possible."[123] The maxim that statutes in derogation of the common law are to be strictly construed, though increasingly disregarded, remains a guide for courts interpreting statutes.

The practice of courts to interpret statutes as they do today—adding to literal meaning, subtracting from it, modifying it, and sometimes just plain ignoring it—is perhaps the most enduring legacy of the common law tradition in our modern age of statutes. Unlike in civil law countries, where statutes are *the* law, statutes in the common law tradition have always been, at most, only "one of the" sources of law, and not the last word at that. In our tradition, the last word is for the courts, for reasons that are purely practical. After all, no legal rule made by a legislature is self-executing. A statute can have force in real life only if somebody does something to give it that force. For many statutes, of course, that "somebody" is the executive branch and its administrative agencies, which are subject in turn to judicial review.[124] For many other statutes, however, that "somebody" is the courts; it is the courts that issue the orders directing government officials to take actions out in the world, the actions that give these statutes their practical force. The effect of this reality is to make the courts a critical gatekeeper. Before such a statute can have real effect "on the ground" it has to pass through, be interpreted by and then be acted on by a judge—who then orders it into actual force. Whether a government official turned up at Mrs. Baldinger's door to cart away *Champs de Blé à Vétheuil* depended very crucially on what the courts decided to do with the words of CPLR §214.

---

[123] *Id.*

[124] Administrative agencies and their regulations are discussed later in this chapter.

HOW STATUTES GET ENACTED

The mechanics of legislative enactment are of interest to lawyers and judges primarily because the "legislative history" of a statute may have a bearing on its proper interpretation. When interpreting a statute, a court's primary consideration is to try to make the statute do what it was meant to do. But whose intention counts, and where do you find it?

A new law normally gets its official start when a member of the legislature introduces a proposal known as a *bill*. The legislator is often not the one who thinks up the need for the new law and almost never does the actual drafting. Instead, some private or governmental interest, looking to benefit itself or its mission, persuades a legislator to *sponsor* the new law and prepares the first draft of its specific language (wording).

After the legislator introduces the bill, it goes to a *committee* of legislators for further consideration and, possibly, hearings. The legislatures of 49 states have two "houses"[125] and, of course, Congress has two—the Senate and the House of Representatives. Each house has its own separate "leadership," controlled by the majority political party. Depending on the local house rules and practices, it may take a bit of politicking, and maybe some rewriting, before the leadership is willing to assign the bill to a committee.

Once the bill is in committee, hearings are scheduled if the committee chair is amenable—and getting the chair to be amenable may require more politicking and more rewriting. At the hearings, typically, the bill's sponsors including the introducer will say on the record what the new law would do (the "intent") and why it is necessary (its "purpose"). Carefully note the two words in parentheses—"intent" and "purpose." They figure significantly in the lore of statutory interpretation. Other members of the committee and outside witnesses will also speak to these matters. Eventually a committee report might be written

---

[125]The sole exception is Nebraska, which has a *unicameral* (one-house) legislature.

by its staff (more "intent" and "purpose" statements). If a majority of the committee members favor the bill, it will be voted out of the committee and "marked up" to the full house. Most bills die in committee, however, often without even a hearing.[126]

Once a bill is "marked up" to the full house, it will be scheduled for debate on the floor, provided the house leadership is amenable. In the floor debate various house members will make still more statements as to what the new law would do ("intent") and why it is necessary ("purpose"). The people making these statements may or may not have a clue what the whole thing is really about. During the floor debate, specific questions are asked and answered on the record. Sometimes this is done for the express purpose of *making* a record — of making legislative history in the hope of influencing future court interpretations. Finally, a vote is taken and the bill is either passed or defeated by the full house.

Since new laws have to be approved by both houses of the legislature, this same process has to be paralleled in the other house, though sometimes the two processes occur more or less concurrently. If there are differences between the bills passed by two houses, the discrepancies have to be hammered out in a "conference committee." It consists of members appointed by the leadership of each house. Then, at last, the harmonized bills go back to their respective houses for a final vote. Following all the rewriting and diverse people inserting bits of their own "intention" and "purpose" into the bill (and into the record), the definitive statutory wording finally emerges.

The last step in the process is approval by the executive (President or governor), who signs the bill into law. If, instead, the executive *vetoes* the bill, it is dead unless the two houses vote to *override* the veto by a supermajority (in Congress, it must be two-thirds). Most new laws are, however, approved by the executive and, in doing so, the executive frequently issues an

---

[126] From here on we will ignore all the ways a bill can be killed, as dead bills are generally of little interest to practicing lawyers.

official message explaining what the law is supposed to do and why it is necessary—more "intention" and "purpose."

There are two big points you should get out of this brief description of the mechanics of legislating: First, the creation of a new statute often involves a lot of politicking and rewriting, providing many occasions along the way when people will make statements for the record of what the new law is supposed to do ("intent") and why it is necessary ("purpose"). Second, these various statements might not always be exactly the same or even remotely consistent, and they might be motivated by "commitments" running no deeper than the exigencies of politics. None of them necessarily represents the viewpoint of the "legislature as a body" (whatever that might mean).

ADMINISTRATIVE REGULATIONS

In addition to statutes, lawyers also must be concerned with their junior counterparts, administrative regulations—formal rules issued by various governmental agencies pursuant to statutory authority. Although administrative regulations are not statutes, they look and operate much like statutes and they tend to be interpreted by the courts in a similar way. The remainder of this section gives a brief overview of administrative regulations and their place in the legal system. For the time being, however, you may wish to scan or skip over the remainder of this section, and go directly to the next section, on page 164, "Interpreting Statutes."

Beginning a little over 100 years ago, people began to recognize that in some areas of life—especially the activities of certain important industries—statutory enactments alone were not up to the task of addressing the detail and complexity of various recurring problems. To meet these new challenges Congress and the state legislatures began creating "administrative agencies" and gave them the job of regulating entire industries in the public interest. The creation of these agencies inaugurated a new phase in governmental administration and in law. No longer were the legislatures and courts alone in generating new legal requirements that people have to observe. Administrative agencies have become, in their quasi-legislative and quasi-judicial functioning, for all practical purposes a "fourth branch" of government, taking their place beside the older executive, legislative, and judicial branches.[127]

The administrative trend started with the railroads and the Interstate Commerce Commission (now defunct); then it moved on to the regulation of energy companies and other utilities. Nowadays administrative agencies have become a popular vehicle for providing a wide variety of governmental services (for example, the Social Security Administration) and protections (for example, the Environmental Protection Agency). By combining expertise and specialization with legions of hierarchically organized employees, administrative agencies have made it possible for government to carry out myriad programs and projects in the public interest (or believed to be such), which could never have been mounted by means of statutes and courts alone. The members of Congress and their legislative staffs could never, for example, muster the expertise or time needed to create a comprehensive and detailed set of clean air and water standards for all of the environmentally varied areas of the country, not to mention keeping the standards up to date. Congress has therefore created the Environmental Protection Agency to do the job instead, leaving it primarily to that agency to figure out what is needed to attain the congressional goals while staying within the general criteria and constraints that Congress has set.

Administrative agencies are usually headed by politically appointed commissioners, boards, or single administrator. Through their staffs (the government "bureaucracy"), they interpret and carry out broad legislative purposes and, in support of this process, they promulgate *regulations* of general application

---

[127] Technically, all administrative agencies fall within one of the three constitutional branches of government, usually the executive. As a practical matter, however, they operate more autonomously than in strict hierarchic subordination.

and issue *rulings* in specific cases. The promulgation of administrative regulations is a *legislative*, or "quasi-legislative," function of the agency. The resulting regulations are binding rules of conduct as well as being general policy pronouncements about how the agency interprets its mandate from the legislature and how it intends to carry out its purposes. It is probably a fair guess that, in terms of pure numbers, the greatest bulk of the governmental requirements in this country is in the form of administrative regulations issued *under* statutes rather than rules directly set out *in* statutes. Take a look sometime at the Code of Federal Regulations (the "CFR") in the law library. It fills many, many shelves. Administrative regulations are technically not, however, "laws." Only the legislature and (arguably) the courts can make laws. While agencies are generally required to go though a process of notice and public comment before they issue new regulations, they are not required to accept the suggestions submitted to them, nor are they otherwise democratically responsible directly to the people in the way that the legislature is. Nevertheless, because their regulations are backed up by statute, the regulations have for all practical purposes the force of law.

Administrative agencies also issue rulings in particular cases, applying the agency's regulations and governing statutes to specific sets of facts. These rulings represent the *adjudicative* (or "quasi-adjudicative") functioning the agency. Normally, such rulings are issued only after providing the affected persons with "due process" in the form of notice and opportunities to submit evidence and legal arguments—often with a hearing before a "hearing officer," much like in a judicial trial. You would be correct to guess that lawyers play a major role in the adjudicative functioning of administrative agencies, and administrative hearings are for many lawyers the dominant (or, even the only) part of their litigation practice. Lawyers also play a key role in the rulemaking process, representing clients' interests in reviewing proposed regulations and making comments on them. And, of course, the agencies themselves employ legal staffs, sometimes very large, to assist in carrying out their agency missions.

Obviously, administrative agencies have considerable power, which, if misused, could cause great mischief. Therefore, the actions of administrative agencies are (with a very few exceptions) subject to *judicial review* on the question of legality. That is to say, if an agency takes any action that is outside its statutorily conferred powers, the persons adversely affected by the action may apply to a court to obtain relief from it. The courts tend to be *deferential* in performing their reviews, not presuming to second-guess the agency's expertise or tactical choices and not undertaking to redo or revise its findings of fact. A court will normally not interfere with the agency unless it is persuaded that the agency's action had no "rational" basis, was "arbitrary and capricious" or, in the case of a factual conclusion, had no "substantial evidence" in support.

INTERPRETING STATUTES

Now that we have taken a look at what statutes are supposed to do in a common law system and the mechanics of how they get enacted, we turn to the question of what things the courts might properly consider when they interpret statutory language. Early in your first year you will encounter the so-called *canons of construction*.[128] There are perhaps 50 or more of these canons, depending on who is counting, but they are not consistent. For almost every one of them, there is at least one other that points to the opposite result. For example we earlier saw the canon: "Statutes in derogation of the common law are to be strictly construed." Well, there is another one that says: "Statutes to remedy the common law are to be liberally construed to achieve their purpose." Go figure. Typically, courts tend to cite the canons that support their desired holding and to be dismissive of or simply ignore the ones that do not.

---

[128] "Construction" is another word for interpretation. It is derived from the verb "to construe."

For now we will focus on three *kinds of considerations* that are recurringly important in judicial discussions of statutory interpretation.

1. The *plain meaning* of the statute
2. The legislative *intent* (what it meant by the words it used)
3. The *purpose* of the legislature (the need being addressed)

Courts often say that, if a statute's *plain meaning* is clear, there is no need to go further. The trouble is that the plain meaning is often not very clear, especially in cases likely to be litigated. A slightly more metaphysical point is that words do not have any meaning *at all* except when used within some context, and their meanings inevitably vary according to the context that the user or reader presupposes as applicable. (You may have heard of this general concept in college under the name "deconstruction.") Suppose, for instance, a state statute forbids the unlicensed possession of guns but it contains an exception that expressly says the rule does not apply to "correction officers ... of any penal correctional institution." Can a federal prison guard be convicted and sent to jail if he carries an unlicensed gun into a bar — on the ground that the statute only applies to *state* prison guards? The New York Court of Appeals thought so.[129] Everything came down to context.

What this all boils down to is this: You cannot know the plain meaning of a statute without some clue to what the legislature was trying to express ("intent") or the need it was trying to address ("purpose"). Phrased differently, any lawyer worth his or her salt can generally transmute an inquiry about plain meaning into a wider-ranging investigation of the legislative purpose or intent. A judge trying to escape the constraints of a statute's plain meaning can do likewise.

---

[129] People v. Marrero, 507 N.E.2d 1068 (N.Y. 1987).

At first blush, a historical investigation into the legislature's *intent* or *purpose* might seem the golden key to interpreting statutes. Many judges and lawyers agree that researching a statute's *legislative history* can be invaluable. Others, however, are highly suspicious, some going so far as to deny that legislative history is ever a proper guide to statutory interpretation. As Oliver Wendell Holmes wrote, "I don't care what their intention was. I only want to know what the words mean."[130] More recently, Justice Scalia wrote:

> The greatest defect of legislative history is its illegitimacy. We are governed by laws, not by the intentions of legislators. As the Court said in 1844: "The law as it passed is the will of the majority of both houses, *and the only mode in which that will is spoken is in the act itself....*" [Citation omitted.] But not the least of the defects of legislative history is its indeterminacy. If one were to search for an interpretive technique that, *on the whole*, was more likely to confuse than to clarify, one could hardly find a more promising candidate than legislative history.[131]

Why this hardnosed view? For one thing, there is the constitutional point. The federal and state constitutions provide that legislatures can create new laws only if both houses vote favorably on the same specific words and the executive signs on to those same words. Any judicial wandering into the legislative record to find "intent" or "purpose" means looking at various *other* words, which were *not* enacted as "law," and possibly making them into law in defiance of the constitutionally prescribed process. Besides, legislative history does not really express a legislature's intent at all but only, at best, the *individual* intents

---

[130] Quoted in [Justice] Felix Frankfurter, *Some Reflections on the Reading of Statutes*, 47 COL. L. REV. 528, 538 (1947).

[131] Conroy v. Aniskoff, 507 U.S. 511, 519 (1993) (Scalia, J. concurring). *See also* Pennsylvania v. Union Gas, 491 U.S. 1, 30 (1989), in which Justice Scalia wrote (concurring in part and dissenting in part) "It is our task, as I see it, not to enter the minds of the Members of Congress—who need have nothing in mind for their votes to be both lawful and effective—but rather to give fair and reasonable meaning to the text of the United States Code...."

of individual legislators, staffers, lobbyists, and so on. And these intents may vary.

> [T]he use of legislative history [is] the equivalent of entering a crowded cocktail party and looking over the heads of the guests for one's friends.[132]

The only thing the legislature ever indubitably intended to do as a body is to pass the statute, and therefore nothing else is the "law." So the argument goes.

Nonetheless, most judges feel it is safe to at least take a peek at *some* expressions of legislative intent or purpose in the legislative history, even if it that history may contain conflicting viewpoints, and even if it is not law. For example, if a court is faced with a statute that prohibits bringing firearms to "banks," it might be immensely informative to know whether the legislator's concerns and discussions were centered around financial institutions or riversides. Such peeks must, however, be done with care, and when others cite legislative history you should always be alert for the possibility that all they did was peer into the legislative record and look around for "friends."

Finally, judges sometimes try to discern the intent or purpose of a statute from the language of the statute itself, and then they turn around and use that (supposed) intent or purpose as the key to unlock some particular obscure provision. Sometimes this is referred to as "reading the statute as a whole" or reading different parts of the statute *in pari materia*. The underlying assumption is that if you can discern some obvious intent or purpose from a "clear" part of the statute, you can reasonably assume that same intention or purpose animated the puzzling portion of the statute as well. The problem is, however, this method only is valid if the puzzling provision was indeed meant to carry forward the same general purpose as the clearer portion, rather than perhaps to carve out an exception.

---

[132] Attributed to Judge Harold Leventhal and quoted in Conroy v. Aniskoff, 507 U.S. 511, 519 (1993) (Scalia, J., concurring).

Everybody knows, for example, that the purpose of income tax laws is to raise revenue for the government, but that doesn't mean the tax codes are not sprinkled through with particular clauses actually meant to reduce government revenue — for the benefit of various groups of taxpayers. That sort of thing happens all the time. There is another problem with reading statutes this way. To quote Holmes again:

> When a rule of conduct is laid down in words that evoke [a certain picture] in the common mind . . . , the statute should not be extended . . . simply because it may seem to us that a similar policy applies, or upon the speculation that if the legislature had thought of it, very likely broader words would have been used.[133]

Maybe the legislature wanted to address only a *part* of a problem because, if the sponsors had tried to address the whole problem, they could not have mustered enough votes to get the statute passed. If this is what happened in the legislature then wouldn't it seem utterly improper for a court to fill in what the law's sponsors specifically politicked away?

INTERPRETING THE STATUTE
IN *DeWEERTH*

Consider the demand and refusal requirement that is "in" the statute of limitations in *DeWeerth v. Baldinger*. Did the legislature intend to require demand and refusal but just "forgot" to write it in? Did it not intend such a requirement at all? Or did the legislature intend merely to re-enact in New York a version of a statute that had been around in the state and, previously, in England for hundreds of years?

Actually, what is the purpose of the three-year statute of limitations on replevin actions? More to the point, what can an

---

[133] McBoyle v. United States, 283 U.S. 25 (1931).

inquiry into that purpose tell us about the propriety of including a "diligence" requirement on the true owner? We will see that the Second Circuit's views about the purpose of CPLR §214 were considerably different from those of New York's own Court of Appeals. To help understand these courts' divergent opinions on the subject (which you will read soon) consider these possibilities:

1. The statute is meant to protect *true owners* by delaying the start of the three-year period until after the true owner makes a demand. It is also meant to keep New York from becoming a haven for stolen art works by preserving true owners' rights to reclaim their property.
2. The statute is meant to protect *innocent buyers* of stolen property by not treating them as wrongdoers until they have had a chance to return the property to its true owner — after demand. It is also meant to discourage people from making stale claims and to protect innocent buyers from fraudulent and groundless claims by setting a "reasonable-time" deadline for claims against innocent buyers.

Do you see how the New York statute can be understood as having *either* of these two purposes? Note, however, that if "1" is the real purpose, then *no* "diligence" requirement should be read into the statute, while if "2" is the real purpose, then the statute probably *should* be read to require diligent efforts in a case like *DeWeerth*. Thus, we have divined two inconsistent possible purposes out of the statute (as previously embellished by the New York courts). Which one is correct?

Do not overlook the possibility that neither of the purposes stated above is quite correct. A third possibility is that statutes of limitations are for the purpose of providing a *balance* between the conflicting interests of true owners and innocent buyers of stolen goods — partially favoring the true owner by not according *immediate* ownership to the innocent buyer, while partially favoring the innocent buyer by denying the true owner a perpetual right to reclaim. Perhaps by stressing one of these interests to the virtual exclusion of the other, *both* the court in Second Circuit and the New York Court of Appeals missed the main point, the balance, and got sidetracked as a result. As you read their opinions in Chapter XV,[134] you decide.

---

[134] Their opinions are on pages 193 (*DeWeerth III*) and 208 (*Guggenheim*), respectively.

THE TRIAL

*d*uring the process of discovery, some of the parties' factual disagreements may be resolved, but others will remain unresolved. Mrs. Baldinger never, for example, conceded that Mrs. DeWeerth ever had any ownership rights in the Monet painting. She also had never conceded that Mrs. DeWeerth (if she ever owned the painting) had not voluntarily transferred it away. The evidence concerning these matters rested largely on the testimony of Mrs. DeWeerth, but even though Mrs. Baldinger had no personal information on these subjects, she would certainly have been ill advised to simply give in on them. These matters present *questions of fact* on which the lawsuit might well turn. The trial is the part of the litigation process in which such disputes about the facts of the case are resolved.

In our adversary system, the trial works basically like this: Each side, in turn, presents the evidence that it chooses, in pretty much the way that it chooses, and each side endeavors to rebut or challenge the credibility of the evidence presented by the other side. Then the finder of fact (the jury or sometimes the judge) decides. In the case of a jury trial, we call this decision of fact by its old name *verdict*, which literally means "truly said." The fact-finder considers the conflicting versions of the story, as presented in the evidence, and then it declares which things were truly said.

Two crucial threshold questions in all this are: Who has the burden of initially coming forward with evidence (the "burden of production"), and who has the burden of persuading the fact-finder what really happened? What if, for example, the jury did not particularly believe the story of *either* Mrs. Baldinger or Mrs. DeWeerth? Or what if it cannot make up its mind?

For every factual issue in a case, either one side or the other has what lawyers refer to commonly (though a bit imprecisely) as the "burden of proof." Judge Broderick, for example, mentioned Mrs. Baldinger's attempt "to shift the burden to plaintiff to prove that the painting was stolen and not sold or consigned" by Mrs. DeWeerth's sister. It is the judge's job to decide (in accordance with law) who has the burden "to prove" each factual point that is in contention — who has the burden of *production* (*i.e.*, who must *produce* evidence in the first instance) and who has the burden of *persuasion*. The way these burdens are assigned (*i.e.*, who has the burden on particular points) can be crucially important and sometimes even affect the outcome of the case.

Take, for instance, the issue of whether Mrs. DeWeerth had ever had the painting in the first place. What if there were no satisfactory evidence on this point at all, *i.e.*, Mrs. DeWeerth had no proof she ever had possessed the painting but Mrs. Baldinger had no proof Mrs. DeWeerth had not possessed it? What happens then? You would be right to assume that in such a situation the court will *simply leave the parties as it finds them*. That is, if Mrs. DeWeerth could not produce evidence of prior ownership or, at least, prior possession of the painting, then Mrs. Baldinger would get to keep the painting — even though she could not prove it was hers, either. In other words, Mrs. Baldinger could conceivably have won the case simply because she did not have the burden to *produce* the evidence on this point. In the actual case, of course, Mrs. DeWeerth did produce evidence of both ownership and prior possession — including inheritance records and an old photograph of the painting in her home. By producing this evidence, Mrs. DeWeerth met her burden of production. That still did not mean she necessarily would prevail on this issue. She also had the burden of *persuasion*. To meet the burden of persuasion she had to convince the fact-finder to accept her evidence as determinative of the issue.

Who has the burden of production and persuasion? In general, the person who is asking the court to do something has the burden of demonstrating that there is a factual and legal basis for the court to do it. Thus, typically, the plaintiff in a case — who is asking the court to grant some remedy — will have the burden of both production (going forward with the evidence) and of persuasion. There are, however, exceptions. We will see more about this a few paragraphs later, when we get into the structure of the trial.

One of the characteristic features of the American legal system is the prevalence of jury trials. In a jury trial the evidence is presented before a group of citizen fact-finders, carefully selected to be impartial. They determine the facts on the basis of the evidence. (The judge, you will remember, determines the law.) In the common-law world *outside* the United States, the jury trial has now become much less usual, even in the jury's birthplace, England, where juries are scarcely ever used except in criminal cases. Oddly, at the same time, some civil-law countries, which once operated without juries, are adopting the practice of using citizen fact-finders, especially for prosecutions of major crimes.

The U.S. Constitution guarantees the right to a jury trial for criminal defendants (except for the least serious crimes) and for many civil proceedings. Even so, juries are often waived in both kinds of proceedings, and in criminal cases the widespread practice of *plea bargaining* has made actual trials (and, hence, trial by jury) the exception rather than the rule. Still, it is fair to say that the American legal establishment remains strongly committed to the jury trial as an important component of the justice process, and the right to *demand* a jury trial remains a hallmark of the American common law system. Furthermore, much of the law and practice governing the conduct of trials, particularly the law of evidence, is based on assumptions about how jurors think and act as fact-finders, even though in many trials the judge performs the fact finding role.

In the actual case of *DeWeerth v. Baldinger* the parties chose to have the case tried to the judge without a jury. However, to give you an idea of the flavor of a jury trial, in the next few pages we will describe some of the high points of how things might have happened if the case had been tried before a jury.[135]

SELECTING THE JURY (VOIR DIRE)

Jury selection is the first trial activity in a jury trial. Originally, jurors were preferred who were already well informed about the case at hand; it supposedly helped them assess the credibility of witnesses. Today the situation is exactly the opposite. The "official" goal is that cases be tried before jurors who are as impartial as practicable (though individual advocates never object to a little bias going their own way). The jury selection process allows the lawyers an opportunity to "challenge" jurors they suspect of leaning (or being disposed to lean) toward the other side, in an effort to cull them out. Here's how it typically goes:

After the parties and judge have taken care of any trial-day preliminaries, a group of prospective jurors is brought to the courtroom and is seated in the spectator benches. This group is called the *venire*. Members of the venire are questioned in court to determine their qualifications to sit as jurors in the case at hand. The process is called *voir dire*. In most federal courtrooms, the voir dire questioning is done by the judge,

---

[135] Most of the material in the remainder of this chapter is adapted from ROGER C. PARK, DAVID P. LEONARD & STEVEN H. GOLDBERG, HORNBOOK ON THE LAW OF EVIDENCE (©1998), reprinted with permission of Thomson West.

with the lawyers having the right to submit questions for the judge to ask. In many state courts, the lawyers are allowed to question the prospective jurors directly, either as a group or individually. Sometimes, as in New York state courts, the judge is not even present. The right of the parties to have prospective jurors questioned directly by their lawyers, rather than through the judge, is one of those differences between the federal system and the states that many lawyers hold dear.

In a typical mode of proceeding, the names of twelve randomly selected venire members are called by the clerk and these twelve file into the jury box. They are then questioned and, based on the questioning, reduced in number. Many jurors are dismissed on the basis of their own self-reports: For some stated reason, they do not think they can be impartial or, for personal reasons, they claim they cannot serve. Others are dismissed in response to challenges made by the lawyers for the parties. (A judge may remove a prospective juror for cause *sua sponte*, but judges rarely do so.) A lawyer may challenge any prospective juror for cause. A challenge for cause will be sustained if the judge finds that the person either does not meet the statutory qualifications for jury service or because the person's *voir dire* responses demonstrate there is a substantial chance the person will not hear the matter impartially. For example, in *DeWeerth v. Baldinger* it may well have been regarded as sufficient "cause" to dismiss a prospective juror if the person had been a victim of a theft, was an art dealer, or harbored generally negative feelings toward foreigners. In addition to challenges for cause a party is entitled to a number of *peremptory challenges*, for which no reason need be given. Although each side has only a limited number of peremptory challenges (fixed by statute or court rules), the lawyers are free to make a peremptory challenge for almost any reason whatever.[136] Generally, more peremptory challenges are permitted in criminal cases than in civil.

---

[136] Except for a reason that is unconstitutional. *See, e.g.*, Batson v. Kentucky, 476 U.S. 79 (1986) (restricting exercise of peremptory challenges based solely upon race).

The number in criminal cases often varies with the seriousness of the charge.

The *voir dire* process continues, calling further venire members to the jury box to be questioned and, potentially, challenged, until the proper number of jurors and alternates has been selected. The jurors thus selected then take their juror's oath and are thus empanelled.

OPENING STATEMENTS

Once the jurors and alternates have been sworn in, the lawyers make *opening statements* to the court, first by the lawyer for the plaintiff, and then by the lawyer for the defense. These opening statements are often mischaracterized in the media as opening "arguments." They are not supposed to be arguments, however, but rather to give the jurors an advance idea about what is coming. Specifically, the opening statements are the place where Mr. Horan and Mr. Sills would describe to the finders of fact the evidence they expect to present during the trial. A lawyer can and should endeavor to describe the evidence in a persuasive manner, but the lawyer is not supposed to draw inferences from the evidence or ask the jury to reach conclusions about it. Needless to say, lines like these are hard to draw and some courts are less than strict in enforcing the prohibition against argument in an opening statement.

In this case, Mrs. DeWeerth's counsel would go first because Mrs. DeWeerth was the party with the burden of persuasion, and the party with the burden — the plaintiff or prosecutor — is the one that makes the first opening statement. (At the end of the trial, in the closing arguments, the party with the burden of persuasion generally gets to go last.) In many jurisdictions, the defendant may reserve making an opening statement until after the plaintiff has presented her main evidence at trial (the plaintiff's case-in-chief). As a matter of practice, however, for the defendant to do this is now rare;

most defendants prefer to seize the opportunity to address the jurors immediately following the plaintiff.

PRESENTING THE TESTIMONY AND OTHER EVIDENCE

Plaintiff's Case-in-Chief. During this portion of the trial, Mrs. DeWeerth's counsel calls witnesses (including Mrs. DeWeerth herself) to testify and produces tangible evidence in support of her cause of action. The testimony of witnesses takes the familiar form of questions and answers, under oath, in the presence of the fact-finder (*see* Appendix A). In order to help assure the reliability of the testimony and other proof that the lawyers provide, there are established *rules of evidence* that limit what the lawyer may ask and the matters the witness may speak about. While a witness is being *examined* at trial, the lawyer for the other side will listen carefully to what is said and must be ready to object instantly if anything is attempted that he or she considers "harmful" and in contravention of the rules of evidence. With rare exceptions, the judge rules on these in-court objections immediately—perhaps following a brief oral argument by counsel, either in open court for all to hear or, less publicly, "at the bench."

During Mrs. DeWeerth's case-in-chief her witnesses would have been questioned first by her own counsel (the "direct examination"), and then they would have been *cross-examined* by counsel for Mrs. Baldinger. Lawyers regard cross-examination as a crucial *testing* process for the credibility of testimony and as one of the most important reasons why adversarial trials can be generally relied on as tools for getting to truth. By means of a probing cross-examination lawyers can frequently bring to light significant weaknesses in the opponent's case. At some point you should take a look at the testimony in Appendix A, which deals generally with Mrs. DeWeerth's prior ownership and possession of the painting, and ask yourself: Are the details of the facts as revealed in that testimony as crisp and clear-cut as they appear from the judicial opinions that are based on those same facts?

Once Mrs. DeWeerth has produced all her evidence in support of her case, her lawyer tells that court that "the plaintiff *rests*." Before resting, however, it is crucial that her counsel be satisfied that she has presented enough to make out a *prima facie* case. That is, it is crucial that the testimony and exhibits presented on her behalf be, taken as a whole, legally sufficient to permit a reasonable jury to find in Mrs. DeWeerth's favor on *every* point for which she has the burden of producing evidence. If sufficient evidence on even *one* of the essential points is missing, then the defendant is entitled to judgment as a matter of law.

You will remember from the decision on the summary judgment motion (*DeWeerth v. Baldinger II*) there were genuine issues of material fact on the questions of whether Mrs. DeWeerth was the owner of the Monet, whether it was stolen from her, and whether she therefore had a superior right to possession of it. Because there were genuine issues of material fact on these questions, it was not appropriate to grant summary judgment for Mrs. Baldinger. Instead, these questions were to be resolved at trial. Now, however, we are at trial, and Mrs. DeWeerth has her opportunity to present evidence on her prior ownership of the painting and the circumstances surrounding its disappearance.

Let's assume that, at the trial, Mrs. DeWeerth's attorney presented no evidence of her prior ownership of the Monet and its disappearance beyond the evidence that was referred to in Judge Broderick's opinion on summary judgment. If that happened, we may safely also assume that Mr. Sills still would not believe that Mrs. DeWeerth has made out a legally sufficient case on her "superior" right to possession. While Judge Broderick also probably has not changed *his* mind on the sufficiency of the evidence either, Mr. Sills should nonetheless move for a "judgment as a matter of law"[137] on behalf of Mrs. Baldinger. His argument for

---

[137] FED. R. CIV. P. 50. In traditional jury practice, this motion is often referred to as a motion for a *directed verdict*.

granting the motion would be that, on the evidence presented so far, no reasonable juror could conclude both that Mrs. DeWeerth previously owned the painting and that it was stolen from her and, therefore, her claim of a right to possess the painting was baseless as a matter of law. The motion may seem futile at this point but it would be necessary to "preserve" the issue, *i.e.*, keep it alive for a later motion and, possibly, for appeal.

Such trial motions are typically made orally, in open court. They are normally ruled on right away — and denied.

Defendant's Case-in-Chief. If the judge has denied the defense motion for judgment as a matter of law (meaning the plaintiff produced sufficient evidence to support a finding in her own favor), it is the defendant's turn to present evidence. Despite the judge's determination that the plaintiff has presented a *prima facie* case, the defendant might choose not to present any evidence. This might happen if defendant's attorney believes that, even though there is sufficient evidence to *support* a finding for the plaintiff, the evidence is still not sufficient to *persuade the jury*. If Mr. Sills had believed that Mrs. Baldinger could obtain a verdict without presenting evidence of her own, he might simply rest without further ado and then make a final argument based upon the evidence in the plaintiff's case-in-chief, including evidence elicited on cross-examination of plaintiff's witnesses. This tactic — rare in civil cases — is possible because of the important difference between the burden of producing evidence and the burden of persuasion. The burden of producing evidence is satisfied if the plaintiff's evidence meets the bare minimum needed to support a jury verdict for the plaintiff, while the burden of persuasion is carried only when the evidence is powerful enough actually to persuade the jury to find for the plaintiff.

In the usual case, the defendant presents the testimony of witnesses and offers exhibits in roughly the same fashion as in the plaintiff's case-in-chief. The defendant's evidence may be offered to establish the defendant's affirmative contentions (the defendant was somewhere else, the defendant has legal title to the property, etc.) or it may be offered to discredit the plaintiff's witnesses or counter the plaintiff's evidence. When the defendant has presented all of the evidence relating to the plaintiff's claim, or any affirmative defenses the defendant may have, the defendant rests.

Plaintiff's Rebuttal and Defendant's Surrebuttal. After the defendant has rested, the plaintiff has an opportunity to offer witnesses and exhibits to rebut matters or discredit witnesses put forth during the defendant's case-in-chief. In general, however, a plaintiff may not present evidence as "rebuttal" unless it relates in some way to the evidence or witnesses that the defendant produced in her case-in-chief. For example, if the defendant presents testimony that tends to discredit the testimony of the plaintiff's second witness, the plaintiff may present rebuttal evidence to support the credibility of that witness's testimony. The plaintiff normally may not, however, present "rebuttal" evidence to support testimony that the defendant has left unchallenged. Similarly, when the plaintiff's rebuttal case is finished, the defendant is allowed a surrebuttal (or rejoinder), but the surrebuttal is normally limited to matters raised in the plaintiff's rebuttal. These limitations on rebuttal and surrebuttal, though generally followed, are not entirely hard and fast, however. The trial judge may allow a departure from the ordinary limited scope of rebuttal and surrebuttal if circumstances and fairness warrant.

MOTIONS FOR JUDGMENT AS A MATTER OF LAW OR JUDGMENT OF ACQUITTAL

When there is no more testimony from either side, and both sides have rested, one or both parties in a civil action may move for a judgment as a matter of law. This motion asks the judge to rule that on all of the evidence presented in the trial, no reasonable jury could find in favor of the other party. The motion is similar in concept to the defendant's motion for a "judgment as a matter of law at the end" of the plaintiff's case-in-chief, discussed earlier. There is, however, an important difference: The defendant's motion for judgment at the end of the plaintiff's case-in-chief is grounded on the theory that the plaintiff has failed (allegedly) to meet its burden of production, *i.e.*, failed to make a *prima facie* case. At the end of all the evidence, however, the judge may enter judgment for the defendant as a matter of law even if the plaintiff has met its burden of production, provided that the judge concludes a reasonable jury could not find, based on all the evidence, that plaintiff met its burden of persuasion. The judge will not grant the motion merely because the judge, in his or her own mind, happens to be persuaded that the moving party ought to win and would have so held if sitting without the jury. Rather, to grant the motion, the judge must be willing to say that, based on all the evidence, *no reasonable jury* could reach any other conclusion. In a criminal case, the defense may move the judge to take the decision away from the jurors and enter a judgment of acquittal, but the prosecution may not move for a judgment of conviction.[138]

Again, to "preserve" the issue for a later motion and possibly appeal, Mr. Sills should move for a judgment as a matter of law on behalf of Mrs. Baldinger, arguing that the evidence does not show a legal basis for Mrs. DeWeerth's claim of a superior right to possess the Monet. And again such motions are typically made orally, in open court, and are ruled on right away — usually denied.

CLOSING ARGUMENTS

After all of the evidence has been presented to the jury, the lawyers have an opportunity to address the jurors. Closing argument is the lawyer's opportunity to sum up the case and to explain to the juror why the evidence presented and the law

---

[138] U.S. Const. amend. VI (guaranteeing a right to trial by jury in criminal cases).

they will hear from the judge should, taken together, lead inexorably to a verdict for the lawyer's client.

In the Southern District of New York and in many state jurisdictions, the party with the burden of persuasion is given the last word to the jury. The defendant's counsel makes the first closing argument and then the plaintiff's counsel, thus allowing the party with the burden to respond to arguments made by her opponent. There are, however, variations among the courts on the order of closing argument: for example, allowing the party with the burden to go first *and* last or giving both parties an opportunity for a rebuttal.

CHARGE TO THE JURY

After all of the evidence is in and the lawyers have made their closing statements, it is almost time for the jury to decide whether to make Mrs. Baldinger return the Monet painting to Mrs. DeWeerth. To make this decision, the jurors will "retire" to the jury room and deliberate in order to reach their verdict. First, however, there remains a most important step. The judge must give a *charge to the jury*. In the judge's charge, the jury receives *instructions* as to the law. That is, the judge tells the jurors what legal rules and standards they should use in deciding the case. The jury's chief job is "fact-finding," but juries are not usually asked to create a recitation of their findings of fact. Rather, they are usually expected to reach "mixed conclusions of fact and law," which means they are to apply the facts (as they find them) to the law that the judge instructs them to use. It is the judge's job to decide what "the law" is for purposes of the case.

Ordinarily the lawyers do not simply leave it up to the judge to figure out what should be the applicable rules and principles of law. Each side submits to the judge written requests for jury instructions on the various points they consider to be important to their respective causes. Mr. Sills, for example, would almost certainly want to request strong instructions on the necessity for positive evidence of ownership or prior possession before a person can be entitled to take a chattel long held by another. Mr. Horan, by contrast, would specifically oppose any instruction implying that the law requires anything more of Mrs. DeWeerth than evidence showing that she actually possessed the painting 35 years before and that it was taken without her consent.

For our remaining review of *DeWeerth v. Baldinger*, we will assume that Judge Broderick gave a charge to the jury that included the following items:

1. The usual "standard" instructions that the judge had developed over the years in order to inform the jurors in his court about their role in the process, to remind them of their responsibilities, and to inform them about such points as the burden of persuasion and the standard of proof, which are similar in most civil cases.
2. Instructions to tell the jurors what specific findings of fact they must make in order to conclude: (1) that Mrs. DeWeerth *ever* had a legal right to the painting currently possessed by Mrs. Baldinger—for example, that she had inherited the painting or otherwise legitimately acquired it and had it in her possession, and (2) that the painting was taken from Mrs. DeWeerth (or the person to whom she had entrusted it) without her consent and against her will.

Concerning the crucial specific findings of fact, the instructions to the jury might have gone something like this:

Before you can reach a verdict that plaintiff DeWeerth is entitled to recover the painting from the defendant, you must find based on credible evidence that plaintiff DeWeerth actually had a superior right to possession of the painting and that she did not make or authorize a voluntary transfer of it.

In this connection, plaintiff DeWeerth has presented testimony and documentary evidence which, if believed by you, would tend to establish that she became the owner of the Monet by inheritance from her father and remained such until the painting disappeared from her sister's home. She has also presented testimony to the effect she neither sold the painting nor entrusted it to anyone else to sell. She has also presented a 1943 photograph of a painting displayed in her residence next to a Rodin sculpture and testimony to the effect that it is the same Monet painting currently possessed by defendant. This evidence, if believed by you, would further support plaintiff DeWeerth's claim of prior ownership of the painting and her superior right to possess it. Plaintiff DeWeerth has, moreover, presented testimonial and documentary evidence which, if believed by you, would support an inference that the Monet painting held by defendant was stolen from the home of plaintiff's sister during the occupation of the latter's house by American soldiers after plaintiff had sent the painting to her sister's home for safekeeping, but with no intention that it be sold. . . .

While defendant Baldinger disputes plaintiff's contentions on these points, defendant has presented no evidence directly contradicting the testimonial and documentary evidence presented by plaintiff in support of her claim of superior title. Therefore, the question comes down to whether you believe plaintiff's evidence concerning her inheritance and prior possession of the Monet painting, and concerning the circumstances of its disappearance.

If you believe the evidence that plaintiff DeWeerth presented to show that she inherited the Monet painting, that she possessed it in her home and that she was deprived of it involuntarily, then you should find that plaintiff DeWeerth has a superior right to possess the painting and render a verdict in her favor. If, however, you do not believe the evidence that plaintiff presented to show she had prior ownership and possession of the painting, or if you do not believe that she parted with that ownership and possession involuntarily, then you should find in favor of the defendant Baldinger and your verdict should be for her.

THE JUDGMENT (AND A MOTION FOR A "JUDGMENT N.O.V.")

```
UNITED STATES DISTRICT COURT
SOUTHERN DISTRICT OF NEW YORK
- - - - - - - - - - - - - - - - - - - - - - - - - - - - - - - - - - -X
                                      :
        GERDA DOROTHEA DE WEERTH,      :       83 Civ. 1233
                       Plaintiff,     :
                                      :
        -against-                     :       JUDGMENT
                                      :
    EDITH MARKS BALDINGER,             :
                   Defendant and,     :
                   Third Party Plaintiff, :
        against                       :
                                      :
                                      :
    WILDENSTEIN & CO., INC,            :
            Third-Party Defendant.[139] :
- - - - - - - - - - - - - - - - - - - - - - - - - - - - - - - - - - -X
```

   This action having been commenced on the 16th day of February 1983 by the filing of a complaint, and a copy of the summons and complaint having been duly served upon the defendant on March 21, 1983, and defendant having filed her answer and counterclaims on April 5, 1983, * * * and the action between plaintiff and defendant

---

[139] Editor's note: When Mrs. Baldinger was sued for the painting, she turned around and sued Wildenstein & Co. Inc. so that she could receive compensation for the painting's

having come on for trial before the Court and jury, Honorable
Vincent L. Broderick, District Judge, presiding, and the issues
having been duly tried and the jury having duly rendered its
verdict, and the court having expressly found no just reason for
delay in the entry of judgment for plaintiff and having expressly
directed the submission and entry of a final judgment pursuant to
Rule 54(b) of the Federal Rules of Civil Procedure.

Now, on motion of Fox Glynn & Melamed, attorneys for plaintiff
Gerda Dorothea De Weerth, it is

ORDERED AND ADJUDGED that plaintiff Gerda Dorothea De Weerth is
the owner of the painting having the dimensions 25-$\frac{1}{2}$ × 31-$\frac{3}{4}$
inches (65 × 81 centimeters) entitled "Champs de Blé à Vetheuil"
and signed and dated "Claude Monet '79" which is the subject of
this action; and it is further

ORDERED AND ADJUDGED that defendant Edith Marks Baldinger, at
her expense, shall within 14 days of service of this order upon her
attorney transfer and deliver the painting having the dimensions
25-$\frac{1}{2}$ × 31-$\frac{3}{4}$ inches (65 × 81 centimeters) entitled "Champs de
Blé à Vetheuil" and signed and dated "Claude Monet '79" which is
the subject of this action to Fox Glynn & Melamed as attorneys for
plaintiff Gerda Dorothea De Weerth at such place and under such
circumstances as they shall direct, and it is further

ORDERED AND ADJUDGED that the Clerk of this court shall tax and
enter a bill of costs and disbursements in this action in favor of
plaintiff and against the defendant.

Dated: New York, New York
         April 27, 1987

                                      [signature]
                                      _____
                                      U.S.D.J.

---

value in case she were to lose it. This action against the seller was all part of the same
lawsuit, but the court ordered that the Wildenstein portion of the case be tried separately,
and later. Mrs. Baldinger's suit against Wildenstein is a complication that formed little
part of the litigation leading up to this judgment, and discussion of it is deferred to the
Postscript.

*t*he verdict having been rendered against her, Mrs. Baldinger had one final opportunity to move for a judgment in her favor. This post-trial motion is traditionally known as a "judgment notwithstanding the verdict" or, for short, a "judgment n.o.v." from the Latin *non obstante veredicto*. Under the modern federal practice, however, the motion is assimilated into the rule on trial motions for judgment "as a matter of law," which we saw in the preceding chapter. This post-trial motion is treated as a *renewal* of the party's requests at trial for judgment as a matter of law, but it is normally filed in writing with the court rather than being made orally in open court.

As with Mr. Sills's previous motions for judgment as a matter of law, this one would be founded on the contention that Mrs. DeWeerth's evidence did not show a legally sufficient factual basis for her claim that she has the superior right to possess the Monet painting. This time, however, the motion comes *after* a jury verdict for Mrs. DeWeerth and, therefore, after a jury has concluded that, indeed, the evidence at trial *did* show that she had a superior right of possession.

Jury verdicts can be overturned by judges but, as you might imagine, it is very difficult to get a judge to do it. The importance attached to the fact-finding role of juries in the common-law system means the bar is set very high for those who would ask a judge to overturn a jury verdict. As Judge Broderick might have explained it in denying Mrs. Baldinger's motion for judgment as a matter of law (or "judgment n.o.v."):

In reaching its verdict for plaintiff DeWeerth, the jury must have found that DeWeerth had a superior right to possession of the Monet painting in defendant's possession. In reviewing a jury verdict, the standard of review is purposely very exacting. A court may not grant a judgment notwithstanding a jury verdict unless "there is no legally sufficient evidentiary basis for a reasonable jury to find for [the moving] party. . . ." FED. R. CIV. P. 50(a)(1).

The jury had uncontradicted testimonial and documentary evidence presented by Mrs. DeWeerth to the effect that:

(1) she had inherited the Monet painting from her father in 1922;
(2) she still had the painting in her possession in 1943;
(3) she sent to painting to her sister's home for safekeeping in 1943; and
(4) the painting disappeared while soldiers were occupying her sister's home.

This evidence easily meets the standard of supplying a "legally sufficient evidentiary basis" on which a reasonable jury could find that Mrs. DeWeerth had a superior right to possession of the painting. There is no basis for a judgment for defendant as a matter of law notwithstanding the jury verdict.

Motion denied.

THE APPEAL

*W*hen Judge Broderick denied Mrs. Baldinger's motion for a judgment notwithstanding the verdict, a new phase of this lawsuit began. Had Mrs. Baldinger done nothing more, she would have lost all chance of retaining *Champs de Blé à Vétheuil*. She would have had to turn it over to Mrs. DeWeerth, and that would be that. Therefore, Mrs. Baldinger now had to decide whether to have her lawyer apply to the proper *appellate* court to review the judgment of the trial court. This process of *appealing* a decision is discussed in Chapter IV, and you might want to look at it again to refresh your recollection.

Mrs. Baldinger did not decide to give up. After consultation with her lawyer, she decided to appeal the case to the United States Court of Appeals for the Second Circuit. This is the federal court of appeals that sits in New York City, in lower Manhattan, and handles appeals from the district courts in Connecticut, New York and Vermont.

Mr. Sills's first step was to file a notice of appeal with the clerk of the federal *district* court that rendered the judgment he is appealing from. The contents of the notice of appeal are prescribed by the Federal Rules of Appellate Procedure, as follows:

UNITED STATES DISTRICT COURT FOR THE
SOUTHERN DISTRICT OF NEW YORK

- X
                                           :
Gerda Dorothea DeWeerth,   :   83 Civ. 1233
                    Plaintiff,   :
    against   :   *Notice of Appeal*
                                           :
Edith Marks Baldinger,   :
                Defendant and   :
                Third Party Plaintiff, :
    against   :

WILDENSTEIN & CO., INC,   :
            Third-Party Defendant.   :
- X

   Notice is hereby given that Edith Marks Baldinger, the
defendant in the above named case, hereby appeals to United States
Court of Appeals for the Second Circuit from the final judgment
entered in this action on the 27th day of April, 1987, and from each
and every part thereof.

                                EDWARD M. SILLS
                                Attorney for Defendant
                                225 Broadway
                                New York, New York 10007
                                Tel. No.: (212) 555-6789

   Once Mr. Sills had filed the notice of appeal, the clerk of the
Southern District sent a copy of it to the clerk of the Second
Circuit and also mailed a copy to Mr. Horan, as counsel for the
Mrs. DeWeerth. Observe that the notice still describes the parties
as "plaintiff" and "defendant." Once the appeal was *docketed* in
the Second Circuit, however, these designations changed. As
parties to an appeal, Mrs. Baldinger became the *appellant* (the
person who brings the appeal) while Mrs. DeWeerth, who is
opposing the appeal, became the *appellee*.[140]

---

[140] Under some rules of practice, the parties' names are inverted at the appeals level if, as
here, the defendant is the one who brings the appeal and thus becomes the *appellant*. In
federal courts of appeal today, however, the practice is to keep the order of the parties'
names the same as it was in the district court. In the U.S. Supreme Court, the name of the
party seeking review always goes first. (Note that this has not always been true in all
federal courts — so you may see the parties' names reversed in older cases.)

Remember that appellate courts do not take evidence, and they concern themselves primarily with questions of law — in particular, they review the appellant's contentions that the court below made an *error* of law affecting the outcome of the case. The appeals court's knowledge of the case comes from the *record on appeal* (for factual matters) and from the formal legal arguments made by the parties' lawyers. The record on appeal is a compendium of documents that includes a certified copy of the docket entries (orders and the judgment), the transcript of the trial proceedings and the exhibits and papers that were filed in the district court. It can be pretty hefty — sometimes running to thousands of pages. The appeals court considers the lawyers' legal arguments in light of this record on appeal and, if no error of law is found, then the judgment is *affirmed*; otherwise is it *reversed* or, sometimes, *modified* (or affirmed in part and reversed in part).

The lawyers' arguments on appeal usually take two forms: written and oral. The written arguments are presented in documents (usually, printed booklets) known as *briefs* — one of the law's great misnomers. Before the days of page limits, briefs were known to go on for hundreds of pages. Today, the federal courts of appeal impose page limits of 30 pages for principal briefs, and tighter limits for supplementary "reply" briefs. Brief writers are, however, wise to remember the admonition once quipped by an appellate judge: "We usually read all of a 15 page brief, and the first 15 pages of a hundred page brief."

In preparing their briefs the lawyers will try to present their respective sides of the case with as much supporting authority (either statutory or judicial) as they can find. The finished briefs are delivered not only to the court but also to the opposing counsel, so that each party will be able to check and countercheck the law that the other side has argued should be applicable. But good lawyers know that it is not enough for the brief to present a "tight" legal argument as to why their side ought to prevail. The lawyers must also strive to make the judge *want* to decide the case in their clients' favor, to show why their side should win not merely as a matter of legal logic but also as a matter of palpable *justice*. Brief writing is an art and skill that you will begin to acquire later this year when you do the "moot court" segment of your first year program

By the way, you may be wondering who gets to hold on to the Monet while the appeal is in progress. This is a very important collateral "detail." If nothing were done about it, the district court's judgment would be in effect during this interim, and Mrs. DeWeerth would be entitled to possession of the painting and to take it back to Germany. However, Mrs. Baldinger had the option of moving for a *stay* of the district court's judgment pending the appeal. Such motions for stays are usually granted, provided that the requester (usually the appellant) posts an appropriate bond to protect the interests of the person who won the judgment below. Thus, by obtaining a stay and posting a bond to protect Mrs. DeWeerth's interests, Mrs. Baldinger was able to retain possession of *Champs de Blé à Vétheuil* while her appeal was under way.

On October 26, 1987, about six months after Judge Broderick rendered his judgment, oral arguments in the appeal of *DeWeerth v. Baldinger* were made before a three judge panel of the Second Circuit. The presiding judge at the oral argument was Chief Judge Wilfred Feinberg, along with Circuit Judges Jon O. Newman and Ralph K. Winter. As often happens, the lawyers who had been primarily responsible for the trial were not the ones who made the oral arguments on appeal. One of Mr. Sills's colleagues, Leslie Gordon Fagen, Esq., made the argument for Mrs. Baldinger, while Joseph D. Becker, Esq., of Mr. Horan's firm, argued for Mrs. DeWeerth.

The oral argument in *DeWeerth v. Baldinger* took place in the handsome courtroom of the Second Circuit at 40 Foley Square. It was the first argument of the day, and each lawyer had 20 minutes to present the case for his or her side. As commonly occurs, however, the lawyers were not permitted to proceed peacefully through their carefully prepared arguments but were, instead, peppered with questions from the three judges of the panel sitting on the "bench" — the dais high above them.

Following the oral argument, the lawyers packed up and went back to their offices. The panel remained to hear other oral arguments set for that day. No decision was rendered on the spot (they almost never are). Then two months later, just before New Year's Eve, Messrs. Sills and Horan and their associates received word that the Second Circuit had issued its decision. The judgment for Mrs. DeWeerth had been reversed.

DeWeerth v. Baldinger
(DeWeerth v. Baldinger III)
836 F.2d 103 (2d Cir. 1987)

JON O. NEWMAN, Circuit Judge:

This appeal concerns a dispute over ownership of a painting by Claude Monet that disappeared from Germany at the end of World War II and has been in the possession of a good-faith purchaser for the last 30 years. The appeal presents primarily the issue whether New York law, which governs this dispute, requires an individual claiming ownership of stolen personal property to use due diligence in trying to locate the property in order to postpone the running of the statute of limitations in a suit against a good-faith purchaser. . . . We conclude that New York law imposes a due diligence requirement, that the undisputed facts show that DeWeerth failed to exercise reasonable diligence in locating the painting after its disappearance, and that her action for recovery is untimely. We therefore reverse the judgment of the District Court.

Background

Claude Monet is, perhaps, the most well-known and widely admired member of the school of impressionist painters active in France in the late nineteenth and early twentieth centuries. . . . The painting in the pending case, Monet's "Champs de Blé à Vétheuil," is one of a series of similar impressssionistic landscapes painted by the artist near the town of Vetheuil, located on the Seine in Northern France. The oil painting, measuring 65 by 81 centimeters, shows a wheat field, a village, and trees. It is signed and dated "Claude Monet '79." The painting is estimated to be worth in excess of $500,000.

[Plaintiff's] father, Karl von der Heydt, the owner of a substantial art collection, purchased the Monet in 1908. DeWeerth inherited the painting in 1922 along with other works of art from her father's estate. She kept the painting in her home in Wuppertal-Elberfeld, Germany, from 1922 until 1943 .... A photograph taken in 1943 shows the Monet hanging on a wall in DeWeerth's residence.

In August 1943, DeWeerth sent the Monet and other valuables to the home of her sister, Gisela von Palm, for safekeeping. ... In 1945, at the end of the war, American soldiers were quartered in von Palm's residence. Following the soldiers' departure, von Palm noticed that the Monet was missing. She informed her sister of the painting's disappearance in the fall of 1945.

DeWeerth contacted several authorities concerning the lost Monet. In 1946, she filed a report with the military government administering the Bonn-Cologne area after the war. The report is no longer extant, but DeWeerth testified that it was a standard government form in which she briefly described items she had lost during the war. In 1948, in a letter to her lawyer, Dr. Heinz Frowein, regarding insurance claims on property she had lost, DeWeerth expressed regret about the missing Monet and inquired whether it was "possible to do anything about it." Frowein wrote back that the Monet would not be covered by insurance; he did not initiate an investigation. In 1955, DeWeerth sent the 1943 photograph of the Monet to Dr. Alfred Stange, a former professor of art and an expert in medieval painting, and asked him to investigate the painting's whereabouts. Stange responded that the photo was insufficient evidence with which to begin a search, and DeWeerth did not pursue the matter with him further. Finally, in 1957 DeWeerth sent a list of art works she had lost during the war to the *Bundeskriminalamt*, the West German federal bureau of investigation. None of DeWeerth's efforts during the period 1945-1957 to locate the Monet was fruitful. DeWeerth made no further attempts to recover the painting after 1957.

In the meantime, the Monet had reappeared in the international art market by 1956. In December of that year, ... Wildenstein & Co., Inc., an art gallery in New York City, acquired the Monet on consignment from Francois Reichenbach, an art dealer in Geneva,

Switzerland. . . . Defendant Edith Marks Baldinger eventually purchased the painting in June 1957 for $30,900. The parties have
stipulated that Baldinger purchased for value, in good faith, and
without knowledge of any adverse claim.

Since 1957, Baldinger has kept the Monet in her New York City
apartment, except for two occasions when it was displayed at public
exhibitions. From October 29 to November 1, 1957, it was shown at
a benefit at the Waldorf-Astoria Hotel, and in 1970 it was loaned to
Wildenstein for an exhibition in its New York gallery for approximately one month.

DeWeerth learned of Baldinger's possession of the Monet
through the efforts of her nephew, Peter von der Heydt. In 1981,
von der Heydt was told by a cousin that DeWeerth had owned a
Monet that had disappeared during the war. Shortly thereafter, von
der Heydt identified the painting in a published volume of Monet's
works, *Claude Monet: Bibliographie et Catalogue Raisonne, Vol. I
1840-1881* (intro. by Daniel Wildenstein . . .), which he found at
[a] Museum in Cologne, less than 20 miles from where DeWeerth
has been living since 1957. The *Catalogue Raisonne* indicated that
the painting had been sold by Wildenstein in 1957 and that Wildenstein had exhibited it in 1970. . . .

DeWeerth instituted the present action to recover the Monet on
February 16, 1983. The District Court adjudged DeWeerth the
owner of the painting and ordered Baldinger to return it. . . .

Discussion

In this diversity action, we must apply the substantive law of
New York, including the applicable New York choice of law rules.
Klaxon Co. v. Stentor Electric Mfg. Co., 313 U.S. 487, 61 S. Ct.
1020, 85 L. Ed. 1477 (1941). [The court discusses various New
York choice of law rules.] In the present case, if DeWeerth's action is
time-barred under New York's limitations law, then the action is
untimely regardless of whether it accrued in New York or Germany.

The New York statute of limitations governing actions for recovery of stolen property requires that suit be brought within three years
of the time the action accrued. N.Y. Civ. Prac. L. & R. §214(3)

(McKinney 1972). The date of accrual depends upon the identity of the party from whom recovery is sought. Where an owner pursues the party who took his property, the three-year period begins to run when the property was taken. [Citation to New York case omitted.] This is so even where the property owner was unaware of the unlawful taking at the time it occurred. [Citations to New York cases omitted.] In contrast, where the owner proceeds against one who innocently purchases the property in good faith, the limitations period begins to run only when the owner demands return of the property and the purchaser refuses. *Menzel v. List,* 22 A.D.2d 647, 253 N.Y.S.2d 43, 44 (1st Dep't 1964), *on remand,* 49 Misc. 2d 300, 267 N.Y.S.2d 804 (Sup. Ct. 1966), *modified on other grounds,* 28 A.D.2d 516, 279 N.Y.S.2d 608 (1st Dep't 1967), *modification rev'd,* 24 N.Y.2d 91, 298 N.Y.S.2d 979, 246 N.E.2d 742 (1969); *Duryea v. Andrews,* 12 N.Y.S. 42 (2d Dep't 1890); *accord Kunstsammlungen Zu Weimar v. Elicofon,* 536 F. Supp. 829, 848-49 (E.D.N.Y. 1981) (applying New York law), *aff'd,* 678 F.2d 1150, 1161 (2d Cir. 1982). Until demand and refusal, the purchaser in good faith is not considered a wrongdoer, *Gillet v. Roberts,* 57 N.Y. 28 (1874), even though this rule somewhat anomalously affords the owner more time to sue a good-faith purchaser than a thief.

In the present case, it is undisputed that DeWeerth initiated her suit within three years of the date her demand for return of the Monet was refused. However, the fact that her action was brought soon after refusal does not end the inquiry. Under New York law, even though the three-year limitations period begins to run only once a demand for return of the property is refused, a plaintiff may not delay the action simply by postponing his demand. Where demand and refusal are necessary to start a limitations period, the demand may not be unreasonably delayed.[141] *See Heide v. Glidden Buick Corp.,* 188 Misc. 198, 67 N.Y.S.2d 905 (1st Dep't 1947) (contract action);

---

[141] By contrast, the unreasonable delay rule, applicable to this case as a substantive requirement, specifies that whenever a demand would be required to start the limitations period, that demand may not be unreasonably delayed. This rule, focusing on the plaintiff's conduct, conceptually starts the limitations period at the point where the plaintiff has had an opportunity to use due diligence in locating the property and making a demand, and has failed to do so.

Austin v. Board of Higher Education, 5 N.Y.2d 430, 442-43, 186 N.Y.S.2d 1, 10-11, 158 N.E.2d 681 (1959) (mandamus proceeding); *Reid v. Board of Supervisors,* 128 N.Y. 364, 373, 28 N.E. 367, 369 (1891) (reimbursement for price of real estate purchased at tax sale); *Kunstsammlungen Zu Weimar v. Elicofon, supra,* 536 F. Supp. at 849 (recovery of stolen art). . . .

Baldinger asserts that DeWeerth's action is untimely because the delay between the painting's disappearance in Europe in 1945 and DeWeerth's demand for its return in 1982 was unreasonable. DeWeerth responds that she cannot be charged with unreasonable delay before learning the identity of Baldinger in 1982 because she could not have known before that time to whom to make the demand. These contentions frame the precise issue presented by this appeal: Whether New York law imposes upon a person who claims ownership of stolen personal property an obligation to use due diligence in attempting to locate the property.

DeWeerth points out that no New York court has ever held that the unreasonable delay rule applies *before* the plaintiff has learned the identity of the person to whom demand must be made. In *Glidden Buick, Reid,* and *Austin,* plaintiffs were barred for unreasonably delaying demands to known defendants. DeWeerth suggests that in the absence of New York authority directly on point, her actions before she discovered that Baldinger possessed the Monet cannot be subject to the unreasonable delay rule. Baldinger responds that New York courts, confronting the issue, would impose an obligation of due diligence to attempt to locate the person in possession of another's property. The District Court did not decide the issue, concluding that plaintiff had exercised due diligence in any event. 658 F. Supp. at 694.

This Court's role in exercising its diversity jurisdiction is to sit as another court of the state. *Guaranty Trust Co. v. York,* 326 U.S. 99, 108, 65 S. Ct. 1464, 89 L. Ed. 2079 (1945). When presented with an absence of controlling state authority, we must "make an estimate of what the state's highest court would rule to be its law." [Citations omitted.] In making that determination, this Court may consider all of the resources that the New York Court of Appeals could use, [citation omitted], including New York's stated policies and the law of other jurisdictions. We determine that in an action for the recovery of stolen personal property, the New York Court of Appeals would not make an exception to the unreasonable delay rule for plaintiff's actions prior to learning the identity of the current possessor. Rather, we believe that the New York courts would impose a duty of reasonable diligence in attempting to locate stolen property, in addition to the undisputed duty to make a demand for return within a reasonable time after the current possessor is identified.[142]

An obligation to attempt to locate stolen property is consistent with New York's treatment of the good-faith purchaser. The purpose of the rule whereby demand and refusal are substantive elements of a conversion action against a good-faith purchaser is to protect the innocent party by assuring him notice before he is held liable in tort:

> The rule is a reasonable and just one, that an innocent purchaser of personal property from a wrong-doer shall first be informed of the defect in his title and have an opportunity to deliver the property to the true owner, before he shall be made liable as a tort-feasor for a wrongful conversion.

Gillet v. Roberts, supra, 57 N.Y. at 34; *accord Kunstsammlungen Zu Weimar v. Elicofon, supra,* 536 F. Supp. at 848. The rule may disadvantage the good-faith purchaser, however, if demand can be indefinitely postponed. For if demand is delayed, then so is accrual of the cause of action, and the good-faith purchaser will remain exposed to suit long after an action against a thief or even other innocent parties would be time-barred. [Citations omitted.] As the court in *Elicofon* observed, the unreasonable delay rule serves to mitigate the inequity of favoring a thief over a good-faith purchaser. 536 F. Supp. at 849. In this case, plaintiff's proposed exception to the rule would rob it of all of its salutary effect: The thief would be

---

[142] We have elected not to submit the unresolved state law issue in this appeal to the New York Court of Appeals pursuant to the recently authorized procedure permitting that Court to answer questions certified to it by . . . a United States Court of Appeals. . . . Though the issue presented by this appeal is interesting, we do not think it will recur with sufficient frequency to warrant use of the certification procedure.

immune from suit after three years, while the good-faith purchaser would remain exposed as long as his identity did not fortuitously come to the property owner's attention. A construction of the rule requiring due diligence in making a demand to include an obligation to make a reasonable effort to locate the property will prevent unnecessary hardship to the good-faith purchaser, the party intended to be protected.

New York law governing limitations of actions also weighs in favor of a duty to attempt to locate stolen property. The New York Court of Appeals has said that

> the primary purpose of a limitations period is fairness to a defendant (*Flanagan v. Mount Eden Gen. Hosp.*, 24 N.Y.2d 427, 429, 301 N.Y.S.2d 23, 248 N.E.2d 871). A defendant should "'be secure in his reasonable expectation that the slate has been wiped clean of ancient obligations, and he ought not to be called on to resist a claim where the "evidence has been lost, memories have faded, and witnesses have disappeared"'" [Citations omitted.] There is also the need to protect the judicial system from the burden of adjudicating stale and groundless claims.

Duffy v. Horton Memorial Hospital, 66 N.Y.2d 473, 476-77, 497 N.Y.S.2d 890, 892-93, 488 N.E.2d 820 (1985) (citation omitted). These policies would be frustrated if plaintiffs were free to delay actions for the return of stolen property until the property's location fortuitously came to their attention. Conceivably, those claiming to be owners, or their heirs, could wait idly for decades or even centuries before any legal obligation arose to pursue their claims. In such cases, all of the problems of lost evidence, faded memories, and unavailable witnesses would undoubtedly be exacerbated. Additionally, fraudulent and groundless claims would be encouraged as defendants would face a heavy burden of refuting proffered testimony related to events of the distant past.

A rule requiring reasonable diligence in attempting to locate stolen property is especially appropriate with respect to stolen art. Much art is kept in private collections, unadvertised and unavailable to the public. An owner seeking to recover such property will almost never learn of its whereabouts by chance. Yet the location of stolen art may frequently be discovered through investigation. *See* F. Feldman & B. Burnham, *An Art Archive: Principles and Realization*, 10 Conn. L. Rev. 702, 724 (1978) (French and Italian authorities credit stolen art registries and investigation efforts for recovery rates as high as 75%). Unlike many other items of stolen personal property, such as jewelry or automobiles, art loses its value if it is altered or disguised. Moreover, valuable works of art, unlike fungible items like stereo components, tend to be easily remembered by those who have seen them. Thus, the owner of stolen art has a better chance than most owners of stolen property in tracking down the item he has lost.

Other jurisdictions have adopted limitations rules that encourage property owners to search for their missing goods. In virtually every state except New York, an action for conversion accrues when a good-faith purchaser acquires stolen property; demand and refusal are unnecessary. [Citation omitted.] In these states, the owner must find the current possessor within the statutory period or his action is barred. Obviously, this creates an incentive to find one's stolen property. It is true that New York has chosen to depart from the majority view. Nevertheless, the fact that plaintiff's interpretation of New York law would exaggerate its inconsistency with the law of other jurisdictions weighs against adopting such a view. At least one other state has recently confronted the limitations problem in the context of stolen art and has imposed a duty of reasonable investigation. *See O'Keeffe v. Snyder,* 83 N.J. 478, 416 A.2d 862 (1980). *See also* Comment, *The Recovery of Stolen Art: Of Paintings, Statutes and Statutes of Limitations*, 27 U.C.L.A. L. Rev. 1122 (1980).

In light of New York's policy of favoring the good-faith purchaser and discouraging stale claims and the approach to actions to recover property in other jurisdictions, we hold that under New York law an owner's obligation to make a demand without unreasonable delay includes an obligation to use due diligence to locate stolen property.

[Standard of Review]

* * * Where, as here, the issue is the application of a legal standard — "reasonable diligence" — to a set of facts, review is *de novo*. See *Utica Mutual Ins. Co. v. Fireman's Fund Ins. Co.*, 748 F.2d 118, 122 & n.3 (2d Cir. 1984) (whether plaintiff's failure to discover a fraud was reasonable is a question of law subject to plenary review); *Reid v. Board of Supervisors, supra,* 128 N.Y. at 373, 28 N.E. at 369 ("What is a reasonable time [to make a demand that starts the limitations period] is *a question of law.* . . .") (emphasis added).

The question of what constitutes unreasonable delay in making a demand that starts the statute of limitations depends upon the circumstances of the case. *Id.; Kunstsammlungen Zu Weimar v. Elicofon, supra,* 536 F. Supp. at 849. When the action is for the return of stolen property, one of the key circumstances is the nature and value of the property at issue. See *O'Keefe v. Snyder, supra,* 83 N.J. at 499, 416 A.2d at 873. It has been recognized that when the property is valuable art, the search efforts that may reasonably be expected of an owner may be more exacting than where the property is of a different kind or of a lesser value. *Id.*

* * * DeWeerth's investigation was minimal. The "reports" filed with the military government and the *Bundeskriminalamt* amounted to no more than a standard form listing personal items lost during the war and a one-sentence letter submitting a list of works "I lost during and after the war." . . . DeWeerth's contacts with the lawyer Frowein and the art expert Stange were no more meaningful. She wrote to Frowein regarding her insurance coverage. She mentioned that the Monet was among the art she had lost and inquired generally, "Is it possible to do anything about it?" It is not clear whether this was a request to find the painting or simply a question about insurance coverage. In any event, when Frowein wrote back that the Monet would not be covered by insurance, DeWeerth let the matter drop. DeWeerth did ask Stange to find the Monet. But, as with Frowein, the investigation never was started; Stange replied that he had insufficient information on which to proceed, and DeWeerth then abandoned the effort.

More revealing than the steps DeWeerth took to find the Monet are those she failed to take. Conspicuously absent from her attempts to locate the painting is any effort to take advantage of several mechanisms specifically set up to locate art lost during World War II. As described in *Elicofon*, one such mechanism was a program initiated by the allied forces in Europe to handle works of art looted during the war. Under this program, Central Collecting Points (CCPs) were established throughout Germany where works of art turned in to the occupying forces were catalogued and stored until claimed by their rightful owners.[143]

Nor did DeWeerth publicize her loss of the Monet in any one of several available listings. . . . Most indicative of DeWeerth's lack of diligence is her failure to conduct any search for 24 years from 1957 until 1981. Significantly, if DeWeerth had undertaken even the most minimal investigation during this period, she would very likely have discovered the Monet, since there were several published references to it in the art world. [The court recites the four published references mentioned in Judge Broderick's statement of facts, set out in Chapter II.] Consultation of any of these publications would likely have led DeWeerth to the Monet. . . .

DeWeerth's failure to consult the *Catalogue Raisonne* is particularly inexcusable. A catalogue raisonne is a definitive listing and accounting of the works of an artist. The Monet *Catalogue Raisonne* depicts each of Monet's works in chronological order and sets forth each work's provenance — a history of its ownership, exhibitions in which it has been shown, and published references to it. The entry for painting number 595, the one here at issue, indicates that Wildenstein sold the painting in the United States in 1957 and that it was exhibited by Wildenstein in 1970. This entry could have easily directed DeWeerth to Wildenstein. Indeed, when in 1981 DeWeerth's nephew learned from a cousin of the lost Monet, he was able to identify it in the *Catalogue Raisonne* within

---

[143] DeWeerth asserts that the CCPs would not have been helpful in her search because, pursuant to the agreement of the allied forces, the collecting points were established to deal with property looted by the Germans in occupied territory and not with property lost in Germany. . . . [Still,] they were a potentially fruitful subject of investigation and ought to have been contacted.

three days, which led to the identification of Baldinger shortly thereafter.*

The District Court suggested excusing DeWeerth's failure to search for the Monet after 1957 on the grounds that she was elderly during this period, that published references to the Monet were not generally circulated, and that as an individual she could not be expected to mount the sort of investigation undertaken by the government-owned art museum in *Elicofon.* 658 F. Supp. at 694-95. But in 1957, when DeWeerth made her last attempt to locate the painting, she was only 63 years old. Moreover, though the published references may not have been generally circulated, they were accessible to anyone looking for them as Peter von der Heydt's quick discovery in the *Catalogue Raisonne* makes clear. Finally, although an individual, DeWeerth appears to be a wealthy and sophisticated art collector; even if she could not have mounted a more extensive investigation herself, she could have retained someone to do it for her.

This case illustrates the problems associated with the prosecution of stale claims. Gisela von Palm, the only witness who could verify what happened to the Monet in 1945 is dead. Key documents, including DeWeerth's father's will and reports to the military authorities, are missing. DeWeerth's claim of superior title is supported largely by hearsay testimony of questionable value. Memories have faded. To require a good-faith purchaser who has owned a painting for 30 years to defend under these circumstances would be unjust. New York law avoids this injustice by requiring a property owner to use reasonable diligence in locating his property. In this case, DeWeerth failed to meet that burden. Accordingly, the judgment of the District Court is reversed.

---

*Editor's note: Perhaps relevantly, however, the *Catalogue Raisonne*'s so-called "definitive listing" did not mention either DeWeerth or her father as previous owners of the painting, nor did it indicate the chain of ownership leading from DeWeerth to Baldinger. Instead, this "definitive listing" had the painting just appearing out of nowhere after WWII. Hmm.

STUDY QUESTIONS

You should be able to answer the following questions based on in *DeWeerth v. Baldinger III.*

1. On what ground did Baldinger assert that DeWeerth's action was untimely?
2. On what ground did DeWeerth contend that she cannot be charged with unreasonable delay?
3. One of the crucial rules relied on by the Second Circuit was, in the court's words: "Where demand and refusal are necessary to start a limitations period, the demand may not be unreasonably delayed." The court cited three New York cases in support of this "no unreasonable delay" rule. Look at the parentheticals accompanying these citations. What were the cited cases about? Were any of them actions to recover stolen property?
4. On what basis did DeWeerth's counsel assert that the New York "no unreasonable delay" cases were distinguishable from the facts in *DeWeerth v. Baldinger*?
5. How did the Second Circuit deal with the fact that there was no "New York authority directly on point" on the question of whether the "no unreasonable delay" rule would apply even when the owner does not know who has her property?
6. According to the Second Circuit, what is the "purpose" of New York's demand and refusal requirement? Whom was it supposed to protect?
7. If the law allowed the demand to be indefinitely postponed how would it work counter to this supposed "purpose"?
8. *Therefore* (from 6. and 7.): Once it found that New York had a policy to protect good faith purchasers, the Second Circuit proceeded ask itself the following question: In light of this policy, would the New York courts hold that the owner must make "a reasonable effort to locate the property"? What did it conclude?

9. Let's be clear here: The choice in cases like these is between two innocent parties—the true owner and the good faith purchaser. Which did the Second Circuit decide that the New York courts would prefer?

10. In deciding whether DeWeerth's delay in making a demand was unreasonable, what "standard of review" did the Second Circuit use?

11. When the Second Circuit applied the legal standard—"reasonable diligence"—to the facts of this case, what did it conclude? Did DeWeerth exhibit "reasonable diligence"?

12. Notice how the Second Circuit dealt with *O'Keeffe v. Snyder*, as compared with the district court. What was different?

And do as adversaries do in law, strive mightily, but eat and drink
as friends.
                                        —*William Shakespeare,*
                        Taming of the Shrew, act I, sc. 2

*U*nder the Second Circuit's interpretation of
the New York statute of limitations, Mrs.
DeWeerth's rights to the Monet were out the
window; the judgment of District Judge Broderick was gone.
The Second Circuit, had consulted the same body of judicial
decisions as Judge Broderick — "the holdings in cases deemed
to be precedents" — but the Second Circuit found it appropriate
to "extract different rules of law" from those precedents, leading
to the opposite legal outcome.

The quoted phrases in the preceding paragraph are (as you
might have already recognized) taken from one of the excerpts
quoted in the chapter "The Common Law." They are from the

passage that explains why many Legal Realists and the Crits believe that law is "indeterminate," that it is *all* open texture. While most would probably say the Realists and Crits go too far, that the law is generally both stable and predictable, here we see in action what the critics have in mind — or, if you prefer, an example of how skilled lawyers can work with the legal materials to further their clients' interests: Two courts, using the same facts and the same body of law, have reached opposite conclusions, and both with good reasons. Indeed, as you read Judge Newman's opinion for the Second Circuit you may have trouble recalling exactly why it was that Judge Broderick ever reached the opposite conclusion in the first place. Judge Newman makes some persuasive sounding arguments about both the law and facts — but then, so did Judge Broderick. It is possible, it seems, to make persuasive legal arguments for *both* sides in the same case. Notice, especially, that the reason the Second Circuit reversed Judge Broderick was *not* that he used the wrong statute, missed a crucial precedent, or overlooked a critical piece of evidence. It was simply that the two courts extracted different legal rules from the precedents and drew different conclusions about the legal import of certain facts. Both of these courts, sitting as federal courts in a diversity case, were supposed to be applying the law of New York, but the two saw that law differently. Which court got it "right"?

Let's see what New York's own highest court had to say. Here is an opinion rendered by the New York the Court of Appeals three years after the Second Circuit overturned Judge Broderick's interpretation:

Solomon R. Guggenheim Foundation v. Lubell
569 N.E.2d 426, 429 (N.Y. 1991)

OPINION OF THE COURT

The backdrop for this replevin action (*see, CPLR art 71*) is the New York City art market, where masterpieces command extraordinary

prices at auction and illicit dealing in stolen merchandise is an indus-
try all its own. The Solomon R. Guggenheim Foundation, which operates the Guggenheim Museum in New York City, is seeking to
recover a [Marc] Chagall gouache worth an estimated $200,000.
The Guggenheim believes that the gouache was stolen from its
premises by a mailroom employee sometime in the late 1960s.
The appellant Rachel Lubell and her husband, now deceased,
bought the painting from a well-known Madison Avenue gallery in
1967 and have displayed it in their home for more than 20 years.
Mrs. Lubell claims that before the Guggenheim's demand for its
return in 1986, she had no reason to believe that the painting
had been stolen. * * *

Mr. and Mrs. Lubell had purchased the painting from the Robert
Elkon Gallery for $17,000 in May of 1967. The invoice and receipt
indicated that the gouache had been in the collection of a named
individual, who later turned out to be the museum mailroom
employee suspected of the theft. . . . On January 9, 1986, Thomas
Messer, the museum's director, wrote a letter to the defendant
demanding the return of the gouache. Mrs. Lubell refused to return
the painting. . . .

The trial court [relied] on *DeWeerth v Baldinger* (836 F.2d 103),
an opinion from the United States Court of Appeals for the Second
Circuit. . . . Because the museum in this case had done nothing for
20 years but search its own premises, the court found that its conduct was unreasonable as a matter of law. Consequently, the court
[held] that the museum's cause of action was time barred. * * *

New York case law has long protected the right of the owner
whose property has been stolen to recover that property, even if it is
in the possession of a good-faith purchaser for value (*see, Saltus &
Saltus v Everett*, 20 Wend 267, 282) [decided 1838]. There is a
three-year Statute of Limitations for recovery of a chattel (CPLR 214
[3]). The rule in this State is that a cause of action for replevin
against the good-faith purchaser of a stolen chattel accrues when
the true owner makes demand for return of the chattel and the
person in possession of the chattel refuses to return it [citations
omitted]. Until demand is made and refused, possession of the
stolen property by the good-faith purchaser for value is not

considered wrongful [citations omitted]. Although seemingly anom-
alous, a different rule applies when the stolen object is in the possession of the thief. In that situation, the Statute of Limitations runs
from the time of the theft [citation omitted], even if the property
owner was unaware of the theft at the time that it occurred [citation
omitted].

In *DeWeerth v Baldinger (supra)*, . . . the Second Circuit took
note of the fact that New York case law treats thieves and good-faith
purchasers differently and looked to that difference as a basis for
imposing a reasonable diligence requirement on the owners of
stolen art. Although the court acknowledged that the question
posed by the case was an open one, it declined to certify it to
this Court *(see*, 22 NYCRR 500.17*)*, stating that it did not think
that it "[would] recur with sufficient frequency to warrant use of
the certification procedure" . . . .
Actually, the issue has recurred several times in the three years
since *DeWeerth* was decided [citation omitted], including the
case now before us. We have reexamined the relevant New York
case law and we conclude that the Second Circuit should not have
imposed a duty of reasonable diligence on the owners of stolen artwork
for purposes of the Statute of Limitations.

While the demand and refusal rule is not the only possible
method of measuring the accrual of replevin claims, it does appear
to be the rule that affords the most protection to the true owners of
stolen property. . . . Other States that have considered this issue
have applied a discovery rule to these cases, with the Statute of
Limitations running from the time that the owner discovered or
reasonably should have discovered the whereabouts of the work
of art that had been stolen *(see, e.g., O'Keeffe v Snyder*, 83 NJ
478, 416 A2d 862; CAL CIV. PROC CODE §338 [c].*)*

New York has already considered — and rejected — adoption of
a discovery rule. [Here the court discusses legislation that was proposed but was ultimately vetoed by the governor on advice of the
U.S. State Department, the U.S. Justice Department and the United
States Information Agency.] In his veto message, the Governor
expressed his concern that the statute "[did] not provide a

reasonable opportunity for individuals or foreign governments to receive notice of a museum's acquisition and take action to recover it before their rights are extinguished." The Governor also stated that he had been advised by the State Department that the bill, if it went into effect, would have caused New York to become "a haven for cultural property stolen abroad since such objects [would] be immune from recovery under the limited time periods established by the bill." * * *

[I]t would not be prudent to extend [the] case law and impose the additional duty of diligence before the true owner has reason to know where its missing chattel is to be found. . . . We conclude that it would be difficult, if not impossible, to craft a reasonable diligence requirement that could take into account all of [the] variables and that would not unduly burden the true owner.

Further, our decision today is in part influenced by our recognition that New York enjoys a worldwide reputation as a preeminent cultural center. To place the burden of locating stolen artwork on the true owner and to foreclose the rights of that owner to recover its property if the burden is not met would, we believe, encourage illicit trafficking in stolen art. . . . [S]hifting of the burden onto the wronged owner is inappropriate. In our opinion, the better rule gives the owner relatively greater protection and places the burden of investigating the provenance of a work of art on the potential purchaser.

* * *

So, what can we say? In *DeWeerth v. Baldinger*, the Second Circuit produced an interpretation of New York law that was bold, insightful, and wrong. It decided that Mrs. Baldinger was entitled to keep the Monet when, under New York law, Mrs. DeWeerth was clearly entitled to have it. Now what?

For Mrs. DeWeerth and Mr. Horan, the next step was pretty clear. Armed with the new and definitive holding from the New York Court of Appeals, it was time to go back to court. After all, remember from Chapter IV that in "diversity cases" the federal court is supposed to apply exactly the same law as would be applied by a court of the state in which it sits. Here's what happened.

DeWeerth v. Baldinger
(DeWeerth v. Baldinger IV)
804 F. Supp. 539 (S.D.N.Y. 1992)

BRODERICK, District Judge

* * * Plaintiff [DeWeerth] has now moved for relief under Rule 60, Fed. R. Civ. P., [which allows judgments to be reopened for certain reasons, such as "newly discovered evidence," as well as "for any other reason justifying relief. . . ."]

For the reasons set forth below, I conclude that the Rule 60 motion must be granted. In summary, the highest court of New York State has now ruled in *Guggenheim v. Lubell*, 77 N.Y.2d 311, 567 N.Y.S.2d 623, 569 N.E.2d 426 (1991), . . . that state law requires—and, according to the state court ruling, would previously have also required—a result which is consonant with my original determination. Because of the primacy of the state courts in determining interpretation of state law under principles of federalism, as discussed in greater detail below, the *Guggenheim* decision, albeit stating that it also reflects prior law, is a new development justifying Rule 60 relief.

* * *

The "ultimate source for state law adjudication in diversity cases is the law as established by the constitution, statutes, or authoritative court decisions of the state." [Citation omitted.] Accordingly, a "federal court sitting in diversity must follow the law directed by the Supreme Court of the state whose law is found to be applicable. . . ." [Citation omitted.]

Primacy of state court interpretation in matters of state law is a constitutional and statutory principle dating back to the founding of the Republic. * * * In *Erie* [*v. Tompkins*], the [Supreme] Court declared that federal courts were bound to follow state law, including the construction of those laws by a state's highest court, on any matter not governed by the federal Constitution or a federal statute. ＊ ＊ ＊

Failure to act on the present Rule 60 motion would deny Mrs. DeWeerth the right to recover her property solely because she initially brought this action in federal rather than state court. Had Mrs. DeWeerth brought suit in state court, her claim would have been deemed timely commenced under the applicable statute of limitations.

Such inconsistency is exactly the type of result that *Erie* was enacted to avoid. ＊ ＊ ＊ The subsequent decision of the New York Court of Appeals in *Guggenheim*, however, provides a construction of New York law which, under *Erie*, is controlling, and which involved an explicit rejection of the Second Circuit's *DeWeerth* approach. ＊ ＊ ＊

This court is "obliged to give full effect to decisions of New York's highest court on issues involving the application of New York law." *Sanchez v. United States*, 696 F.2d 213, 216 (2nd Cir. 1982). ＊ ＊ ＊

In order to prevent the working of an extreme and undue hardship upon plaintiff, to accomplish substantial justice and to act with appropriate regard for the principles of federalism which underlie our dual judicial system in this extraordinary case, I hold plaintiff is entitled to similar relief here.

＊ ＊ ＊

I find that plaintiff has asserted valid grounds for relief pursuant to Federal Rule of Civil Procedure 60(b)(6). . . .
SO ORDERED.

＊ ＊ ＊

So based on the District Court's application of New York law, it looks as though Mrs. DeWeerth has won once again. Here is the response of the Second Circuit:

DeWeerth v. Baldinger
(DeWeerth v. Baldinger V)
38 F.3d 1266 (2d Cir. 1994)

WALKER, Circuit Judge:

[T]he district court . . . abused its discretion in ordering relief from the final judgment based on Rule 60(b). * * *

Based on the New York Court of Appeals' opinion, the district court determined that DeWeerth would have prevailed in this case had she originally brought her suit in the New York state courts. It then held that *Erie Railroad Co. v. Tompkins*, 304 U.S. 64, 82 L. Ed. 1188, 58 S. Ct. 817 (1938), and its progeny entitled plaintiff to a modification of the final judgment in this case to avoid this inconsistency. It determined that the countervailing interest of both the parties and the courts in the finality of litigation was outweighed by the need "to prevent the working of an extreme and undue hardship upon plaintiff, to accomplish substantial justice and to act with appropriate regard for the principles of federalism which underlie our dual judicial system." 804 F. Supp. at 550.

* * * While acknowledging that Judge Broderick engaged in a scholarly and thorough discussion of the issues, we think that his decision inappropriately disturbed a final judgment in a case that had been fully litigated and was long since closed. In our view, *Erie* simply does not stand for the proposition that a plaintiff is entitled to reopen a federal court case that has been closed for several years in order to gain the benefit of a newly-announced decision of a state court. * * *

DeWeerth argues that this case is distinguishable because the state court did not announce a "change in the law," but rather clarified that New York law is — and always was — contrary to what the federal court held it to be. While we agree that *Guggenheim* did not involve a "change in the law" in the sense that it adopted a rule different from one that previously existed, we do not agree that *Guggenheim* stated that the question decided by the *DeWeerth* panel had long been settled in New York. The *Guggenheim* court stated only that New York's demand and refusal rule was well established; it did not state that the question of whether a due diligence requirement should be added to this rule was clearly settled. In fact, no earlier New York case had addressed this issue. The earlier *DeWeerth* panel noted that this question was an open one. . . .

When confronted with an unsettled issue of state law, a federal court sitting in diversity must make its best effort to predict how the state courts would decide the issue. * * *

It turned out that the *DeWeerth* panel's prediction was wrong. However, by bringing this suit, DeWeerth exposed herself to the possibility that her adversaries would argue for a change in the applicable rules of law. By filing her state law claim in a federal forum, she knew that any open question of state law would be decided by a federal as opposed to a New York state court. The subsequent outcome of the *Guggenheim* decision does not impugn the integrity of the *DeWeerth* decision or the fairness of the process that was accorded DeWeerth. * * * The very nature of diversity jurisdiction leaves open the possibility that a state court will subsequently disagree with a federal court's interpretation of state law. However, this aspect of our dual justice system does not mean that all diversity judgments are subject to revision once a state court later addresses the litigated issues. Such a rule would be tantamount to holding that the doctrine of finality does not apply to diversity judgments. . . .

We conclude that the prior *DeWeerth* panel conscientiously satisfied its duty to predict how New York courts would decide the due diligence question, and that *Erie* and its progeny require no more than this. . . . There is nothing in *Erie* that suggests that consistency must be achieved at the expense of finality. . . .

We believe that the district court abused its discretion in ruling that the important interest in the finality of the judgment in this case, which was more than four years old[144] at the time of that ruling, was outweighed by any injustice DeWeerth believes she has suffered by litigating her case in the federal as opposed to the state

---

[144] Editor's note: The judgment was actually only a little over three years old at the time or the ruling (12/30/87 - 2/14/91). Why do you suppose the Second Circuit exaggerated the age of the judgment in making this point?

forum. Accordingly, we reverse the district court's decision granting her motion under Rule 60(b)(6).

* * *

OWEN, District Judge:[145]

I respectfully dissent
The majority recognizes that in dismissing Mrs. DeWeerth's action
on New York statute of limitations grounds, the prior *"DeWeerth*
panel's prediction was wrong." * * * While the doctrine of finality
of judgments does address an important interest, it should not deter
us from using Rule 60 today to do justice because we may have to
deal hereafter with the Rule's invocation in unworthy cases. * * *

Accordingly, contrary to the majority, I . . . would affirm on the
scholarly and thorough opinion of Judge Broderick below.

* * *

"We are not final because we are infallible, but we are only infallible because we are final."   —*Justice Robert Jackson*[146]

STUDY QUESTIONS

1. The Second Circuit thought it would be unacceptable to have
   "all diversity judgments . . . subject to revision once a state
   court later addresses the litigated issues." What would be so
   bad about that?
2. The Second Circuit agreed that the New York Court of Appeals
   did not "change" the law in *Guggenheim*, but it insisted

---

[145] Editor's note: The Honorable Richard Owen, United States District Judge for the
Southern District of New York, sat on this appeal "by designation," *i.e.*, as a temporary
assignment.
[146] Brown v. Allen, 344 U.S. 443, 540 (1953) (concurring).

nevertheless that the New York court "settled" a question of law that was "open." What's the difference, and why should that difference matter to a federal court sitting in a diversity case? Isn't the bottom line that Mrs. DeWeerth would have been deemed the owner in a New York court, but the Second Circuit, though supposed to follow state law, simply got it *wrong*?

3. After the *Guggenheim* case, it was about as clear as any legal point can be who had been the painting's true owner under New York law. That being so, is it nevertheless proper for a lawyer to make a play for the property by trying to persuade a proud court to invoke "finality" rather than let its mistakes be "corrected" by a lower court judge? Is that what happened here?

4. More generally from question 3, suppose a sharp-eyed lawyer spots a possibility of persuading a court to take away somebody's property and give it to somebody else, namely, to the lawyer's own client. As long as the lawyer sees a way to carry this off without actually breaking any laws, is it all right to try it? Would it violate the lawyer's duty of loyalty *not* to try it?

* * *

On May 4, 2001, the Second Circuit cited its own opinion in *DeWeerth V* as support for its conclusion that finality should *not* prevent a judgment from being reopened:

> A district court may "relieve a party . . . from a final judgment, order, or proceeding for . . . (6) any other reason justifying relief," Fed. R. Civ. P. 60(b), if the movant can demonstrate "extraordinary circumstances" or "extreme and undue hardship." DeWeerth v. Baldinger, 38 F.3d 1266, 1272 (2d Cir. 1994). We have held that Rule 60(b)(6) "should be liberally construed when substantial justice will thus be served." Radack v. Norwegian America Line Agency, Inc., 318 F.2d 538, 542 (2d Cir. 1963).

LeBlanc v. Cleveland, 248 F. 3d 95 (2d Cir. 2001). Judge Walker (the same judge who wrote the opinion in *DeWeerth V*), wrote the opinion in *LeBlanc*.

POSTSCRIPT

"[T]o question a reputable dealer about his title would be an 'insult' ... perhaps, but the sensitivity of the art dealer cannot serve to deprive the injured buyer of compensation for a breach which could have been avoided had the insult been risked"[147]

So in the end, Mrs. Baldinger got to keep Monet's *Champs de Blé à Vétheuil*, and Mrs. DeWeerth got nothing. This was not an overall happy solution, but then this was not a case with any obvious "win-win" possibilities. Both women had understandable reasons to be deeply attached to this Monet. One had inherited it from her father in 1922; the other had it in her home since the 1950s. It had been a big part of both of their lives. The facts presented the classic legal conundrum of true owner vs. honest buyer, where one of two innocents must suffer. There were no "halfway" solutions under the law as it stands. Either Mrs. DeWeerth was still the owner of the

---

[147] Menzel v. List, 246 N.E.2d 742, 745 (N.Y. 1969).

painting, or Mrs. Baldinger had become the owner—and that was that.

Before finishing up, however, we ought to consider one final point, one we have so far paid little attention to. There was an additional party to this lawsuit, Wildenstein & Co., Inc., the art gallery that sold the Monet to Mrs. Baldinger. After Mrs. Baldinger was served with her summons, she turned right around and sued Wildenstein, in the very same proceeding. By *impleading* Wildenstein, Mrs. Baldinger sought to assure that, if she lost the painting to Mrs. DeWeerth, then Wildenstein would be immediately available to compensate her for its value, over $500,000. As a result of the impleader, Mrs. Baldinger was not only the defendant but also a "third-party plaintiff" in the same lawsuit—she was the third-party plaintiff against Wildenstein, and Wildenstein became a "third-party defendant."

The reason that Mrs. Baldinger had an action against Wildenstein is that in every sale the seller is deemed by law to give the buyer an "implied warranty of title" (unless the seller affirmatively excludes it). The purpose of this warranty is to give the buyer a right to compensation in case the seller's ownership turns out to have been faulty. According to New York case law, the amount that the breaching seller owes the buyer is equal to the value of the object at the time the buyer is forced to surrender it to the true owner.[148] In short, Wildenstein was facing the possibility of paying a $500,000-plus judgment on a picture it originally had sold for only $30,900.

Even though Baldinger was suing Wildenstein, the gallery was essentially "on her side" throughout the various stages of *DeWeerth v. Baldinger*. They both hoped to prevent Mrs. DeWeerth from winning back the painting. As long as Mrs. Baldinger retained the Monet, Wildenstein would not be liable for breach of warranty and would not be liable for the $500,000-plus compensation. Furthermore, the district court ordered that the DeWeerth-Baldinger part of the case was to be tried separately from the Baldinger-Wildenstein part of the

---

[148] *Id.*

case. This order had the effect of removing Wildenstein and its "deep pocket" from the focus of unwanted attention while the DeWeerth-Baldinger dispute was considered. Such a move made it perhaps a bit harder to decide the main case for Mrs. DeWeerth. With Wildenstein on the sidelines, it would not have been so obvious that any loss to Mrs. Baldinger would be made up by Wildenstein. But then, you might ask, why should the Wildenstein gallery be left holding the bag?

Maybe it would not have to. Recall that Wildenstein acquired the Monet on consignment from Francois Reichenbach, an art dealer from Geneva, Switzerland. Although Reichenbach was apparently still alive, neither Wildenstein nor Mrs. Baldinger called Reichenbach as a witness to clarify where he got the painting. As Judge Broderick wrote:

> The trail back from Mrs. Baldinger leads through Wildenstein to Reichenbach, and stops there. There is no evidence before me with respect to how Reichenbach came into possession of the Monet.

Perhaps if Mrs. DeWeerth had been allowed to get her property back (as called for by New York law), and Wildenstein had been liable to Mrs. Baldinger, then Wildenstein would have taken a keener interest in pursuing Reichenbach, asserting its right to indemnity under *his* implied warranty. If only that had happened, we might have found ourselves led to the truth about the origins of the painting. As it was, however, the Second Circuit let Wildenstein off the hook and thereby helped—for this case, at least—make New York "a haven for cultural property stolen abroad" by declaring the Monet "immune from recovery," exactly the sort of thing that New York policy was trying to prevent.[149]

In summary, even if the Wildenstein gallery was as innocent as the other parties in this case, there are reasons why it — more than either Baldinger or DeWeerth — might more appropriately have shouldered the loss. The gallery was the one participant, probably the only participant, in a good position to resolve the

---

[149] *Guggenheim*, 77 N.E.2d at 627.

questions about the painting's provenance. If only it had asked before taking the consignment from Reichenbach. It is almost certain that *somebody* back there in the chain of possession bought the Monet from a fishy character and put it on the legitimate art market and, by doing so, that somebody is responsible for creating this whole mess. As the case turned out, however, Mrs. DeWeerth lost her painting, Mrs. Baldinger suffered "considerable personal distress and anguish,"[150] and somebody got away scot-free.

---

[150] DeWeerth v. Baldinger, 658 F. Supp. at 696.

EXTRACTS FROM TESTIMONY
OF GERDA DOROTHEA DeWEERTH

BY MR. EPSTEIN [counsel for Wildenstein & Co., Inc.]:

Q: Mrs. De Weerth, I am now going to ask you some questions about your father's acquisition of the painting by Monet. You have stated, at paragraph 5 of your affidavit, that the painting was purchased between 1902 and 1908, to the best of your recollection. How do you recall those dates?

A: This is, in fact, based on a statement by my sister, who said that the painting was acquired well before her marriage, which took place in 1909. I personally would probably not have remembered the date as accurately, because I am so much younger than my sister. After all, I was only born in 1894.

Q: Do you know why your sister identified the year 1902, as the earliest date on which the picture was purchased?

A: No, I don't know.

Q: So you do not know whether it was purchased in 1902, or not?

A: No, I don't.

Q: Now the first sentence from paragraph 5 states that your father purchased a painting between 1902 and 1908, to the best of your recollection. Is your testimony now that you have no recollection of the purchase?

A: I accepted the word of my sister. I accepted what my sister said.

Q: Do you remember the painting being delivered to your home?

A: I don't, perhaps, recall the actual delivery, but I do remember my father showing me the painting as a new acquisition.

Q: Do you recall who delivered the painting to your home?

A: No, I don't.

Q: It is true, is it not, that your father purchased many paintings?

A: Yes, it is.

Q: Do you recall where the painting was hung in your father's home?

A: I seem to remember that it was first placed on a sort of tripod in a large living hall where we were living at the moment.

Q: Is that the only location in the home where it was hung?

A: I think so, yes.

* * *

Q: Now after your father died, how many paintings did you inherit—excuse me, paintings and other art objects—did you inherit?

A: I am afraid I don't know this by heart.

Q: Can you approximate the number? Was it closer to ten or closer to one hundred?

A: Well, it definitely wasn't a hundred.

Q: Was it closer to ten?

A: Yes.

* * *

Q: Did your sister also inherit paintings from your father?

A: Yes.

Q: Did she inherit approximately the same number of paintings that you did?

A: Most probably, yes.

Q: Did your mother inherit any paintings from your father?

A: I don't think so.

* * *

Q: Mrs. De Weerth, with respect to those paintings [of your father's] that you do not have, are those paintings that your sister inherited?

A: Yes.

Q: Did your father have a will?

A: The split up, or the division, of those works and objects of art had already been agreed upon among us, before his death.

Q: Let me ask the question again: Did your father have a will?

A: I think so, yes.

Q: Is a copy of that will still in your family's possession?

A: I don't know.

Q: Would you have any way of finding out?

A: I—at least, I do not know whether the last valid version of his will is still around, is still available. . . .

It would certainly be difficult to find out, the notary public who we employed for that task, is dead. He died a few years ago. And after all, my father died in 1922, and that's sixty years ago.

Q: Do you have any recollection of reading your father's will at any time after his death?

A: Most probably, I did read it, but the list of paintings had been, as I said, agreed upon beforehand among us and to the best of my recollection, it was not included in the will.

Q: Does that mean that you took—you and your sister took—possession of the paintings before your father died?

A: No.

Q: So that possession of the paintings was transferred to you and your sister after your father's death?

A: Yes. The answer is yes.

Q: Do you recall whether the will made any reference to the disposition of the paintings to you and your sister?

A: I don't think so.

* * *

Q: Mrs. De Weerth, you have testified that agreement was reached as to the division of your father's art works before he died. How was that agreement reached?

A: In writing, my mother wrote it down.

Q: So am I correct that your mother decided which daughter would get which works of art?

A: No. It was not my mother alone who decided this. We did, in fact, consider this, think about this, together.

Q: Do you recall having one or more conversations with your mother and sister about how the works were to be divided?

The Witness (in English): Several conversations, yes.

Q: Do you recall anything of what was said during those conversations?

A: Well, we talked about the works of art.

Q: Do you have, in your possession, the document created by your mother dividing the paintings?

A: I don't know whether it still exists.

Q: When did you last see it?

A: Well, it was not really a document, in the strict sense of the word, it was more the jottings in a sort of copybook. And I probably last saw it when I received the paintings in my home in Elberfeld. But I do not know for sure.

Q: So that you last saw the document sometime after your father's death, is that correct?

A: Yes, that is true.

Q: Do you have, in your possession, any document that transferred title of any of your father's paintings to you?

A: I don't know, but I don't think so. But it has always been decided that the Monet would belong to me.

* * *

Q: When you acquired the painting, after your father's death, did you obtain insurance on it?

A: We has a general household insurance policy, but the painting was not specifically mentioned in the policy.

Q: Is that statement correct with respect to the entire period during which you possessed the painting, that is, from your father's death, until 1943?

A: Now whether I did have a general household insurance policy at Wuppertal-Elberfeld, I do not know exactly. I may

have done, but I don't know. But certainly, my mother did have such an insurance at the time.

Q: At the time during your possession of the painting, was it specifically identified in an insurance policy, either taken out by you, or by another member of your family?

The Witness (in English): No, I don't think so.

BY MR. EPSTEIN:

Q: During the same period, this 1922 to 1943, did you specifically identify any of your paintings or art objects in insurance policies?

A: No, I don't think so.

Q: Do you retain copies of any of those old insurance policies?

A: For which year?

Q: Any of the years between 1922 and 1943.

A: No, no. I haven't got any.

Q: Why did you decide to send the painting to your sister in 1943?

A: The reason was the war. And the danger of destruction of valuable items by bombs. And it appeared to me that these items would be safer at Oberbalzheim. And also, I had the opportunity of using a furniture van, at the time, which was available to me. And therefore, I took this opportunity to send a few items, to send a few things, away. Incidentally, many people were doing that at the time.

Q: How many works of art did you send to your sister in 1943?

A: I don't know the exact number. There weren't many.

Q: So that you retained many of your works of art in your
own home at this time?

A: Yes. And the supplement to the previous question: It
was definitely below ten.

Q: Did you send any items, other than works of art, to
your sister?

A: Yes, a variety of household items.

Q: Did you keep an inventory or list of what you sent to
your sister in 1943?

A: I may have had one at the time, but I certainly don't
possess any such list now.

* * *

Q: Did you give your sister permission to dispose of any
of the possession you gave her?

A: No.

Q: Did your sister dispose of any of the possession you
gave her?

A: No.

Q: After the war, did you receive everything you had
given her, save the Monet?

A: Yes, I think so. I do think I got everything back,
with the exception of the Monet.

* * *

BY MR. EPSTEIN:

Q: Mrs. De Weerth, after you sent the Monet in the furniture van in 1943, you never saw it again, is that
correct?

A: That is correct. I never saw the painting again.

Q: You never saw it in Oberbalzheim?

A: No.

* * *

Q: When did your sister advise you that the Monet was
missing?

A: She informed me soon after she, herself, found out.
But I do not recall the exact date.

Q: You have stated in paragraph 11 of your affidavit that, to the best of your recollection, she informed you some time in late 1945. How did you recall this date?

A: It is probable that my sister gave me that information

Q: So that you are stating here not your recollection but your sister's recollection of when you were informed?

A: To some extent, yes. But I was also told at the time that the information was reliable enough for me to sign it. [Apparently meaning the affidavit? Ed.]

Q: How did your sister notify you that the painting was missing? I mean, by letter or by conversation?

A: Yes, I did ask that before, and that's the trouble. I don't know. It was probably by letter.

Q: Am I correct, that if it was by letter, you do not still possess the letter?

A: Quite right. I don't possess that letter anymore.

* * *

Q: Did you at some time begin to maintain a file, or a collection of documents, that pertained to this painting?

A: No. Well, just in this last year or so, but not previously.

* * *

Q: Now in paragraph 15 of your affidavit, you have stated that you wrote to Dr. Alfred Stanger with respect to the missing Monet. Do you recall writing to Dr. Stanger?

A: Yes. I do remember that. And I also remember his response, his reply.

Q: Before I get to that letter, let me ask you, Mrs. De Weerth: Did you take any steps to locate the Monet between 1948, when you wrote to Dr. Frowein, and 1955, when you wrote to Dr. Stanger?

A: That's so many years really that I can't say this with any amount of certainty, but apparently, there is no evidence to suggest that I did. And once Dr. Stanger had written to me in such a negative and discouraging

vein, saying that it was really rather pointless to
pursue the matter, I think I—I think I did not make
any further efforts in that matter.

Q: With respect to Dr. Stanger, had he been an acquaintance of yours prior to 1955?

A: To the best of my recollection, I only made Dr. Stanger's acquaintance then and there. He was recommended to me—people advised me to consult him as an
art expert, but then, nothing much came of that, anyway, because he thought that the small picture which
I had was really too little to identify the Monet with
any amount of certainty. And he also said that Monet
had painted several similar scenes in that region,
which are not all that similar, but I only know this
now after having seen the catalogue. So
Dr. Stanger's comments were really, really quite
misleading at the time.

Q: Do you recall who recommended Dr. Stanger to you?

A: No.

Q: Did you have other acquaintances, at this time, who
were art historians or art experts?

A: I don't remember.

* * *

Q: Subsequent to your correspondence with Dr. Stanger,
did you ever speak, at any time, to another art his-
torian or art expert about locating the Monet?

A: I don't think so.

Q: If I can, now, draw your attention to paragraph 16,
Mrs. De Weerth, you refer there to a report you filed
with the Bundeskriminalamt. Can I ask you what the
Bundeskriminalamt does, and how it functions?

A: I can't do that. That's really beyond me. That's
asking a bit too much.

Q: Is it the police force?

A: No. This is different from the police.

Q: Is it some sort of investigative agency?

A: Yes. That is probably the way you can describe it.
There still is a Bundeskriminalamt today, so
you'll just have to try and make investigations as
to its functions. I am afraid I can't tell you.

Q: Why did you file a report with the Bundeskriminalamt
in 1957?

A: Perhaps, somebody told me that that was another avenue open to me.

Q: Did you hope that they would conduct an investigation into the loss of your works of art?

A: Well, I hoped that something would come of it.

Q: Did you keep a copy of the report you filed with the
Bundeskriminalamt?

A: No, I haven't. If it's not with the files here, then
there is none.

* * *

Q: After this report was filed, did you receive any
response from the Bundeskriminalamt?

A: I don't recall.

Q: Do you recall being interviewed by any investigator
from the Bundeskriminalamt?

A: No.

Q: Do you recall receiving a letter from the Bundeskriminalamt?

A: No.

Q: Did you request an interview with anyone at the
Bundeskriminalamt, after you submitted this report?

A: The answer was no.

Q: In paragraph 16, you state that you had lost so many
things in the war and its aftermath that you were
involved in pursuing a number of avenues to try to
recover damages. My question is: What were those
number of avenues you were pursuing?

A: Now, forty years later, of course, I don't recall the
exact details. But possibly, they were addresses
that people gave me, addresses that I should write
to. But I don't know, now, after forty years.

Q: So that when you signed this affidavit last year, you
did not recall what the avenues were that were mentioned here?

A: No.

* * *

Q: Between 1957 and 1981, did you contact any investigator agency with respect to the Monet?

A: I don't know exactly. I can tell you with some measure
of accuracy and reliability that I did not do so in

the last few years. Whether I did so immediately after '57, I can't really say with any measure of reliability.

Q: Did you contact any agency of the German government, between 1957 and 1981, with respect to the Monet?

A: Again, the answer is: I don't know.

Q: Did you contact, again, between 1957 and 1981, did you contact any agency of the American government with respect to the Monet?

A: No.

Q: Did you retain any lawyer, between 1957 and 1981, to search for the Monet?

A: Again, I don't know.

Q: Did you contact any private investigator, in search of the Monet, between 1957 and 1981?

A: No.

Q: Did you contact any are historians or art experts, between 1957 and 1981, with respect to the Monet?

A: Again, for the years immediately after 1957, I can't say with any measure of certainty. It's such a long time ago.

Q: Did you contact any museums, either in Germany or elsewhere, between the years 1957 and 1981, with respect to the Monet?

A: The same answer. . . .